Howard A. Patten is Teaching Fellow in the Department of Middle East and Mediterranean Studies, King's College London. He holds a PhD from King's College London and an MPhil from the University of Cambridge.

ISRAEL AND THE COLD WAR

Diplomacy, Strategy and the Policy of the
Periphery at the United Nations

HOWARD A. PATTEN

I.B. TAURIS

LONDON • NEW YORK • OXFORD • NEW DELHI • SYDNEY

I.B. TAURIS
Bloomsbury Publishing Plc
50 Bedford Square, London, WC1B 3DP, UK
1385 Broadway, New York, NY 10018, USA

BLOOMSBURY, I.B. TAURIS and the I.B. Tauris logo are
trademarks of Bloomsbury Publishing Plc

First published in Great Britain 2013
Paperback edition first published 2019

A catalogue record for this book is available from the British Library.

A catalog record for this book is available from the Library of Congress.

ISBN: HB: 978-1-8488-5808-4
PB: 978-1-7883-1490-9

Series: Library of International Relations, volume 57

Typeset by NewGen Publishers, Chennai

To find out more about our authors and books visit
www.bloomsbury.com and sign up for our newsletters.

For My Mother,
Elaine

CONTENTS

Acknowledgements   viii

Abbreviations   ix

Introduction   1

1. From the Margins to the Centre: Israel's Policy
   of the Periphery, Pre-1955   4

2. Iran and Israel, 1956–72: Calculated Ambivalence?   36

3. Iran and Israel, 1973–82: From Consolidation to Revolution   59

4. Turkey and Israel, 1956–72: Alignment and Ambivalence   81

5. Turkey and Israel, 1973–82: Rejection and Realignment   98

6. Ethiopia and Israel, 1956–72: From Partner to Pariah   116

7. Ethiopia and Israel, 1973–82: Pressure and Resistance   141

8. The Policy of the Periphery   155

Conclusion   164

Notes   166
Bibliography   219
Index   229

ACKNOWLEDGEMENTS

I would like to thank members and associates of Kibbutz Bet Zera, in particular the Klass and Church families, whom, apart from being dear friends, have supported me in many, many ways. For her unsurpassed patience and wisdom, I thank Georgia Cameron-Clarke. Thanks also go to Maria Marsh for her guidance and understanding.

I reserve special thanks for Professor Rory Miller, who has proved to be an outstanding supervisor and unfaltering friend, and Professor Efraim Karsh, whose eminent professionalism and expertise have enriched my work over the years. To them both, I owe an immense debt of gratitude.

Finally, I would like to thank my mother Elaine, whose support has been unquestionable and who has made this book, and so much more, possible. Recognising her here is hardly enough of an appreciation, but it is, nevertheless, a start.

ABBREVIATIONS

AIOC	Anglo-Iranian Oil Company
BOAC	British Overseas Airways Corporation
BP	British Petroleum
CIA	Central Intelligence Agency
ES	Emergency Session
GMT	Greenwich Mean Time
IAF	Israel Air Force
IDF	Israel Defence Forces
MECOM	Middle East Command
MEDO	Middle East Defence Organisation
NATO	North Atlantic Treaty Organisation
NIOC	National Iranian Oil Company
NSP	National Salvation Party
OAU	Organisation of African Unity
OPEC	Organisation of Petroleum Exporting Countries
PLO	Palestine Liberation Organisation
SAVAK	*Sazmani-Amniyat Va Kisvar*
UAR	United Arab Republic
UK	United Kingdom
UN	United Nations
UNEF	United Nations Emergency Force
UNGA	United Nations General Assembly
UNRWA	United Nations Relief and Works Agency

UNSC	United Nations Security Council
US	United States
USSR	Union of Soviet Socialist Republics
UNTSO	United Nations Truce Supervision Organization in Palestine

INTRODUCTION

We have begun to strengthen our ties with neighbouring countries on the outer circle of the Middle East: Iran, Ethiopia and Turkey, with the purpose of creating a powerful dam against the Nasserist-Soviet torrent. We have established friendly relations and an attitude of mutual trust with the government of Iran and the Emperor of Ethiopia. Recently, our ties with the Turkish government have become more intimate, above and beyond our normal diplomatic relations. Our purpose is the creation of a group of states, not necessarily an official and public pact which ... will be capable of standing firm against the Soviet expansionism with Nasser as its middleman, and which may be able to save the independence of Lebanon; perhaps, with time, that of Syria as well. This group will include two non-Arab Moslem countries (Iran and Turkey), one Christian country (Ethiopia) and the State of Israel.[1] (David Ben-Gurion, 1958).

Israel is the sole Middle Eastern state that has been systematically excluded from regional political and economic alliances[2] due to its boycott by the majority of the Arab League Member States.[3] Consequently, it has had restricted access to regional actors,[4] leading the Jewish state to search for alternative ways to establish and consolidate itself, gain international legitimacy, help overcome Arab seclusion and to enable it some form of role in the Middle Eastern system. Thus, Israel made various attempts to join Western defence and economic organisations.[5]

Israel also began to develop contacts with states on the periphery of the Middle East that shared its concerns over the perceived dangers of Nasserist expansionism, Arab nationalism and regional Soviet penetration.[6] David Ben-Gurion, Israel's first prime minister, expressed particular concern over possible Communist subversion in Iran, the threat to Ethiopia's independence by Eritrea and moves by Nasser on black Africa.[7] For Ben-Gurion, these people were potential allies for Israel and, moreover, the Jewish state sought to pursue ties with non-Arab ethnic minorities within Arab countries. As a result, links with the non-Arab indigenous population in Sudan, the Iraqi Kurds, the Lebanese and Syrian Druze and the Maronite Christian community in Lebanon were developed at various stages.[8]

This concept came to be known as the Policy of the Periphery and began to be institutionalised in Israel's foreign policy framework in the mid 1950s.[9] It was intended, *inter alia,* to create the perception, both in the region and the world, that the Middle East was not solely Arab, or Islamic, but rather a region with a diversity of peoples, religions and languages.[10] The policy was also a proactive attempt by Jerusalem to dislocate Egyptian President Gamal Abdel Nasser's theory of Egypt as the centre of the Arab, Islamic and African worlds; a theory that saw Egypt as the dominant power in the region.[11] The objective of the Policy of the Periphery was to disrupt this dynamic by forging an outer ring of states, thereby promoting a more diverse representation of the region.[12]

The policy was the brainchild of Reuven Shiloah, the first director-general of Mossad, the Israeli intelligence agency.[13] Shiloah had conceived the idea in 1931, whilst on assignment in Kurdistan for the Jewish Agency, the pre-state Jewish authority.[14] During this time, he established significant contacts with the stateless Kurds and realised that, for the Zionists, there were significant benefits in forging covert links with non-Arab peoples in the region.[15]

Ben-Gurion believed that the dynamic created by cultivating pockets of allies around the Middle East could gradually convince the majority of the Arab states to temper their position towards Israel. He stated that

The Middle East is not an exclusively Arab area; on the contrary, the majority of its inhabitants are not Arabs. The Turks, the

Persians, and the Jews – without taking into account the Kurds and the other non-Arab minorities in the Arab states – are more numerous than the Arabs in the Middle East, and it is possible that through contacts with the peoples of the outer zone of the area we shall achieve friendship with the peoples of the inner zone, who are our immediate neighbours.[16]

In addition, Ben-Gurion was aware that the United States (US) had significant interests in the Middle East and would look favourably upon this policy.[17] In fact, the Policy of the Periphery was merely a single element in a wider strategic vision that Shiloah envisaged for Israel. After returning from the Israeli Embassy in Washington to take up a position at the Israeli Foreign Ministry, Shiloah called for a strategic alliance with the US and Europe, which could potentially alleviate the rejection Israel faced from the surrounding states and allow it to assume its place in a Western-led strategic bloc.[18] As he explained to Golda Meir, such a stance would 'increase the level of our involvement in Western security arrangements'.[19]

CHAPTER 1

FROM THE MARGINS TO THE CENTRE: ISRAEL'S POLICY OF THE PERIPHERY PRE-1955

Israel and Iran

Iran voted against the United Nations General Assembly (UNGA) partition plan on 29 November 1947.[1] The vote came at the culmination of a frustrating time for the Iranian delegation at the United Nations (UN). Indeed, at the Ad Hoc Committee on Palestine, on 11 October 1947, Iranian Representative, Mostafa Adl said that, 'in the absence of a reasonable and workable solution, and since other members of the Committee had not shared his views … had accepted as an intermediary solution the minority plan for the establishment of a federal state', but it was imperative that the Assembly not support the 'imposition on Palestine of a government which would satisfy neither party'.[2]

The conclusion of the Iranian delegation was that 'the two States recommended in the majority plan would not be viable, but would become a liability of world concern'. Adl clarified, though, that the Iranian position was not 'based on any lack of sympathy for the Jewish community or on a pro-Arab spirit, but only on the principles of the Charter'. The diplomat announced that Palestine should be left 'to the Palestinians, irrespective of whether they were Moslems, Jews or Christians' and the inhabitants of Palestine should 'determine their own fate'. Adl also stated that the Iranian delegation would 'support a solution for partition only if it were supported by the majority of the peoples of Palestine'.[3] This statement revealed the Iranian concern for regional stability that would reappear at the UN frequently.

Three days before the vote on partition, Adl had claimed that, 'to partition a country into two different States, an Arab State and a Jewish State ... will not be viable', and 'will probably be still-born'. He continued, 'The solution proposed to you has no foundation in law' and he believed that partition 'suggests the open violation of the principle enshrined in Article 1, Paragraph 2, of the Charter, which gives all Members the right to govern themselves freely, without any kind of foreign vote or pressure and the right to choose the form of government which best suits them'.[4]

So concerned was Adl over regional stability, that he stated partition would 'result in exposing not only the Near and Middle East, but perhaps the whole world, to fire and slaughter.' Iran, he added, would vote against partition 'in loyalty to the principles of the Charter and conscious of the respect which is due to them'.[5] At the vote on partition, Adl declared that the 'Arab world wishes at all costs to avoid a conflict which might have regrettable consequences' and that 'it [the Arab world] is ready to abandon its position of intransigence and even make concessions.'[6] Keen to delay the vote, preserve Iran's ties with the Muslim world and to prevent the creation of a Jewish state, which could scupper Iran's relations with the Arab world, he then requested an adjournment of 'not more than a few weeks,' in order to 'prepare the plan for the future government of Palestine' and stated that UNGA could be 'convened in Special Session to decide on the question'.[7]

Iran was becoming aware that its border with the Union of Soviet Socialist Republics (USSR) made it a front-line state in the developing Cold War. This heightened the Iranian fear of further Soviet penetration of the Middle East throughout the late 1940s and early 1950s[8] and, as Israel abandoned its policy of non-alignment and moved towards the West, Iran became more interested in pursuing bilateral ties, seeking concomitantly to develop relations with the US. However, in Iran at the time, there were two major political forces opposed to relations with Israel: the pro-Soviet and anti-Zionist Tudeh Communist party, and the Shi'a fundamentalists.[9] These two forces were able to take advantage of the fact that many Iranian centrist intellectuals and nationalists were concerned with the struggle against perceived British dominance over Iran, via the Anglo Iranian Oil Company (AIOC).[10] Thus, R.K. Ramazani's definition of Iran's relationship with Israel between 1948–50 as 'calculated ambivalence'[11] is appropriate, particularly as Iran, after having recognised Israel *de jure*, voted against its admission to the UN.[12]

The Israeli move away from non-alignment and the cultivation of relations with Tehran was championed by the Israeli Embassy in Washington as a means for Israel both to overcome its political isolation and to negate the perception that it was a foreign entity in the Middle East. Jerusalem tacitly adopted the precedent forged by the embassy and ties with Iran became a strategic goal for Israel from October 1949.[13] In addition to the stratego-political aspect of these ties, for Israel there was the added catalyst of potential immigration. Iran's Jews, however, had not been persecuted by the regime, even after the birth of Israel and the subsequent war, and within the Iranian Jewish community, there was little awareness of the need to immigrate to Israel.[14] Indeed, the Shah claimed to encapsulate the Iranian position towards all its citizens, including Jews,

> We have never believed in discrimination based on race, colour or creed, and have often provided a haven for oppressed peoples of backgrounds different from our own. For example, it was characteristic of Cyrus the Great that, when he conquered Babylon, he allowed the Jews, who had been exiled there by King Nebuchadnezzar after the conquest of Jerusalem in 597 B.C., to return to Palestine with their sacred vessels and rebuild their destroyed temples.[15]

In fact, it was concern over the fate of Iraqi Jews that helped to facilitate the expansion of ties between Israel and Iran.[16] *Aliyah Bet*, the organisation for the clandestine immigration of Jews to Palestine between 1920 and 1948 and precursor to the Mossad, had established links with

the Iranian government during the 1948 war, with the specific purpose of aiding in the evacuation of Jews from Iraq. Israel, with Iranian
support, successfully established an infrastructure for this purpose.[17]
There were harsh restrictions on the lives of Iraqi Jewry; Zionism was
declared a crime in 1948 and there was no form of legal emigration
until 1950. To circumvent this obstacle, Israel turned to Iran, which
became an alternative, albeit low-key, route for Jewish emigration.[18]
In response, Iraq pressured Iran to close its border in order to prevent
the passage of Jews, and Iran initially acquiesced, though subsequently
performed a *volte-face* in the face of Israeli pressure.[19]

Domestically, Iran was encountering complications, particularly
in the spheres of agriculture and technological development, areas in
which Israel had expertise and was willing to offer the services of its
technicians and engineers.[20] These contacts led to a deepening of the
relationship and, consequently, there followed additional co-operation
in areas such as planning co-ordinated positions over political development.[21] This, in turn, made military co-operation between the
two countries increasingly likely. Indeed, Israel had initially attracted
Iranian interest largely due to its high level of economic development,[22]
and it has been revealed that both Israel and the US worked together
in order to develop the Iranian secret police, the SAVAK.[23]

Co-operation between the senior political echelons of both countries was also notable. This was carried out with the minimum of
exposure, with the Iranian diplomatic presence in Israel based in the
Swiss Embassy and the Israeli presence in Tehran officially termed
a trade mission.[24] In essence, the Iranian Representative arrived in
Israel in 1949 without either consent from the Israeli foreign ministry,
or a clear designation, but promptly began dealing with reparations
for Iranian families who had been affected by the 1948 war.[25] After
Iran's *de facto* recognition of Israel in March 1950, the Shah allowed
Jerusalem to maintain a low level presence in Tehran.[26]

While covert relations between Iran and Israel were developing, at
the UN, the Iranian stance was openly critical of Israeli policies. Indeed,
speaking of the 1948 War of Independence, Iranian Representative
Ghassemzadeh stated that 'the desire of the Arabs to return to their
homes was based on a natural, sacred and inalienable right, consecrated

by the Charter, which all Member States of the United Nations had signed' and that the 'Government of Israel was, however, unwilling to fulfil the obligations imposed upon it by the relevant resolutions of the General Assembly'. He continued, that the 'General Assembly should instruct the Government of Israel to comply with the provisions of United Nations resolutions by permitting Arab refugees to return to their homes and by compensating them for property losses.'[27]

With this appeasement of the Arab bloc at the UN, Tehran, coinciding with its recognition of Israel, stated that it would be willing to accept an official Israeli diplomatic delegation on 16 March 1950, following the Shah's return from a trip to Pakistan.[28] Israel believed that the reception of such an official diplomatic team would begin to institutionalise the relationship between the two countries, and render any sudden Iranian withdrawal of recognition impracticable.[29] As a result of the meeting, Iran's official Representative in Jerusalem became its special envoy.[30] However, the formal exchange of missions was beset by difficulties, which largely stemmed from Iran's inability to withstand both internal and external pressures over its relationship with Israel, and culminated in the closure of the Iranian Consulate-General in Jerusalem on 7 July 1951.[31] The closure, damaging as it was for the Israelis, was explained by the Iranians as the result of a crisis between Britain and Iran over the future control of Iranian oil. In addition, Iranian Prime Minister, Mohammad Mossadeq, heading a nationalist coalition formed around opposition to the AIOC, which was nationalised in 1951, was facing considerable internal opposition to Iran's ties with Israel.[32] This was an interesting event indeed as, now, the Iranian government was attempting to allay Israeli fears over the ostensible worsening of the relationship between the two countries and not solely attempting to placate the Arab bloc at the UN.

To counter some of this pressure, the Iranian delegation at the UN presented a mollifying stand on the Arab-Israeli dispute. Representative Dr Djalal Abdoh explained that 'while Iran was bound to the Arab States by cultural and religious ties, it had no animosity towards Jews'. To emphasise this, he added 'the best proof being that the Jews were represented by a Jew in the Iranian parliament' and that 'recently a group of Iranians imbued with Nazi ideology had been legally prosecuted'. Moreover, the diplomat believed that, since 1947, the dynamic between Israel and the Arabs had changed, as in 1947 'the Arab states had opposed the partition of Palestine and the internationalisation of Jerusalem; today, they were ready to negotiate with Israel ... ' Finally, Abdoh noted that 'a state could not live in peace and prosperity so long as its neighbours did not have friendly feelings towards it' and that Israel should 'take a realistic attitude and recognise that it was surrounded by Arab States which had made great concessions to it'.[33]

From 1951, the US, under Truman, decided that Mossadeq was a threat to both Iran's domestic interests and those of the US.[34] This was confirmed for Washington in 1953, when Mossadeq turned to the USSR for economic aid in order to counter the hardship faced by Iran after western oil companies placed an embargo on Iranian oil in response to the nationalisation of the AIOC. As a result, the US administration, through the CIA, facilitated a *coup d'etat* against Mossadeq, which returned power to the Shah and succeeded in reducing the political power of the Iranian elected assembly.[35]

The reaction of the US to the re-installation of the Shah was unequivocal. As early as September 1953, the US issued an emergency grant to Iran and aid continued to the tune of US$23 million for 1953. Subsequently, grants increased, with Iran receiving US$85 million in 1954, US$76 million in 1955 and US$73 million in 1956. Official American data reveals that US economic aid to Iran for the years 1953–57 totalled some US$366.8 million, the bulk of which was delivered after the removal of the Mossadeq regime. US military aid also increased: for the years 1949–52, Iran received US$16.6 million in military grants. Over the next five years, the figure reached US$133.9 million.[36]

Thus, Iranian relations with the West acquired a new vitality; the Shah envisaged a framework for alliance with the US as an attempt to curb Soviet backed Nasserist expansionism, and there was a desire to strengthen Iran's economic sector through agricultural aid in the form of Israeli expertise.[37] He also declared the main cause of Iran's domestic and external difficulties to be the lack of military security, and defined the greatest threat to the country as Soviet penetration, potentially facilitated by Iranian Communists, aided by the Soviets.[38] Essentially, the Shah promoted the belief that military preparation was essential for Iran's social and economic welfare and external security. In this context, ties with Israel were seen as a foil to the increasing power of the USSR in the Middle East.

However, at the UN, the Iranian delegation vocalised concern over the plight of the Palestinian refugees. Representative Dr Ali Gholi Ardalan noted that 'on the basis of two nutritional surveys ... many children between six months and two years of age were suffering from chronic intestinal disorders due to a diet deficient in proteins', though he added that, 'It was gratifying to note that the proportion of refugees living in tents had been reduced to 32 percent in March 1954, as compared with 87 percent in March 1951'.[39] This said, the majority of UN Member States voiced their concerns over the plight of the Palestinian refugees, including those with more pro-Israel tendencies. For the recently re-installed Shah, such statements served to mollify Arab UN Member States, concerned over the growing relationship between the US and Iran.

The Shah then began to counter the revolutionary Arab states, led by Egypt, with his own policy of positive nationalism.[40] In this sense, the Cold War within the Arab world was joined by an Iranian-Arab Cold War, which saw Iran defending pro-Western concerns.[41] Iran, though ostensibly continuing to sympathise with Arab nationalist concerns, such as the Palestinian refugees, was perturbed by the Soviet disposition increasingly adopted by the Arab world. The Egyptian Revolution of 1952 aggravated this and by 1955, as Nasser gained support for his pan-Arab worldview, Iran and the Shah's policy of positive nationalism became an increasingly important target for Cairo. As the Shah revealed

> We are not intimidated by anybody who tries to tell us whom we should have for our friends, and we make no alliances merely for the sake of alliances or of vague principles, but only in support of our enlightened self-interest. We cultivate the friendship of all, and are prepared to take advantage of every country's technical skills if to do so does not prejudice our interests or

our independence. This gives us great freedom of action – much more than that enjoyed by any dogma-ridden state.[42]

The same year, 1955, also saw Iran take its seat as an elected member of the United Nations Security Council (UNSC)[43] and, some three months later, it took this opportunity to support UNSC Resolution 106.[44] This resolution was conceived as a result of the Israeli Defence Forces (IDF) engaging Egyptian forces near Gaza on 28 February 1955. The resulting battle left 39 dead, 32 wounded and destroyed several military installations.[45] The resolution, *inter alia,* condemned Israel for the attack and called upon it to prevent further attacks.[46] Referring to the incident, Iranian Representative Nasrollah Entezam noted, 'we know upon whom the heavy responsibility rests for an act of aggression which caused the death of about 40 persons and the wounding of a similar number'.[47]

However, he continued, 'I am aware of the fact that there exists in this area a state of tension which often provokes attacks that are difficult to prevent. But the existence of that tension could never justify a premeditated and organised attack carried out by the forces of the regular army'. The Iranian delegation wanted Israel punished. As Entezam noted, 'We could have wished that the Council would go further and recommended effective measures to punish the aggressor and prevent the recurrence of such acts'.[48]

Iran voted in favour of UNSC Resolution 107,[49] which called for Israel and Egypt to co-operate with the Chief of Staff of the United Nations Truce Supervision Organization in Palestine (UNTSO).[50] Iran also voted in favour of UNSC Resolution 108, concerning the maintenance of the cease-fire.[51] Iranian disquiet was further highlighted by Representative Abdoh, who stated, 'I should like to refer to an event of the utmost seriousness, which ... occurred on 31 August, when six United Nations military observers and three other members of the United Nations staff were detained by the Israel authorities in Beersheba ...' Abdoh believed that such actions would, 'not only ... obstruct the work of the Truce Supervision Organisation, but also ... damage the prestige of the United Nations'. The diplomat added that he 'should like to try to believe that this act was committed without the knowledge of the Government of Israel'.[52] Thus, the UNSC, like the UNGA, was used by the Iranian government to express its concerns over actions on the Middle East, although ensuring that the rhetoric, whilst serving as a sop to the Arab bloc, did little to adversely affect its relationship with Israel.

The budding alliance between Jerusalem and Tehran also began to develop economically. For the three years preceding the 1956 Sinai Campaign, Israel had received approximately 30 per cent of its oil from the USSR. The oil was paid for in significant part by Israeli exports[53] and created a highly advantageous balance of payments for Israel.[54] Indeed, a diplomat from the British Foreign Office, C.A.E. Shuckburgh, in a meeting with Platt, a managing director of Shell, mentioned that British Petroleum (BP) and Shell had been under pressure from the Israelis to lower their prices. To Platt, it seemed that, 'The obvious solution ... was to supply from Persia, which would effect a reduction in cost of £1 per ton even if the oil was shipped around the cape'. However, Shuckburgh expressed, there was a concern that, 'empty tankers which had called at Haifa might be prevented by the Egyptians from passing through Suez or even seized'. Platt also endeavoured to find out whether shipments 'could not be made from Persia to "Cape Town for orders" and not direct to Haifa'.[55]

Moreover, the British Embassy in Tel Aviv noted that Horowitz, then head of the Bank of Israel, had expressed his hope that the British government would 'do their best to encourage the transaction, not only because supplies of Persian oil, even if they were shipped round the Cape, would save Israel a substantial amount of foreign currency', but it would also make clear to all that the British government 'were opposed to any extension of the Arab boycott'.[56] Furthermore, the British revealed that, in February 1955, 'Representatives of the Israel Fuel Corporation were in Tehran pressing the Persian Government to agree to the purchase of some of the 12.5 per cent free oil'. The Economic Counsellor believed that this was a political issue for Iran, as it was likely to impact on Persian-Arab relations.[57] The Israeli Representatives appeared to tire of waiting for the Iranian government to reach a decision concerning their requests and left the country. The British Embassy in Tehran revealed that before the men had left, however, they had 'mooted the idea of arranging for oil shipments from Persia through Swiss intermediaries'. The embassy also stated that 'the Israelis hoped to buy 750,000 barrels a year from Persia'.[58]

The British were content to allow Iran to sell oil to Israel. In fact, D.L. Stewart of the British Foreign Office noted that the oil sales would not 'damage the market in Israel of our major oil companies'. This was largely due to the belief that 'In general, Persian-Arab relations are of no very great concern to us.' However, the British thought, this would change were Iran to join a 'Middle East defence organisation'.[59]

In Jerusalem, though, Iran was considered to be preferable to the USSR as a future supplier of oil, as gases for fertilisers and chemicals could be extracted from Iranian oil, whereas Soviet oil had a weak chemical content.[60] Moreover, the stable supply of Soviet oil was not guaranteed for both logistical and political reasons, while Iranian production far exceeded that required for Iran's domestic use.[61] Furthermore, Israel was interested in the potential strategic value of Iranian oil, specifically its impact on the Suez Canal blockade. Rising economic relations between the two countries were not solely beneficial to Israel, though; Iran required buyers for its oil and the proceeds generated were essential in funding its economic development.[62]

Thus by 1955, the relationship between Israel and Iran, although not reaching the level of residential diplomatic delegations, nevertheless, was extraordinary and the continuing Israeli presence in Iran allowed Jerusalem a vital channel of communication with a key nation in the Muslim Middle East that would soon prove its worth. In Jerusalem, eyes began to look towards another country in the region that had been identified as a potential element to Israel's Policy of the Periphery. Turkey, it was hoped, would translate its mutual interests with Israel into a bi-lateral relationship.

Israel and Turkey

It is well documented that Turkey voted against the UNGA partition plan in November 1947.[63] Relations between Turk and Jew over the future of the *Yishuv,* the pre-state Jewish community in Palestine, though, had far preceded this historical event. Indeed, in the early

1880s, Sultan of the Ottoman Empire, Abdul Hamid, had identified the potential benefit of a Jewish revival in Palestine, chiefly as a prospective source of income for the economically troubled Ottomans. But Hamid was unwilling to allow another diverse national group access to lands in his empire. He was aware that the Jews, were he to permit their immigration to Palestine, would be in propinquity to Jerusalem, Islam's third holiest site. Cautious not to exacerbate existing tensions with the Armenian population, Hamid was also conscious of the possible effect on the various separatist movements in the Balkans and East Anatolia.[64] As a result, he prohibited Jewish immigration.[65] This prohibition, although symbolically damaging to Jewish nationalist aspirations, was inefficiently enforced due to both Zionist determination to create a National Homeland and a lacklustre approach by the Ottomans and, in 1900, the Jewish population of the *Yishuv* had doubled to some 50,000, the preponderance of whom were new immigrants.[66]

Ultimately, it was Theodore Herzl, the founder of political Zionism, who, in June 1896, succeeded in convincing the Sultan to give his implied consent to the Zionist enterprise in Palestine. Herzl arrived in Istanbul and although not granted an audience with the Sultan, was nevertheless asked on his behalf to aid in promulgating the Ottoman cause overseas, a cause gravely tarnished in the aftermath of the Armenian massacres, and to organise a substantial loan of some T£2,000,000 for the financially strapped Ottomans.[67] Subsequently, in a meeting with the Sultan five years later, on 19 May 1901, Herzl presented a tailored financial plan that would direct control of the Ottoman Public Debt Administration away from the European elites, and into the hands of the Sultan. The plan would essentially involve the purchase of Ottoman debt by a Jewish collective, within a number of years. This would be done, Herzl stated, in return for an Imperial Charter for the Colonisation of Palestine.[68] The plan was particularly attractive to the Sultan, as the moribund state of the Ottoman economy upon his ascension to power had facilitated its control by Europe, and, as a result, Hamid was determined to forge a new economic policy, driven by the need to repay the debts and regain control of the economy.[69] The Sultan was intrigued, but did not acquiesce to Herzl's proposition.

Additional visits to the Sultan by Zionist Representatives in 1904 and 1907[70] also failed in obtaining the Charter. In 1909, the Young Turks, a group of army officers who favoured the reformation of the Ottoman Empire, toppled Hamid, and, on 20 September 1914, they rescinded the 'Red Slip', the temporary residence permit to Palestine, and icon of Ottoman opposition to immigration, and ultimately abolished all restrictions on Jewish settlement in Palestine.[71]

This attitude towards the Jews remained constant throughout the period of transition from Ottoman Empire to Turkish Republic. However, there were two central issues, albeit conspirational in nature, which served as potential spoilers for closer ties between Turk and Jew: the first was that Jews were seen by some in Turkey as having behaved treacherously towards the Ottoman Empire in its final years, deliberately facilitating its disintegration in order to ascertain the creation of a Jewish state.[72] The second told of the Jews, along with other minorities, being predominant in the Turkish trade and finance sectors, an issue which fuelled latent and internecine unease, eventually spilling over into anti-Jewish violence, witnessed in the events of Thrace in 1934, when many thousands of Jews fled to Istanbul in order to escape pogroms and anti-Jewish violence, causing the government to send military forces to the area in an attempt to maintain order.[73]

However, Kemal Atatürk, himself considered by some to be a *donme*, a Jewish convert to Islam who clandestinely practised Judaism,[74] was known by many Jews of the Turkish Republic as 'El Gadol', 'The Great' in Ladino. This was largely due to his removal of Islam from Turkish politics, the abolition of the Caliphate, and his belief that the Jews, as loyal citizens of the Turkish Republic, should live freely. In addition, he ceased the jurisdiction of Sharia courts, ensured that the state took control of education, nationalised devout foundations and closed religious orders and brotherhoods; potential bases of power for his opponents.[75]

Moreover, Atatürk appointed the first Jewish member of the Turkish parliament, Abravaya Marmarah, in 1935. The same year also saw a delegation of Turkish Jews competing in the Maccabi games in Palestine in 1935; Turkish involvement in the Levant Fair in Tel Aviv in 1936, which had been organised by Zionist figures and 1938 saw

Representatives from the *Yishuv* participate in the International Fair in Izmir.[76] Allowing Jews to live freely, though, was not a new phenomenon. Indeed, under Ottoman tradition, every non-Muslim minority was granted autonomy in running its own institutions and the proclamation of the *Hatti Humayun* in 1856, deemed all Ottoman citizens to be equal in law. Additionally, in 1926, Turkey adopted the Swiss Civil Code, after which the Jewish community renounced its minority status.[77] And it was Atatürk in 1933, who allowed several Jewish professors to escape Nazi Germany and settle in Turkey. During the Second World War, the Jews of Turkey were safe.[78] Indeed, a number of Turkish diplomats aided in saving the lives of Jews during the war, in particular, the Consul of Rhodes from 1943–44, Salahattin Ülkümen, who became the first Muslim to be recognised as a Righteous Gentile by the Yad VaShem Holocaust memorial in Jerusalem.[79]

After the collapse of the Ottoman Empire, which had ruled for some 400 years, Turkey attempted, in short order, to forge a foreign policy that would ensure its freedom from entanglement in potential geo-political mires, both within the regional Soviet sphere of influence, and within the Muslim world.[80] The combined threats of Nasserist expansionism, Arab nationalism and regional Soviet penetration were cause for significant concern in Ankara, but it was the mutual fear of communism which initially served to complicate the embryonic relationship between the Jewish state and Turkey and led Turkey to vote against partition.

Over the years, however, the tensions that characterized Turkish-Arab relations, a Kemalist foreign policy and geo-political factors contrived to facilitate the Israeli-Turkish relationship. Indeed, both Arabs and Turks used the Ottoman Empire, particularly its collapse, as an issue for mutual antagonism; many Arabs regarded Turkey as an imperial power and many Turks insisted that the Arabs betrayed Turkey through their involvement in the so-called Arab revolt of the First World War.[81] In addition, there were mutual land claims, with Turkey claiming the province of Mosul from Iraq, and Syria, the Turkish district of Hatay, which Turkey had annexed in 1939. The latter issue, in particular, served as proof to many Arabs that Turkey was collaborating with the West, as France had agreed to the annexation of Hatay.[82]

It was due to the tension between Moscow and Ankara that one of Turkey's immediate national interests had been ensuring a continued British presence in the Middle East after London had transferred the Palestine question to the UN. The prevailing belief in Ankara was that the newly born Jewish state would be vulnerable to Communist infiltration,[83] a belief strengthened by the Kremlin's support of the partition plan, by the fact that many of Israel's political leaders had come from an Eastern European political culture and because many of them had been involved with the, essentially Communist, kibbutz movement.[84]

To be sure, this fear was disseminated to the Turkish public via several of the country's newspapers, all convinced that the USSR would move swiftly to any area of the globe where chaos reigned, or political vacuum appeared. This concern was further heightened by reports in a Turkish newspaper that officers from the Yugoslav army were on their way to aid the Jews in fighting, proof if any were needed, that the Communists were determined to subvert the political direction of the Jewish state. There were also statements emanating from British and Arab sources, claiming that many of the Jews fleeing Eastern Europe for Palestine were, in fact, Communists, sent to lay the foundations for a Communist state. Moreover, there were rumours asserting that the Jews were being aided in their struggle by Soviet officers.[85]

A relationship between the Jewish Agency and Turkey had begun to flourish in 1938, when then president of the Agency, Chaim Weizmann, travelled to Turkey and held meetings with Prime Minister Bayar and then minister of national economy, Ismet Inonu. It was during these meetings that several Turkish statesmen revealed their admiration for the successful economic and social development of the Zionist movement in Palestine. Indeed, Bayar suggested that American Jews import Turkish items, paying for them in dollars, in order to allow Turkey to wean itself from its economic dependence on Germany. Moreover, during the dark times of the Second World War, Turkish officials had allowed the Jewish Agency to operate under the auspices of the British Embassy in Turkey, allowing many Jews to be spirited via Turkey, to Palestine.[86]

There was additional contact between Turkey and the Jewish Agency, particularly when the Foreign Trade Institute, created by the Agency and the Palestine Manufacturers' Association, opened a branch in Turkey. As well as participating in the Izmir International Fair in 1938, the Agency was present at the fairs of 1939 and 1943, during which the Zionist flag was raised, along with those of Turkey and Britain; the Star of David being the only non-state flag present at the event. After the discussions concerning the status of the Jewish Agency, Turkey named the experienced diplomat, Selim Sarper as its permanent Representative to the UN. Sarper, a man who apparently had access to Inonu and enjoyed his support in political matters, was well known amongst the members of the Jewish Agency, many of whom respected his role, in particular, in rescuing Jewish children from the Nazis in Europe and transporting them to Palestine.[87]

The Turkish diplomatic position *vis-à-vis* the partition of Palestine was enunciated in a speech made by Turkish UN delegate and ambassador to Washington since 1945, Hüseyin Ragip Baydur, in May 1947,

> In the Middle Ages, Jews who had been turned out of certain European countries sought refuge in Turkey. Since then, a considerable Jewish colony has been living in Turkey prosperously and in full possession of all civil liberties...a Representative of the Jewish Agency...came to see me to express to me the appreciation of the Jewish Agency for humane help and treatment afforded by the Turkish Republic to the Jews who had been the victims of oppression in certain European countries during the Second World War. These two instances, one remote and the other immediate, illustrate the attitude and the feeling of the Turkish people toward the Jews.[88]

That said and careful not to alienate the Muslim bloc at the UN, Baydur revealed,

> On the other hand, the Turkish nation has a long common history with the Arabs ... we lived and worked together with the Arabs for centuries with mutual respect for each other's national

feelings and social rights. As a result of historical evolution in the lives of the nations, they have now attained their independence. Although our frontiers are separated, our hearts are still united. The Turkish nation sincerely desires to see the new Arab States happy and prosperous.[89]

Turkey was conspicuous by its silence at the majority of UN debates concerning the Palestine Question, both prior and subsequent to partition. At the second Special Session of the UNGA, meeting from 16 April to 14 May 1948, Turkey's behaviour is of interest, particularly as the Turkish delegation offered a partial explanation for its rejection of partition. Representative Kural stated on 1 May 1948, that while he was 'unwilling to support any proposal for the establishment of trusteeship over a people completely capable of self-government', nevertheless believed that 'some measure was necessary to stop bloodshed and to calm the disquiet created'. He 'did not consider that the decision on partition, which his delegation had voted against, was a solution to the problem'. Kural believed that 'a trusteeship, or rather a provisional regime, provided that its temporary character was stressed ... might lead to satisfactory results'.[90]

On 30 June 1948, although yet to recognise its independence, Ankara signed a postal agreement with Israel. This was justified as a humanitarian act for the 10,000 Turkish citizens living in Israel at the time. Moreover, the Turkish government rescinded a travel ban in September 1948, initially put in place to ensure that Turkish citizens did not enter the war zone and Ankara radio declared that all Turkish citizens were able to immigrate to any destination they desired. Turkey's Jews seized this opportunity and, in the initial years of statehood, some 40,000 moved to Israel.[91]

During the 1948 Arab-Israeli war, Turkey remained neutral, proactively preventing both Turks who wanted to fight on the side of the Arabs and a number of Turkish Jews who wanted to aid Israel, from entering the war zone.[92] After the war, Turkey voted in favour of UNGA Resolution 194 (III) of 11 December 1948, calling for the establishment of a Palestine Conciliation Commission (PCC),[93] which, in the face of Arab opposition, joined as a member, in the company of the US and

France. Of the members of the commission, it was believed that the US would be pro-Israel, France would be neutral and Turkey would represent Muslim sentiment, thereby creating political equilibrium. However, the Turkish delegate was not only anti-Communist, but also visited Israel.[94]

As a result of the war, Israel was unable to produce the food needed to sustain its population; a situation that worsened as new immigrants arrived to the Jewish state from various parts of the world. Turkey agreed to export produce to Israel, and in May 1948, a Turkish ship bound for Israel was captured by Syrian forces, the crew imprisoned and the food confiscated. It was not an isolated incidence and resulted in Israel offering war risk insurance and the use of its own transport ships in future trade dealings with Turkey.[95]

Furthermore, in March 1949, Turkey became the first Muslim state to grant *de facto* recognition to Israel.[96] In May of the same year, it abstained in the vote over Israel's admission to the UN,[97] and diplomatic relations between the two countries were established at the level of legation in March 1950,[98] with a Minister Plenipotentiary appointed to Tel Aviv and an Israeli legation established in Ankara. Following its decision to recognise Israel, Turkey was castigated by the Arab states for betraying the spirit of Islamic solidarity. The Turks, though, effectively countered this claim by stating that they were among the last of the Western European states to recognise Israel[99] and that the Egyptian-Israeli Armistice Agreement of February 1949, in addition to the contacts transpiring between Israel and other Arab states, were proof that these countries had recognised Israel prior to Turkey doing so.[100] Moreover, Ankara hoped, recognising Israel would aid in defeating anti-Turkish perceptions in the West and encourage Western nations to offer it support, particularly important for Turkey in the context of the developing Cold War.[101]

For Israel, diplomatic relations with Turkey were of the utmost strategic significance and this was manifested by Jerusalem's insistence on a *military attaché* to its legation in Ankara.[102] Moreover, Jerusalem was aware that Turkey was a nascent international power, actively seeking multi-lateral defence agreements, including NATO membership.[103] This, *inter alia*, led Israel to believe that developing ties with Turkey would draw it closer to the West.[104] In addition, Jerusalem saw the potential in developing ties with a Muslim state as a means of preventing the Arab-Israeli conflict being perceived as a purely religious-ethnic struggle.[105]

Turkey's desire to belong to the Western camp continued after the Turkish elections in 1950, when the Democratic Party, under Adnan Menderes, came to power. Menderes criticised his predecessors for failing to obtain Turkish membership in NATO and, in July 1951, his foreign minister Fuat Koprulu stated that 'The defence of the Middle East is necessary for the defence of Europe as regards strategic and economic matters. Therefore, after joining NATO, we will enter into . . . negotiations with interested parties in order to execute the role due to us in the Middle East'.[106]

The character of the formal initial diplomatic steps between Israel and Turkey was one of wariness and uncertainty. The Israeli Foreign Ministry's Middle East Department had initially attempted to construct an outline for the development of mutual relations based on non-alignment. The dilemma for Israel was in trying to reconcile its desire to maintain, concomitantly, strong ties with East European Jewry and develop ties with Turkey.[107]

For the former, Jerusalem was required to maintain diplomatic channels with the governments of various East European countries, anathema to Turkish foreign policy.[108] Moreover, the fact that Israel, *ipso facto*, was unable to adopt a policy of open hostility towards the USSR signalled to Turkey that the Jewish state was already filled with Bolsheviks.[109] For Israel, convincing Turkey that it was not a Communist state became a matter of urgency.[110]

To this end, Ankara received instruction from Jerusalem on the political system of Israel, which emphasised the weakness of the political hard-left in the Israeli Knesset.[111] The Israeli government also elaborated on the predicament of Soviet Jewry, a plight unlikely to endear Israeli Jews to communism, and revealed that Israel was receiving aid from the US. In Jerusalem, this fact alone was thought to be enough to convince the Turks of its Western orientation.[112] The Turkish disquiet was further augmented by a number of religious factors: several aspects of Islam had been repressed under Kemalism in the name of modernisation and statism.[113] But with the rise to power of Turkey's Democratic Party in 1950, some restrictions were lifted: the Arabic call to prayer was legalised, there were Koran readings over the radio, the Religious Ministry had its budget vastly increased,[114] and there was a *laissez-faire* approach from the political elite towards the appearance of traditional Muslim dress and the use of the Arabic alphabet.[115] The atmosphere in Turkey had changed and Islam was no longer proscribed, with Islamic sects, although remaining illegal, no longer actively pursued and harassed.[116]

Moreover, the Islamic weekly *Sebilurresad* conducted a campaign during the winter of 1950–51, against what it perceived as the three dangers: the black menace (Christianity), the yellow menace (Judaism and Freemasonry), and the red menace (Communism and Atheism).[117] These attacks reached a dramatic climax when the editor of the newspaper was arrested after attempting to disparage Kemalism, by blaming it for Turkey's ties with Israel. However, the dominant belief amongst Turkish policy makers was that the powerful Jewish political lobby in Washington and pro-Israel sentiment in Congress could help to overcome the sizeable Greek and Armenian lobbies, which were growing in influence and were seen as inherently hostile to Turkish interests.[118] For Turkey, such support could potentially solve existential issues, such as the precise location of the Western line of defence against Soviet aggression, a matter of some concern for Ankara as 'out of area' definitions did little to clarify Turkey's significance in NATO contingency plans.[119]

Bilateral trade also cemented the relationship. Indeed, throughout the period 1946–49, Israel was Turkey's third largest export market.[120] Israel sold Turkey technological products and expertise and, in return, Turkey sold Israel agricultural produce, such as wheat, eggs and raw materials. This had special significance for Israel, as the implementation of the Arab boycott had prevented it from importing foodstuffs from its neighbours. Moreover, by the beginning of the 1950s, Turkey was keen to find alternative trade partners to Germany, then its main source of imports, due to its rising trade deficit with Bonn.[121]

Consequently, Turkey began to import greater quantities of industrial products from, *inter alia*, Spain, Yugoslavia and Israel. Israel, in particular, was proficient in refining oil and the Israeli company, *Solel Boneh,* the construction arm of the *Histadrut,* Israel's General Federation of Labourers, was constructing apartments and airfields in Turkey,[122] while Turkey provided a ready market for the budding Israeli manufacturing sector in refrigerators and other electrical appliances.[123]

The Korean War of 1950–53 was a watershed in Israel's evolving ties with Turkey, with Israeli opposition to the Communist invasion of Korea serving as a vehicle to further develop the relationship.[124] Turkish forces had seen action in Korea, with some 5,200 Turkish military personnel losing their lives,[125] and the Turkish perception was that the war had been a setback for the US. Moreover, returning Turkish soldiers had anecdotal validation of a lack of fighting prowess amongst US forces. The immediate concern for Turkey was that the US had apparently failed to protect Korea, even with a military presence in Japan: what could be expected of it were Turkey under threat?[126]

During the Korean War, a central political issue in Turkey was its admission to NATO, particularly because of the potential Arab-Soviet threat emanating from the south. Also, the Turkish Democrat party had started to distribute state land to the poorest amongst the landless peasants; US foreign aid was used to purchase tractors and many Turks began to see the first fruits of modernisation.[127] The Democrats saw an opportunity to synthesise this modernisation, with stronger ties with the West. Consequently, in 1950, Turkey applied for membership to NATO and it was the fighting prowess shown by its soldiers in the Korean War, coupled with unease in the West over regional stability, which ensured Turkey's acceptance to the organisation in 1952.[128] For the US and Israel, the potential of the Turkish military in countering Soviet and Arab regional designs was of great strategic significance. In particular, NATO saw its southern flank extend to the eastern Mediterranean, covering Turkey's Black Sea coast, through which the USSR had access to the Mediterranean.

To further cement the evolving relationship between Israel and Turkey, in 1952, Jerusalem adopted its formal policy on Cyprus.[129] In essence, the Greek desire was to see *enosis,* or unification of the island, while Turkey wished to see the continuation of the *status quo*. In order to ensure the adoption of the Turkish line, Israeli diplomats in Jerusalem urged that 'the consideration of our relations with Greece should not burden us excessively'.[130] In fact, Israel strove to ensure that *enosis* was disparaged, portraying it as artificial and the work of the Greeks of Cyprus, where, it was maintained, communism was rife.[131] In this way, Jerusalem saw no need to align itself with a movement which would again allow Turkey to call into question Israel's political hue.

Concurrently, at the UN, the Turkish delegation adopted a mollifying stance on the Arab-Israeli dispute. Indeed, Representative Ilhan Savut noted at a meeting of the Ad Hoc Political Committee, chaired by Selim Sarper that 'the Conciliation Commission for Palestine had been established in order to make a United Nations organ available to assist the parties concerned to settle the differences outstanding between them'. He added 'unfavourable political circumstances had prevented the Commission for Palestine from carrying out its task'.[132] This approach was reiterated by Savut, two weeks later, when, talking of the Palestinian refugees, he claimed 'Two steps should be taken by the United Nations at once. First, it should continue to provide direct assistance' and second, 'ways and means must be found to provide the necessary economic setting in which the refugees would be able to support themselves'. Moreover, Savut emphasised his country's empathy with the Palestinian refugees. Turkey, he noted, 'had made what contributions it could, either directly or via the Turkish Red Crescent' and that Turkey 'had received nearly 155,000 refugees since 1950, about 2,500 of whom had come through arrangements with the International Refugee Organisation'.[133]

With American support, Turkey and Greece signed an agreement on Friendship and Co-operation with Yugoslavia on 28 February 1953. This agreement became the Balkan Defence Pact, when it was signed by the three countries in Bled, Yugoslavia, the following year.[134] Israel was enticed by the potential benefits of these agreements. Indeed, the Israeli Foreign Ministry argued that 'it (is) incumbent on us ... to approach this group of states'.[135] Moreover, Israel believed that, were Ankara focused on these new agreements, it would have less time and inclination to involve itself in the Middle East and, as a result, would be less susceptible to Arab attempts to embroil it in the region. In fact, an Israeli diplomat opined that the relationship between Turkey and Israel would be unlikely to be adversely affected by an increase in Arab influence, but rather by complications in *Solel Boneh's* operations in Turkey and the continuance of three-way business deals, where Israel was deemed to make too large a profit.[136] Israeli overtures towards joining the signatories were comprehensively rejected.[137]

Furthermore, Israel was disconcerted by what it deemed to be Turkey's *Ostpolitik*. Jerusalem believed that any Turkish pact with Pakistan and Iraq would weaken its relationship with Ankara, due to Pakistan's opposition to Israel,[138] and that it would be expedient for Turkey to follow its Balkan policies, rather than look eastwards. Nevertheless, what would eventually evolve into the Baghdad Pact[139] was instigated by the visit of John Foster Dulles, then US Secretary of State, to the Middle East in 1953, in order to estimate regional support for a Western-led federation of states, which would provide a bulwark against the spread of communism.[140]

In Israel, the belief was that Turkey had little to gain from these alliances. However, Turkey saw the potential in Iraq, which had a considerable Communist movement and suffered from internal instability due to communal differences between Sunnis, Shiites and Kurds. Moreover, Iraq was positioned at the centre of the triangle with Turkey and Iran and, although Ankara was not enthused with possible links with Pakistan, it was aware that Pakistan had airfields within striking distance of Siberia and the Soviet military industries located therein, thereby revealing its strategic importance to the West.[141]

The Israeli government, though, feared that arms supplied to Iraq and Pakistan would eventually find their way to the Kurdish rebels in Turkey and might be used by the Iraqi regime against Israeli interests.[142] Moreover, neither Iraq nor Pakistan was overtly anti-Communist and the Iraqi military was weak. Israel maintained that the ideal solution would be to invade and conquer Iraq in the event of a regional conflict involving the Superpowers. However, Ankara remained steadfast in its desire for *rapprochement* with Iraq and deemed all those opposing it as potential enemies.[143]

Thus, Israel began to consider the improbable: potential Turkish aid to Iraqi forces in a military confrontation between Israel and Iraq.[144] In fact, Israeli concerns over such Turkish actions were relayed by the British Embassy in Tel Aviv, which, in a telegram to Whitehall, noted that, 'in the press of July 8 ... Turkey had assured Israel ... that there was no room for any apprehension by Israel that the relations of friendship between the two countries had diminished in any way'.[145]

Moreover, the embassy produced a document stating that 'The more intelligent Israeli' would see 'a chance that the pact will split the Arab League, drive Egypt and Iraq apart, and so diminish the combined political and military strength of Israel's enemies'. Furthermore, 'he hopes ... that Turkey ... may be able gradually to influence Iraq, and through Iraq some at least of the other Arab States, to adopt a constructive policy towards Israel'.[146]

Conversely, the document told of the Israeli fear of Turkey abandoning the Jewish state in order to facilitate the agreement between itself and Iraq. Furthermore, the British believed that, even if the Arab League were divided, some Israelis would 'argue that Egypt will seek support in the Arab States by stepping up her hostility towards Israel, and that Iraq ... will ... compete'. A final, nightmare scenario for the Israelis, according to the British, was that Iraq, after signing a pact with Turkey, would 'proceed to realise her dream of a Greater Syria, which would bring Iraq right up to Israel's frontier'.[147]

In 1955, Turkey assumed its seat as an elected member of the UNSC.[148] The Turkish delegation took this opportunity, like Iran, to vote for UNSC Resolutions 106,[149] 107[150] and 108.[151] Talking of the Gaza incident between Israel and Egypt, Turkish Representative Sarper, president of the UNSC at the time, stated that 'according to the resolution adopted by the Egyptian-Israeli Mixed Armistice Commission on 6 March 1955, it appears to have been a "prearranged and planned attack by the Israeli authorities" and "committed by Israel regular army forces against the Egyptian regular army force"'. He also added that, 'the Security Council cannot overlook the gravity of this particular incident, nor can it withhold its blame for the use of force in violation of the armistice agreement'.[152]

This reaction to the Gaza incident is partially explained by Sarper's remarks to the delegation of the USSR. He stated that,

> Leaving aside the question of the Gaza incident and other adjacent problems, he [the Representative from the USSR] made a statement to the effect that tension in this area results from the policy of certain States, inasmuch as these States pursue a policy in the Near and Middle East not of strengthening peace and cementing friendly relations ... but of forming military blocs, which is bound to create a threat to the national independence and security of those countries.[153]

In response to this attack from the USSR on the Policy of the Periphery, Sarper retorted, 'The only reason for the existence of the present tension, not only in the Middle East but in the entire world, is the very extensive bloc formed by the Soviet Union in pursuance of its aims for domination'. Moreover, he continued, 'This propaganda manoeuvre against so-called military blocs is aimed at the disintegration of the common security front erected by the free nations as a vital necessity for preserving their very existence' and 'These efforts against the formation of such a front of peace and security ... are a clear indication that the Soviet Union has an interest in thwarting the establishment of peace and stability in this region'.[154] The Turkish delegation ended 1955, like Iran, with expressions of concern over the plight of the Palestinian refugees, with Representative Menemencioglu stating that 'the problem of the refugees was a matter of deep concern' because 'Turkey had many ties with the Arab countries and also because the problem directly affected the peace and security in the Near East'.[155]

This period succinctly reveals the tensions that Turkey was experiencing, especially at the UN, over its desire to maintain and develop ties with both the Arab world and Israel, whilst, at the same time, confronting the USSR, whose existence in the Middle East was a source of great concern. The Suez War would intervene, though, with its own consequences for Turkey and the region.

Israel and Ethiopia

Although the Sinai Campaign of 1956 and its immediate aftermath marked the crystallisation of the Policy of the Periphery, special relations had been forming between Israel and Africa, particularly Ethiopia, for some years before that.[156] Israel's Africa Policy was initially designed both to complement the Policy of the Periphery in an attempt to overcome the rejection facing it in the Arab world and to present a formal demonstration of its non-aligned status.[157] The prevailing logic in Jerusalem dictated that, were Israel to recognise the emerging African states and aid in their development, it would attain their appreciation and benevolence.[158] Moreover, Israel's diminutive size allowed the view that its aid would not be coercive, rather altruistic.[159]

African states emerging from colonial rule and requiring political and economic aid, welcomed Israeli support as a fellow new state which had recently encountered similar socio-economic problems.[160] Israel believed it could make itself relevant to such states and provide something more than the large-scale technology offered by the Powers.[161] As Ambassador Yaakov Shimoni, a senior diplomat at the Israeli Foreign Ministry explained, Israel could offer 'something connected with building a nation. How do you build a society, an administration? In that sense, first Asian countries and later African countries thought that they saw in Israel some elements which they could use'.[162]

There were also political connotations. Ben-Gurion addressed the issue of friendship amongst Israel, Africa and Asia by emphasizing the similar backgrounds and political experiences of all these countries.[163] 'We have faced and tackled many of the problems of development which face them; our experience with such problems is recent; and we have registered major successes with comparatively meagre resources.'[164] As a senior Israeli Foreign Ministry official explained, 'Africa is a battleground between Israel and the Arabs. It is a fight of life or death for us'.[165]

Jerusalem believed that the history of Arab involvement in slave trading would encourage African states to pursue a relationship with Israel and there was also significant Israeli interest in gaining the support of the smaller African states in order to offset the hostile Arab and Muslim voting blocs facing Israel at the UN.[166] As an Israeli Foreign Ministry official explained,

> Africa's friendship has banished the spectre of Israel's isolation in the Third World. The vigorous stand taken by African leaders in advocacy of peaceful settlement of conflicts has strengthened Israel's conviction that the states of Africa are able and willing to play a central part in bringing about permanent peace in the Middle East. President Nasser in his 'Philosophy of Revolution' insists that the way to Africa leads through Cairo. Everything today points to the likelihood that the way to Cairo may lead through Africa.[167]

The sole political condition attached to aid given by Israel was that the recipient government diplomatically recognise the Jewish state.[168] As Ambassador Shimoni explained,

> We were particularly interested to be accepted by the emerging group of nations to which we thought we belonged. We knew, of course, that there were difficulties on the way. These were two kinds. One kind was the doubt about the legitimacy concerning the birth of Israel and the nature of Israel. There is no sense in glossing that over. We cannot close our eyes to that. Some nations, certainly our Arab neighbour nations, some Asian and later some African nations, had doubts about the legitimacy of the birth of Israel; some even totally objected to the event. They regarded the whole process of our emergence into independence and nationhood as something unjust, unjustified, illegitimate.[169]

The potential benefits of overcoming Arab efforts to both isolate Israel in the world and to portray it as a bulwark of imperialism and communism in the Middle East were significant. Thus, Israel, working through the *Histadrut* and other non-governmental channels, established non-official contacts amongst African nationalists in colonial territories, with a view to aiding them in the transition to independence, and thus, facilitating inter-governmental relations.[170]

Golda Meir, described as the 'architect of Israel's Africa policy',[171] explained Jerusalem's attitude towards Africa in the following terms,

> Like them, we had shaken off foreign rule; like them, we had had to learn for ourselves how to reclaim the land, how to increase the yields of our crops, how to irrigate, how to raise poultry, how to live together and how to defend ourselves. Independence had come to us as, it was coming to Africa, not served up on a silver platter but after years of struggle, and we had had to learn-partly through our own mistakes-the high cost of self-determination.[172]

She went on to reveal that 'We did what we did in Africa not because it was just a policy purely of enlightened self interest-a matter of *quid pro quo*-but because it was a continuation of our own most valued traditions and an expression of our own deepest historic ties'.[173]

Interestingly, such statements echoed the sentiments of Theodore Herzl, the founder of political Zionism, in his novel Old-Newland (*Altneuland*) where one of the characters, Steineck, says gravely,

> There is still one problem of racial misfortune unsolved. The depths of that problem, in all their horror, only a Jew can fathom. I mean the Negro problem ... Think of the hair-raising horrors of the slave trade. Human beings, because their skins are black, are stolen, carried off and sold. Their descendents grow up in alien surroundings despised and hated because their skin is differently pigmented. I am not ashamed to say though I be thought ridiculous, now that I have lived to see the restoration of the Jews, I should like to pave the way for the restoration of the Negroes.[174]

During the 1950s, the Middle East was experiencing the end of imperialism and the fervour of aspiring independence. At the centre of this dynamic was Egypt under the leadership of Nasser. It appeared that Nasser was attempting to underplay the concept of 'Egyptianism' for the sake of Pan-Arabism and Cairo positioned itself at the centre of the drive for radical change in the region.[175] Moreover, in October 1955, Nasser signed a mutual defence treaty with Syria, and, in the following year, finalised a five-year, trilateral military alliance with Saudi Arabia and Yemen.[176]

Nasser continued his Pan-Arab drive by engaging in more subversive acts. Pro-Nasserist protesters in Jordan forced the resignation of the entire Jordanian cabinet in December 1955, as a reaction to the country's desire to enter the Baghdad pact. Nasser then turned his attention to Africa, where, through the use of propaganda, he attempted to incite the Mau Mau fighters in Kenya and Islamic minorities in Eritrea and Ethiopian Somalia.[177]

The most significant of the African countries for Israel, though, was Ethiopia. Aside from the religious ties that connected Israel and Ethiopian Jews, known as the *Falasha* and *Beta Israel*, there were a number of additional factors which served to create intimate ties between the two countries: Haile Selassie considered himself to be the 'Lion of Judah' and a direct descendant of the Jewish people.[178] Moreover, Selassie and his family had spent time in Jerusalem during the Italian conquest of Ethiopia in 1936 and it was upon his return that he decided to pursue bilateral ties with Jerusalem.[179]

In addition, during the Second World War, a number of Jewish soldiers from Palestine served under British officers in the reconquest of Ethiopia. In fact, it was in Ethiopia that one British Officer, Orde Wingate, saw considerable action, eventually leading guerrilla forces in the country. His unit was known as Gideon Force and in January 1940, it was sent into battle. Wingate had initially been recommended for action by Leopold Amery, then British Secretary of State for India, who believed Wingate's previous experience in guerrilla warfare in Palestine would be useful in the struggle against Italian forces in Abyssinia.[180]

Throughout the entirety of the Abyssinian campaign, Wingate was forbidden to return to Palestine, a fact which angered him immensely, but also facilitated in directing his energies to returning Haile Selassie to the throne. Wingate's military operations were performed under the personal patronage of Selassie and he escorted Selassie back to the capital, after uniting the *Hazara* and *Galla* tribes, traditional enemies, in support of the Emperor.[181]

At the UN vote over the partition of Palestine, the Ethiopian stance was one mindful of possible repercussions from both Israel and the Arab world. As a result, Ethiopia abstained and Representative, G. Tesemma, was keen to explain why. He noted that the Ethiopian delegation had 'remained silent throughout the course of the debate on this very difficult and complex problem of Palestine ... I hope that this complete silence on the part of my delegation has not been interpreted to mean an attitude of indifference or disinterest'. Tesemma revealed that it was his 'duty to state that the Ethiopian delegation finds itself unable to subscribe to the principle of partition involved. We cannot agree that a solution to the problem of that geographical, historical and economic unity known as Palestine should be sought through a partition drawn along religious or other lines'.[182] In an attempt to display an even-handed approach to the Palestine question, Tesemma stated that the

> Ethiopian delegation, for its part, particularly conscious of the intimate and historic ties which bind the people of Ethiopia to both the Arab and the Jewish peoples, feels that no plan which has been heretofore presented affords adequate protection to the opposing interests concerned ... We have been, however, unwilling to adopt a purely negative attitude or to stand in the way of any proposal which might gain the requisite majority vote of this General Assembly. Consistent with that policy, therefore, as in the past, we must reluctantly state that, as it is unable to vote in favour of the present proposal for partition, the Ethiopian delegation will abstain from voting.[183]

After gaining political control of Eritrea in 1952, Ethiopia became locked in a secessionist conflict with Eritrean rebels desiring independence. Israel saw the Eritrean movement as potentially threatening to its strategic interests in the Horn of Africa, and was keen to see Ethiopia prevail in the struggle. The Israeli fear was that an independent, Muslim Eritrea may collude with other Muslim countries to prevent Israeli shipping from using the Red Sea.[184]

Whilst the Israelis were concerned over this issue, the Ethiopian stance at the UN had begun to focus on the problem of the Palestinian refugees. It had been noticeable in 1953, when Ethiopian Representative, Medhen, stated that Ethiopia 'had had some experience of the refugee problem and could sympathise with the Palestinian refugees. It was an urgent problem and a speedy solution should be found for it'. He noted that 'there was violent opposition between the views of the parties concerned, and no grounds for agreement had yet been found despite the efforts made', though he 'still hoped that a compromise might be reached'.[185] In practical terms, however, the Ethiopian delegation, through Representative Dawit, noted that although Ethiopia 'had been among the first to contribute to the relief fund for Palestine refugees ... Ethiopia had recently undertaken a number of reforms and construction works which required all its available resources, it would unhappily be unable to make any further contribution'.[186]

This concern for the Palestinian refugees continued and some two years later, Representative Ato Zaude Heywot revealed his country's belief that 'while development programmes aimed at making the refugees self-supporting would partly alleviate their plight, a sound educational programme would be the best method of contributing to their overall welfare in the region as a whole'. The solution to the worsening problem, he believed, would arrive when the 'Governments directly concerned ... live up to their national traditions and co-operate to eliminate a situation that had become an international and religious disgrace'.[187]

For the US, Britain and Israel, the Ethiopia of the 1950s, an isolated Christian state on the east coast of Africa overlooking the approaches to the Red Sea, leading to the Suez Canal and Eilat, was a relatively stable, pro-Western country and, apart from a brief period in the sixteenth century, Ethiopia's Muslim population had never achieved political power and influence in Ethiopian politics. With its Red Sea shoreline, Ethiopia was a nautical aperture to the rest of Africa for Israel and a buffer zone against Egypt and Somalia along its passage to Asia.[188]

Israel believed that a stable Ethiopia could exert a positive influence over the Horn of Africa and, therefore, was keen to prevent any outside attempt at its subversion. The Straits of *Bab el Mandeb* were vital to Israeli shipping as they ensured freedom of passage through to the Red Sea and for the US, a significant presence on the Red Sea and the Indian Ocean was vital for the maintenance of Western economic security; regional stability and security; the prevention of a possible Soviet blockade of Western oil lanes and ensured that the Red Sea and Indian Ocean remained accessible to Israeli, and Israeli-bound shipping.[189]

Ethiopia also found itself in an ongoing dispute with Egypt over the waters of the Nile, with the Ethiopian government expressing the need to utilise more of the Blue Nile water at its source, in Ethiopia. Thus, in 1955 Emperor Haile Selassie tentatively turned to Israel for aid in various fields including irrigation, a controversial matter, given the dispute over the ownership of the Nile waters[190] and the same year saw the first Israeli diplomatic contingent arrive to celebrate Selassie's Silver Jubilee, followed by the opening of an Israeli consulate in 1956.[191]

These diplomatic breakthroughs in the evolving relationship between the two countries were accompanied by a more moderate tone by the Ethiopian delegation at the UN. Indeed, Representative Aklilou noted that

Today the expression 'Middle East' has taken on its true meaning-the link between Eastern and Western worlds. For instance, Ethiopia, which belongs at once to Africa and the Middle East, is bound to Yugoslavia, a European Power, by ties of friendship and mutual understanding, upon which continued co-operation in this Assembly has set the seal.[192]

Almost as an afterthought, Aklilou noted that,

Another subject of future concern should be assistance to the refugees driven from their homes by the unfortunate events in Palestine. They have suffered for too long. Following on its intervention in the Palestine question, it is the duty of our Organisation to take active steps to solve this heart-rending human problem.[193]

By the end of 1955, the Policy of the Periphery was in effect and offered the countries involved the potential for further co-operation and development. The mutual interests and threats had been identified. The continuing Israeli presence in Iran allowed Jerusalem essential access to a major player in the Middle Eastern system and Iran had aided the Iraqi Jews to immigrate to Israel. Turkey, although loathe to jeopardise its ties with the Arab world and expressing concern for the Palestinian refugees, offered Israel a further influential prop in the region and believed that a close alliance would draw both countries closer to the West. For Israel, the 'numbers game' at the UN was beginning to bear fruit. Specifically, the diplomatic cornerstone of the relationship between Israel and Ethiopia had been cemented by the opening of the Israeli mission in Ethiopia and the Ethiopian stance at the UN became more accommodating towards Israel. However, the political situation in the Middle East from 1956–67 would present the budding alliance with considerable challenges.

CHAPTER 2

IRAN AND ISRAEL, 1956–72: CALCULATED AMBIVALENCE?

The Suez War[1] began on 29 October 1956. A central catalyst to the hostilities had been the decision by Nasser to nationalise the Suez Canal on 26 July of the same year. With this move, France and Britain, who had acquired a concession to operate the Suez Canal for 99 years after its opening, ending in 1968, found themselves dependent on Nasser's goodwill for their oil requirements. Both countries saw a potential ally in Israel for a military operation designed to restore the pre-nationalisation *status quo*.

For many of Israel's enemies, its involvement with Britain and France in the Suez Campaign was unequivocal proof that it was a tool of both imperialism and oppression. Consequently, the Jewish state found itself in danger of being ostracised by a significant number of the new and emerging nations which had, hitherto, offered diplomatic potential. The gravity of the situation was succinctly described by David Ha Cohen, former Israeli Ambassador to Burma. Describing the atmosphere at an Asian socialist conference at the time of the Suez War, he revealed, 'the faces around us, even the faces of some devoted friends of Israel, were stern ... It was a wrathful atmosphere ... when even our best friends were liable under pressure of circumstances to join our opponents and to expel us unceremoniously from the organisation we ourselves had helped to establish ...'[2]

At the time of the Suez Campaign, Iran was an elected member of the UNSC and was reticent in condemning the tri-partite action taken against Egypt. Iranian Representative, Entezam, stated that he did not wish to 'say anything at present' which could 'aggravate a situation already exceedingly serious'.[3] Moreover, he revealed a certain exasperation towards the UN in his statement 'it is very difficult to find words' which have not been used 'over and over again in the Council'. Furthermore, Entezam acknowledged that 'we have come to a point where statements are no longer sufficient'. The Representative took his dissatisfaction a step further when he stated that, should a draft resolution sponsored by the US not 'produce any concrete results', then 'the Council must not hesitate any longer to assume the responsibilities incumbent upon it under the Charter'.[4]

Entezam's condemnation of events in Egypt in 1956 was more vociferous at the 750th meeting of the UNSC later that day. Then, he stated 'Two days ago, when we were discussing the Hungarian question, I clearly set forth the position of my delegation by saying that we were opposed to the presence of foreign troops on the territory of another state'.[5] Furthermore, he revealed that his country should like the governments of Britain and France 'to realise the responsibilities which they are assuming in committing acts which are without precedent in the annals of the United Nations'.[6]

Iran voted for US sponsored draft resolution (S/3710)[7] calling for the withdrawal of Israeli forces from Egyptian territory, on 30 October.[8] However, Britain and France, both permanent members of the UNSC, opposed the draft resolution, thereby defeating it. As a result, the UNSC, unable to reach a unanimous decision, proposed referring the issue to the UNGA Emergency Special Session. The motion was adopted by seven votes, including Iran's, to two, with two abstentions. Both Britain and France opposed the motion. However, within the UN Uniting for Peace framework, it was sufficient for seven members of the UNSC to support a draft resolution in order for it to be adopted.[9]

Consequently, the motion was referred to the UNGA Emergency Special Session on 30 October 1956. The attitude of the Iranian delegation at the Special Session remained consistent with that previously presented at the UNSC. In fact, the Iranian Representative waited until 7 November 1956, to comment on the ongoing crisis in Egypt. In addition, Iran supported all UNGA resolutions pertaining to an immediate end to hostilities, the withdrawal of non-indigenous forces and the establishment of a United Nations Emergency Force (UNEF).

Iran's position *vis-à-vis* draft resolutions A/3308 and A/3309 was supportive. Draft resolution A/3308, though, called for the creation of an advisory committee comprising Representatives from Brazil, Canada, Colombia, India, Iran, Norway and Pakistan, which would oversee the UNEF contingent. Iran, while supporting the draft resolution, rejected the notion of Iranian involvement on the committee. Thus, the Iranian Representative stated 'My delegation wholeheartedly supports the draft resolution [A/3308] ... and will vote in favour of it',[10] but he suggested that 'Ceylon should replace Iran.'[11] Consequently, Iran succeeded in distancing itself from proactive involvement in the Suez crisis and the Iranian delegation ensured it would not jeopardise its relations with the US, Israel, or the Arab states.

On 2 February 1956, Entezam alluded to the stance of the Shah towards Iran's relations with Israel in a speech extolling the virtues of a pragmatic approach to international affairs, 'We must all respect the high principles of the Charter ... However ... it is impossible to find a solution which is 100 per cent satisfactory to all ... If we wish to remain realistic ... we must be satisfied from time to time with half measures ... the best is often the enemy of the good'.[12]

In 1957, Israel became largely dependent on Iranian oil, after the USSR halted its supply to Haifa. For Iran, Israel was the largest *per capita* consumer of oil in the region and also offered Iran an alternative route for exporting oil, should Nasser decide to influence its transit through the Suez Canal. To this end, Israel developed a modest fleet of oil tankers and began using a narrow-gauge pipeline to carry crude oil from Eilat, via Beersheba, to Haifa.[13] The precise amount of crude oil that reached Israel from Iran is difficult to verify, but in July 1960, Egypt spearheaded the Arab League in accusing Iran of having supplied Israel with some 8.25 million tons during the Suez War alone.[14]

In April 1957, the British Embassy in Tehran relayed to the British government that, according to foreign reports, a tanker carrying large quantities of oil had reached the Gulf of Aqaba. The British Foreign Ministry made enquiries as to the origin of the oil and came to the conclusion that, as there was no oil deal between Israel and the National Iranian Oil Company (NIOC), a European country had purchased the oil to be shipped to Africa. However, in order to avoid a potentially embarrassing situation between Britain and its 'friends', the British instructed the NIOC to refrain from any oil deal with Israel and 'to ensure that its oil customers act according to their undertakings'.[15]

Some two weeks later, the British Foreign Office revealed that representatives from BP had visited, in order to discuss the supply of Iranian oil to Israel. The representatives told of the 'Kern Hill', a ship which left Iran on 19 April and would arrive in Eilat on 3 May. The ship sailed after the report of the previous delivery of oil. The BP representatives stated that this action was part of a contract that Israel had with NIOC for the supply of 500,000 tons of oil. In addition, British officials learnt from BP that there was another tanker, the 'British Fame', carrying oil *en route* to Haifa, where it was due to arrive on 26 May.[16]

At some time between September and October 1956, by invitation of the Israeli government, two leading Iranian newspaper owners and a Tehran university professor spent a fortnight in Israel. One of them, Muhandes Vala, then owner of Iran's most popular weekly paper, *Tehran Musavvar*, revealed that he had been impressed by what he had seen in Israel and had visited an atomic energy centre.[17] Vala added that he had made the trip to Israel with the Shah's knowledge and that it was the Iranian government's intention to develop ties with Israel.[18] However, Vala is also reported to have emphasised the constraints on Iran *vis-à-vis* its relations with Israel; namely the threat of opposition from the Arab League and the fear of antagonising radical Islamic elements in Iran.[19]

The role of Israel in supporting Iran against regional Soviet aggression was enhanced after the 1958 Iraqi revolution, when the subsequent Iraqi exit from the Baghdad Pact appeared to have brought revolutionary Arab politics to the borders of Iran.[20] Nasser relished the fact that Iraq was retreating from the West, while Iran saw itself becoming more isolated, along with Israel, in the region. This feeling of isolation was not ameliorated by the breakdown of talks over a non-aggression pact between Tehran and Moscow and by Iran signing a defence agreement with the US in 1959.[21]

The Iraqi revolution had caused concern in both Jerusalem and Tehran over the spreading influence of Arab radicalism. To this end, Iran and Israel made a tactical decision to arm the Kurds in the north of Iraq, in order to keep Iraqi forces engaged, thereby preventing them from exerting pressure, both along the Iranian border and Israel's eastern flank. To facilitate this plan, a meeting was arranged between Kurdish leader Mullah Mustafa Barazani and senior officials from the Israeli Ministry of Defence.[22] It was during this meeting that the two countries decided to support the Kurds in a large-scale offensive against the Iraqi army, rather than wage a campaign of guerrilla warfare. Israel began to train Kurdish fighters and 1965 saw the first training course for Kurdish officers run by Israelis in the mountains of Kurdistan.[23]

From 1956–59, there was a decline in Iranian exports to Israel: in 1956–57, Iran exported approximately 67.4 million rials' worth of goods to Israel, 58.4 million in 1957–58, and a mere 3.2 million in 1958–59. However, the same years saw an increase in Israeli exports to Iran: 1956–57 saw 1.7 million rials' worth of goods, 1957–58, approximately 9 million and 1958–59 a significant 25.3 million.[24] In addition, between 13–21 May 1959, a parliamentary group from Iran visited Israel, a visit that the British Embassy in Tel Aviv described as having 'no precedent'.[25] The parliamentary group consisted of several Iranian notables: Senator Khan Baba Biani, President of the State Academy of Teachers, Dr Mohammad Shahkar, Chairman of the *Majlis* Law Committee and Dr Shaibani, Chairman of the *Majlis* Agriculture Committee.[26] The visitors expressed their desire to see greater development of ties between the two countries.[27] Furthermore, some months later, F.J. Leishman from the British Embassy in Tehran, had occasion to ask Sultan Husain Sanandaji of the Iranian Foreign Ministry, whether he believed there would be a resumption of diplomatic relations between Iran and Israel. The official replied that he and, he thought, his ministry were strongly in favour of the proposal and that India and Israel 'were the two countries in the general area of the Middle East whose interests, both political and commercial, coincided the most closely with those of Iran'.[28]

Until 1960, neither the Iranian, nor the Israeli government openly admitted to their diplomatic ties, but in July of that year, the Shah revealed in a news conference that the relationship between the two countries was continuing and that Iranian *de facto* recognition of Israel had never been revoked under the Mossadeq government.[29] In Egypt, Nasser used this as an excuse to break ties with Tehran and to launch vociferous attacks on the growing ties between Israel and Iran.[30] Nasser stated, 'Now that the Shah has loudly proclaimed that he recognised Israel, America is pleased and so are Britain, Zionism and Israel'.[31]

The Iranian government expelled the Egyptian Ambassador to Tehran and described Nasser as a 'light-headed Pharaoh who is ruling by bloodshed'.[32] Nasser attempted to include other Arab countries in his quest to ostracise Iran on this matter, but they, and Iraq in particular, accepted the Shah's explanation that Iran had recognised Israel in the past and that, essentially, nothing had changed. An important reason for this behaviour was the Arab fear of Nasser and his intentions in the region. As a result, Nasser found himself isolated in the Arab League over the issue of Israel.[33]

There followed a tense period of anti-Iranian rhetoric emanating from many parts of the Arab world, particularly from the United Arab Republic (UAR), finally culminating in the expulsion of the UAR Ambassador in Tehran.[34] The over-riding concern for Nasser was that the Shah would eventually manoeuvre himself into a position where he would be able to build a non-Arab, Muslim coalition in the Middle East[35] and thereby threaten Egypt's position of dominance. Indeed, Iraq and Syria supported the independence movements of Iran's Arab population, particularly in an area close to a major oil reserve, which they renamed 'Arabestan', refusing to call it by its hitherto accepted name of Khuzestan and Nasser renamed the Persian Gulf the 'Arabic Gulf'.[36]

In fact, the British believed that Iran, particularly after Iraq left the Baghdad Pact, had no reason necessarily to continue appeasing the Arab world in its refusal to openly renew its ties with Israel.

Whitehall estimated that such a change in policy would show the Arab world an Iranian statement of intent and an assertion of its independence of policy.[37] Moreover, in 1965, the Syrian cabinet formally claimed the province of Khuzestan as part of the Arab homeland. The Shah saw this as a direct threat to Iran's national security, promptly recalled Iran's Ambassador to Syria, and broke off diplomatic relations.[38]

Reacting to this situation, Ben-Gurion stated in the Knesset that 'The Egyptian dictator broke off relations with Iran because of the friendly relations ... that exist between Israel and that country ... and that friendship continues to exist because it is founded on the mutual advantage that the two countries derive from their co-operation'.[39] In order to protect this mutual advantage, Iran was prepared to deflect a certain amount of Arab pressure. A primary example came in 1960, when an Israeli delegation took part in the third Iranian National Jamboree. The Pakistani delegation threatened to boycott the Jamboree unless the Israeli delegation was removed, to which the Shah countered, the Pakistanis could either stay or leave, but the Israeli delegation would be staying.[40]

In August 1960, a delegation of five scientists, headed by Professor Ali Azad, Rector of Tehran University, was present at the Rehovot Science Conference held in Israel. The professor expressed an interest in Iranian atomic energy for peaceful purposes and revealed that the Israeli Atomic Energy Commission and the University of Tehran had held preliminary talks concerning the training of Iranian students in Israel and the employment of Israeli scientists to operate a nuclear reactor in Iran. Moreover, *Solel Boneh* won a contest for a role in the construction of the Abadan road in Iran, in October, 80 cows were sent from Israel to Iran in order to improve Iranian cattle herds and Israel set up a station in Iran for advising on the use of Israeli fertilisers.[41]

The Shah was quick to see Israel as a valuable supplier of agricultural and water resources, and throughout the 1960s, Israeli experts advised the Iranians on these issues.[42] In April 1961, *Vered,* the Israel Water Resources Development Company, began installing a central sewerage system in Isfahan, taking sole responsibility for the initial stage of the project, at a cost of approximately US$1.25 million.[43] The same year saw some Iranian notables visit Israel: the ex-Deputy Prime Minister Mustafa Alamouti, ex-Minister of Justice Dr R Human and Princess Safiel Firouz, President of the Iranian Council of Women.[44] Other Iranian dignitaries to visit at the time were: Ex-Senator Ebrahim Khajeh-Nuri and Dr Ahmad Human, a professor of Rural Economy and a lawyer. They were joined by the former Under-Secretary in charge of Iranian State Railways, Hassan Shaqaqi. Their visit was arranged by a Jewish contracting firm, Schulman, and according to the ex-senator, the delegation felt it was almost the guest of the Israeli government.[45]

Such interaction reached its zenith in 1962 when, after an earthquake in the Qazvin area of Iran, *Tahal*, Israel's water planning company, undertook a large scale project involving the introduction of improved methods of cultivation and irrigation.[46] The Israeli team on the project successfully involved the majority of the local population throughout its implementation and planning stages, especially useful for the Israelis when attempting, and eventually succeeding, to convince the local farmers of the superiority of modern, deep wells, over the ancient *qanat* wells.[47]

The Shah elaborated on this issue in an interview with the author E.A. Bayne. In reply to Bayne's comment that a national administration of water resources in Iran could have been successful, depending on the administration, the Shah stated, 'Of course, everything boils down to that. They have this in Israel. They have to'. This idea of administering water resources had been supported in a meeting the Shah had held the previous week with the director of the Israeli *Mekorot* Water Company, jointly owned by the Israeli government and the *Histadrut*.[48]

The area for which the Israelis won the development contract totalled some 123,500 acres and was largely inhabited by impoverished farmers. The leader of the Israeli team, Arie L. Eliav, had abundant experience in developing Israeli land south of Tel Aviv and west of the Dead Sea and his appointment as project leader saw him bring this experience to the task. His development plan for Qazvin was based on water development, agricultural redevelopment, community development and local infrastructure.[49] This year saw six Israeli experts involved in the project and, in 1964, the number rose to twenty.[50] Moreover, then Israeli Minster of Agriculture, Moshe Dayan, spent ten days in the country as the guest of his Iranian counterpart, Hassan Arsanjani, causing almost as much speculation as when David Ben-Gurion spent the night at the Shah's private villa in December 1961.[51]

Dayan's trip would have been of particular interest to Major-General Hasan Akhavi, formerly Iranian minister of agriculture and Brigadier Ghulam Reza Yavari. These retired army officers were establishing a cattle-rearing facility near Tehran, which they wanted stocked with Israeli Holstein cattle; a project that had been arranged by the Israeli representatives in the area. The men could also have benefited from the experience of Major-General Ansari, a retired Chief of Police, who had already succeeded in building such a facility.[52]

The same year saw an improvement in Iranian ties with Moscow. There was a new Soviet military doctrine, emphasising nuclear deterrence, which, in turn, lessened Moscow's concern over US support for conventional forces in Iran. In addition, the increased US capability to strike Soviet targets from submarines deployed in the Mediterranean reduced the Iranian fear of Soviet regional penetration.[53] Consequently, in 1962, Iran pledged to Moscow that it would no longer allow its territory to be used to house foreign military bases which could be used to target Soviet assets.[54] This event though, did not appear to alter the military aspect of the Israeli-Iranian relationship. Indeed, the British Embassy in Tehran, on 17 January 1962, was strongly suspicious that General Mirjahangiri, head of the Iranian J3 Branch Supreme Command, which dealt with, *inter alia*, operations and training, left Tehran for Tel Aviv on a British Overseas Airways Corporation (BOAC) flight that morning.[55] This suspicion was corroborated less than a week later, when the British Embassy in Tel Aviv revealed that an Iranian officer had indeed arrived in Israel on 17 January, on BOAC flight BA 309, but the man in question was General Jahanguir, not Mirjahangiri.[56]

According to the British government, the Israeli office in Tehran at this time called itself the 'Israeli Agency'. It was run by a man called Doriel, who claimed to be an economic counsellor. In addition to Doriel, there was a second-in-command in the office, known as Rinot, a German Jew, who was also an economic counsellor and a young Second Secretary from Tel Aviv, an Iranian Jew, known as Ezri. The British believed these facts pointed to the developing ties between Iran and Israel. Furthermore, the British Embassy in Tehran stated that the Iranian New Year, falling on 21 March 1962, would see an increase in the numbers of Iranian Jews travelling to Israel. This was in addition to the decision of the Iranian Workers' Social Welfare Bank to employ an Israeli expert to advise them on instigating Workers' Industrial Co-Operatives.[57]

It was not long before the civilian co-operation between the two countries began to penetrate the military sphere. In January 1964, then Israeli Chief of Staff, Yitzhak Rabin and the Director-General of the Israeli Ministry of Defence, Asher Ben-Nathan, visited Tehran for two days in order to meet with the Iranian Chief of Staff, General Hijazi and to sell the Israeli Uzi sub-machine gun.[58] Although still some way short of Ben-Gurion's dream of the two countries coming to each other's aid in the face of an Arab attack, the alliance was nevertheless, developing steadily.

Moreover, both the Mossad and Savak established offices in the Iranian port city of Khoramshahr, to facilitate aspects of their mutual intelligence gathering. This was usually done through use of the Iranian-Arab population, which would cross the border into Iraq, infiltrate military and political establishments and, upon their return, relay the data acquired to their handlers.[59] Through these offices, the two services were able to trace Soviet military supplies to Iraq, in particular, details of MiG aircraft, information which was then passed on to members of NATO and CENTO.[60]

During the mid-1960s, the Shah suggested that a new Iranian foreign policy be conceived, based on the principles of his domestic reform programmes, known collectively as the 'White Revolution of the Shah and the people'.[61] It was an attempt to remove both feudalistic and unpatriotic policy makers from the Iranian political system.[62] Moreover, the Shah reversed his policy of military preparedness being essential to counter the Communist threat and to bolster the economic well-being of Iran after the downfall of the Mossadeq government in 1953, and began to emphasise co-operation and multi-lateral ties between states,[63] thereby creating a political framework for further ties with Israel. There were a number of external forces that allowed the Iranian regime to embrace this change in policy: foremost, was the removal of the monarchist regime in Iraq. For Iran, the concern was that its own regime would be perceived as too Western in its approach and may experience the same fate and there was the Kennedy administration's desire to see aid recipient regimes help themselves and become increasingly self-reliant.[64]

In addition, there was an increase in Iran's oil production through the land reform programme and a growing government confidence. The multilateral hue of the new Iranian foreign policy also emphasised the desire to maintain equidistance between the two Superpowers. Though in reality Iran did not lean away from the West, the statement of intent was clear; Iranian national interests were paramount in any foreign policy considerations.[65]

Until the advent of the Iraqi revolution, the West had identified the main regional threat to their interests as emanating directly from the USSR. But after the revolution, with the removal of Iraq as a buffer zone between Iran and the anti-Shah regimes of Cairo and Damascus, Tehran became concerned over the association of radical Arab states with Moscow and began to identify a direct link between Moscow and the Arab radicalism that the Iraqi revolution had brought to its borders.[66] This concern was heightened by a British announcement in 1968 concerning the removal of British troops and bases from the eastern Suez area.[67] However, the 1962 military bases pledge disinclined the Iranian regime to talk openly of a Soviet threat to the region. Tehran had also identified Soviet logistical and moral support to the anti-Shah Dhofari rebels in Oman as a strategic concern.[68]

The Six Day War

On the morning of 5 June 1967, the Israeli Air Force (IAF) launched a pre-emptive strike against predominantly Egyptian, Syrian and Iraqi military targets. Israel conveyed a message to King Hussein of Jordan, requesting that his country stay out of the conflict. Hussein, however, having signed a defence pact with Egypt on 30 May, joined the fight. By 7 June, Jordanian troops were retreating across the Jordan River. Israel then moved its forces to the Golan Heights to engage Syrian forces. At the culmination of the war, the Arab forces were routed and Israel found itself administering the newly acquired territories of Judea, Samaria, Gaza, the Golan Heights, the Sinai Peninsula and a unified Jerusalem.[69]

At the fifth Emergency Special Session of the UNGA, Iran's voting pattern revealed a certain ambiguity. This was first apparent in a speech made by Iranian Minister for Foreign Affairs, Ardeshir Zahedi, on 21 June 1967. It appeared that the minister was as dismayed at the failure of the UN to prevent the Six Day War, as he was concerned with the political and military consequences of it. Indeed, Zahedi stated,

> It is not as if there had not been enough signals of what was coming. Nevertheless, those who bore the primary responsibility for the maintenance of international peace and security were not prepared to close ranks in the name of the international community in whose behalf they are supposed to act to prevent the calamity that has overtaken us.[70]

This dismay was restated in the same speech when Zahedi remarked, 'We should, I suppose, be grateful that the Security Council finally brought about a cease-fire, but ... only after tens of thousands of lives had been lost.'[71]

It was with this perception of the failure of diplomacy that Iran voted in favour of the non-aligned powers draft resolution, A/L 522/Rev.3.[72] This draft resolution called, *inter alia*, for Israeli forces to withdraw to positions held prior to 5 June 1967. However, Iran abstained in all four of the separate votes concerning the four paragraphs of draft resolution A/L 519, thus showing that, while it favoured the withdrawal of Israeli forces, it did not accept the terms of the draft resolution, which condemned Israel's actions and called for Israel to compensate the UAR.[73] Iran's abstention was brought into relief by most Arab states voting in favour of all four paragraphs. This vote set a precedent for Iran, as it began to differentiate between issues of Arab and Islamic natures.

Though perhaps not a surprise, as Iran is not an Arab country, this approach, nevertheless, became codified to a greater extent at the UN in this period.[74]

Moreover, the vociferous nature of the Albanian draft resolution, A/L 521, also failed to find favour in the eyes of the Iranian Representative. The draft condemned Israel's aggression; condemned the US and the UK for their perceived aid in the aggression; demanded that Israel compensate the UAR and declared that the UAR alone should decide whether to allow safe passage to Israeli shipping through the Gulf of Aqaba. Iran voted against the resolution,[75] again refusing to adopt the line taken by many Arab states, which voted for the draft resolution, and revealing that the government of the Shah was reticent to condemn the US for any alleged involvement in the conflict.

The Iranian aversion to the more pro-Arab draft resolutions is puzzling when one examines Zahedi's speech. There is a pro-Arab/ Muslim thread running throughout his opening remarks, 'events in the Middle East ... have caused the people and the Government of Iran much anxiety ... at the results of the outbreak of violence which has afflicted the peoples of the area ... with most of whom we have ties of faith, culture and fraternity'.[76] In the following paragraph, Zahedi spoke of 'these affinities which bind us to the Arab peoples, there is small wonder that we look with anguish at the losses and dislocation that have come to them through the clash of arms ... my government has rushed to help the people of Jordan and Iraq in binding up the wounds of war'.[77]

Iran abstained in the vote over the relatively moderate Latin American draft proposal, A/L 523/Rev.1, *inter alia*, calling on all sides to end the state of belligerency and demanding the withdrawal of Israeli forces.[78] The Arab states voted against the draft resolution. Iran then voted in favour of draft resolution A/L 526 and Add.1–3, (2252) which it co-sponsored, calling for humanitarian assistance to the refugees and welcoming UNSC Resolution 237.[79] Zahedi had raised the status and welfare of the refugees previously, explaining, 'we are appalled by the addition to the already large numbers of refugees who have remained unsettled for nearly two decades of new refugee victims of the recent trial of arms'.[80] Moreover, in an attempt to draw a parallel between the fate of the Jews in the Second World War and the aftermath of the Six Day War, Zahedi pointed out to the government of Israel that 'its people have known what it means to be refugees'.[81]

In the wake of the war, Israel's petroleum situation fundamentally altered, which had implications for the relationship between the Jewish state and Iran in the energy sector. Israel began developing Egyptian oil production on the Gulf of Suez side of the Sinai Peninsula, and from July 1967, began pumping 100,000 barrels a day from its origin at Abu Rudeis, to Eilat, the terminus of Israel's pipelines to Ashkelon and Haifa. As a result of capturing the thirty-mile long Abu Rudeis oilfield in 1967, Israel was able to satisfy approximately three quarters of its domestic oil requirements, totalling some 2,500,000 tons a year.[82]

Furthermore, Israel was in favour of opening the east bank of the Suez Canal in the belief that it would reduce the Egyptian desire to renew aggression. However, Egypt refused to accept a cease-fire when the reopening of the Suez appeared to be postponed indefinitely. As a consequence, Israel and Iran entered into a joint venture and constructed a pipeline from Eilat to Ashkelon. It was agreed that each country would have a 50 per cent equity interest in the pipeline and, on 5 February 1970, Israel revealed that the pipeline had been completed, at a cost of approximately US$136 million.[83]

However, concern over the plight of the Palestinian refugees, displaced as a result of the fighting, prompted Iran to vote in favour of UNGA Resolution 2443 (XXIII) of 19 December 1968, which established the 'inalienable rights' of those refugees and established a Special Committee to Investigate Israeli Practices Affecting the Human Rights of the Population of the Occupied Territories.[84] In addition, Iran voted for draft resolution A/SPC/L 166 and add.1,[85] draft resolution A/SPC/L 198 and draft resolution A/SPC/L 231.[86] Here, Iran voted with the Arab countries, aiding Palestinian refugees, thus ensuring a largely unified Muslim/Arab vote on the matter.

Iran was also keen to promote the internationalisation of a solution to the evolving Arab-Israeli conflict and, as a result, voted in favour of draft resolution A/L 527/Rev.1, (2253) which it co-sponsored, rejecting all measures taken by Israel to change the status of Jerusalem.[87] It also voted for draft resolution A/L 528/Rev/1 (2254), which it co-sponsored, calling for Israel to desist in attempting to alter the status of Jerusalem,[88] thus revealing that the centrality of Jerusalem was not only confined to the Arab states, whose UN Representatives voted in favour of both draft resolutions, but was of import to the larger Muslim world, and was also a central tenet of the Iranian diplomatic approach.[89]

In 1969, Zahedi spoke of 'deep shock and repulsion at the burning of the Al Aqsa mosque,' by an Australian tourist, in August of that year and spoke of the 'anger and sense of indignation of people throughout the Moslem world,' again highlighting Iran's ostensible pan-Islamic diplomatic credentials, at least on the subject of Jerusalem. In an apparent attempt to demonstrate the importance of the issue, Zahedi offered the assistance of the Iranian government in the 'rebuilding and repair of the mosque'.[90] Finally, Iran abstained in the vote over draft proposal A/L 529/Rev.1 (2256), defying Arab opinion, which was against the draft proposal, but it is unclear how it voted *vis-à-vis* draft proposal A/L 530 (2257).[91]

As a response to the Iranian perception of UN inertia, Iranian Representative Ghafari, revealed that the government of Iran had pledged a total of 450,000 rials to the United Nations Relief and Works Agency (UNRWA)[92] for the year 1967; had provided food aid to Syria and stated that camps with facilities for approximately 5,000 people had been established in Zizia, near Amman, Jordan. In addition, the Iranian government re-iterated its determination to contribute to any humanitarian rescue operation undertaken by the governments of the host countries in the region.[93] In 1970, the camp in Jordan, apart from its medical centre, was handed over to the Jordanian authorities, and in April 1972, Iran advanced US$40,000 for the construction of a laboratory and the enlargement of the camp's school facilities.[94] Though this aid was significant, it must be noted that Iranian concern over the plight of the Palestinian refugees was no greater than that voiced in the West at the time.

Some three years later, Princess Ashraf Pahlavi, the sister of the Shah, stated that, 'the war of June 1967 added a new wave of refugees to those who had already been leading a precarious existence for over twenty years'.[95] The princess's words came in a year which saw significant developments take place in the relationship between Israel and Iran. Indeed, according to the British Foreign Office, a meeting took place between Israeli Foreign Minister, Abba Eban, and the Shah, in August 1970. The meeting lasted four hours and was organised by SAVAK.[96] Eban's visit to Iran coincided with a report by British diplomatic officials, which noted that 'the Iranian presence here [in Israel] is a good deal less visible than the Israeli presence at Tehran'.[97] The same document noted the presence of an Iranian man named Bashi, who spoke openly of his 'quasi diplomatic status' in Israel whilst at a function. The author of the letter, however, was unsure as to the exact status of Bashi, whether he was a 'regular diplomatist or something less conventional'.[98] Indeed, the signs of an Israeli presence in Iran in 1970 were not entirely hidden: 'shops shut on Saturday, Shalom in the bazaar, Israeli citrus advisers were on the Caspian and water engineers on the plateau.'[99]

However, the British Ambassador to Tehran, D.A.H. Wright, noted in a despatch of the same year, that there was a 'sizeable Iranian diplomatic office in Tel Aviv with an "Ambassador", a Counsellor, a Military *Attaché* and two Representatives of SAVAK. In Tehran, the despatch continues, the Israeli presence was much the same. The Israeli "Ambassador" was, in fact, a Persian Jew from Isfahan, who saw the Shah regularly. Moreover, Wright mentioned that EL AL aircraft flew frequently to Tehran, which was "one of the few boarding points for Israel"'.[100]

The default Iranian stance on the aforementioned issues was one of ambiguity; official denials to new foreign journalists that an Israeli Embassy existed and that EL AL had offices in the country on the one hand while, on the other, Iranian officials attended a memorial service for Levi Eshkol, the former prime minister of Israel, in Tehran Synagogue the previous year.[101] The diplomatic opinion on these matters was that the level of trade between the two countries at the time was deliberately kept quiet and, as a result, other ties were downplayed. Iran was only admitting to one percent of its foreign trade being with Israel, but the document clearly states that, although there was apparently no official Israeli government investment in Iran, money nevertheless entered the country via the Jewish private sector and the Shah made use of the services of two Jewish men, Mourad Aryeh, who had aided the Shah financially when he fled to Rome in 1953 and Habib el Ghanaian. Furthermore, to the British, it was clear that a number of Israeli experts were working in the Iranian Ministry of Natural Resources.[102] In addition, it was revealed that one could, quite frequently, come into contact with 'Iranians in the co-operative and local government field who have been trained in Israel'. Moreover, co-operation in the private sector between the two countries was evolving, with Israeli construction firms involved in the construction of the Darius Khabir dam at Shiraz and at least two Israeli firms were producing agricultural pesticides and poultry food, whilst managing three large chicken farms. The produce of this last venture could be seen in the grocery shops of Tehran, with large boxes stamped 'Hatching Eggs – produce of Israel'.[103]

This year also saw the development of the military aspect of the relationship. The British Foreign Office revealed that the Iranian Parachute Brigade Artillery Battalion was equipped with Israeli 120mm mortars and Israeli made parachutes; the Iranian Imperial Guard was equipped with Israeli machine guns and the Iranian Air Force had sent their fleet of F86 aircraft to Israel 'for some years' for repair, whilst an Israeli aircraft came 'regularly' to Tehran with Sidewinder missiles for servicing.[104]

The British Embassy in Tehran told of a meeting between Colonel Duval, the US Military *Attaché* in Iran and the British Military *Attaché* in Iran, who said that Duval 'was absolutely certain ... there had been contacts between the Iranian and Israeli Armies for the purposes of training the Iranian Special Forces'. He also noted that 'it was possible that the Israelis were using a Phantom simulator in Iran, but Colonel Duval had no evidence to prove or to disprove this'. The Colonel, though, was 'absolutely positive that "Israeli" money had been given to Barazani through Iran, in order to support the Kurds'. Finally, the Colonel stated that the Iranian army officers were 'almost to a man behind Israel and saw Israel as a potential ally in fighting against Iraq and Egypt'.[105]

Moreover, the British Embassy in Tehran revealed to Whitehall that it had a report from its Military *Attaché* who had met the Iranian Chief of Staff, General Djam. The general had revealed that he was in 'regular correspondence' with the Israeli Chief of Staff and that 'the Israeli Army were very worried by the SAM 3 air defence system being installed by Egypt'. The Israeli concern was not solely due to the efficiency and threat posed by the missile systems, but also because the system would 'bring confrontation with the Russians even closer'. The general also believed that it would be a disaster, were Israel to 'go under' and that opening the Suez Canal would only benefit the Russians and Egyptians.[106]

In addition, the Shah sent high ranking members of his army to the 'last Israeli National Day Reception'. Those attending included General Djam, the Chief of the Supreme Command Staff and Admiral Rasa'i, the Commander of the Imperial Navy. There was no Representative from the Foreign Ministry. Furthermore, Wright divulged that the Chief of the Supreme Commander's Staff revealed to his Military *Attaché* that he had 'regular correspondence' with the Israeli Chief of Staff. Additionally, the head of the IAF had visited his opposite number in Tehran the previous year; General Moshe Dayan arrived in Tehran, for the second time, some months prior to the despatch being written and the Iranian general in charge of military procurement went to Israel 'frequently'.[107]

The despatch noted that the most sensitive area of the relationship between Israel and Iran was the export of oil, which Iran had done by camouflaging its oil shipments and selling it via a Swiss company, thereby obscuring much of the data. Since 1961, though, tankers had been reported leaving Abadan every fortnight 'that could only be for Eilat'. The document alleged that the Shah had invested a certain amount of his own money into the 42-inch Eilat-Ashkelon pipeline and that, since its opening, crude oil had been shipped from Kharg to Eilat, at the rate of approximately 50,000 tons a week.[108] Interestingly, this oil does not appear on any Iranian account and Iran denied that the oil was shipped to Israel. In fact, the orders for the oil were processed using the innocuous term 'to sea for orders'. The Iranian stance on the issue was encapsulated by an NIOC director, who stated that the 'NIOC sends no oil through the Eilat pipeline, but it sells oil to Eastern European nations ... it is up to the customer to arrange transport which is none of our business'.[109]

The British Embassy in Tehran, in a letter to Whitehall, noted that they knew from NIOC's own statistics, the quantity of oil that was being exported on its own account to Eastern Europe. The despatch noted that, for the first six months of 1970, this amount totalled over one million tons. The British believed that this amount was a fraction of the total being exported to Israel, but were unable to obtain definitive data. However, D.F. Murray, from the British Embassy in Tehran, learnt from a meeting with an employee of the NIOC that some 40,000 tons of oil a day were being exported to Israel from Iran. The British took this figure as an unproven estimate.[110]

Also highlighted were some areas of Iranian society which were not supportive of the ties between the two countries. For example, at the Iran-Israel football matches of June 1968 and April 1970, one could hear chants of 'back to Auschwitz' from some elements in the crowd. Furthermore, during times of student unrest, there were anti-Israel slogans in evidence and synagogues were sometimes targeted in disturbances. It was also thought that the Iranian left-wing intelligentsia was basically anti-Israel, though perhaps this was an attempt to construct an opposing policy to that of the Shah, rather than being anti-Israel *per se*.[111]

The same year, at the UN, Iran, along with the Arab states,[112] voted in favour of draft resolution A/L 602 rev.2 (2628), which concerned respect for the rights of the Palestinians. This echoed the Iranian Foreign Minister's statement at the Islamic Conference in Jeddah in March 1970, when he declared full support for the 'legitimate rights of the Palestinian people'.[113] Iran subsequently voted in favour of draft resolution A/L 650 Rev.1 (2799), which it co-sponsored.[114]

It was this type of statement which led the British to believe that a continuation of the Arab-Israeli conflict was not in the national interests of Iran. The belief of Whitehall was that, after British withdrawal, the main Iranian concern would be Soviet penetration through Iraq, and the Arab-Israeli conflict, by keeping the Iranian regime occupied, would facilitate such penetration.[115] Also, it was thought, Iran was interested in cementing its position as the hegemon of the Persian Gulf, and the Shah could not afford to isolate himself totally from Arab policies. To this end, the British believed that the Shah ought to maintain his friendship with King Faisal of Saudi Arabia in order to 'stabilise the southern shores of the Gulf'.[116]

Moreover, the British believed that the Shah was becoming 'exasperated' with Israel's position over both the withdrawal of its forces and the status of Jerusalem. This was not helped by either the Shah's purported belief that Jordan and Egypt were interested in separate peace settlements, or his fear of the 'Arab guerrilla movement'.[117] The reported mood of Israeli Embassy officials in Tehran at this time, though, was of a 'phlegmatic' nature. There existed the potential, it was believed, for Iranian Jewry to 'suffer a bit', were the Iranian irritation with Israel to worsen, and it was not surprising for Whitehall to learn that the Iranian police had been advising Iranian shopkeepers of Jewish descent not to display the Star of David in their shop windows.[118]

Reflecting this theme at the UN, Iranian Representative, Abbas-Ali Khalatbari, stated in 1971,

> President Anwar El-Sadat declared his country's willingness to sign a peace agreement with Israel provided that Israeli armed forces are withdrawn from occupied Arab territories. The President of ... Egypt ... offered to reopen the Suez Canal as the first step towards a settlement ... These overtures ... met with Israel's negative response.[119]

This theme was further elaborated upon by Representative Fereydoun Hoveyda, who in 1971, stated that, 'President El-Sadat has taken a number of initiatives and made numerous efforts ... But these overtures, which have won the approval and esteem of the vast majority of the international community, were met with a kind of point-blank refusal on the part of Israel'.[120]

However, the Iranian delegation was not afraid to disregard the *en masse* voting style and vehement anti-Israel stance of the Arab bloc. The distinction between issues of an Arab nature and those of a

Muslim one provided the Iranian delegation with a useful method of not adversely affecting the development of ties with either Israel, or the Arab world, and, concomitantly, provided it with an ideological stance of, at least superficial, sincerity.

One of the first actions of the new government in Iraq, after the 1968 *coup*, however, was to commence subversive activities against Iran. To this end, Saddam Hussein invited the former head of SAVAK, General Teymour Bakhtiar,[121] to Iraq in order to finalise plans for the overthrow of the monarch in Iran, along with the leaders of the Tudeh party aligned with the Ayatollah Ruhollah Khomeini, a radical, anti-Shah cleric, exiled in Iraq from 1965 until 1978. At the same time, the new Iraqi regime initiated a campaign of harassment and persecution of Iranians living in Iraq. During this period, thousands of Iranians were removed from their homes, many of which were confiscated, and relocated to Qasr-e-Shirin.[122] For Iran, the final proof of Iraqi enmity was the signing of the Treaty of Friendship with the USSR on 9 April 1972. The Treaty was a 15 year military and economic commitment on behalf of the USSR, to Iraq.[123]

In the same year, the Shah, in a meeting with Golda Meir, agreed with the Israeli Prime Minister that *détente* would be beneficial for both countries. The Shah also enunciated the tenets which he believed to be the foundation for ties between Jerusalem and Tehran: clandestine operations against radical Arab elements, obtaining Israeli arms and selling petroleum to Israel. However, he maintained that the relationship should remain secret, in order to prevent further animosity in the Arab world towards Iran.[124]

While the relationship was being kept secret, the Iranian delegation at the UN allowed itself the freedom to vocalise its position on the situation in the Middle East in no uncertain terms. Representative Khalatbari stated that 'the situation in the Middle East has taken a turn for the worse, especially during recent weeks'. He then launched a thinly veiled attack on Israel, stating that 'The latest armed interventions against Syria and Lebanon have further endangered peace and security in the area'. In accordance with the Shah's desire not to aggravate Iranian ties with the Arab world, Khalatbari went on to say that, 'The Arab republic of Egypt ... has made successive peace overtures to Israel ... these efforts have, however, met with no positive response and have failed to persuade Israel to withdraw from the occupied territories'.[125]

One factor sure to anger the Arab world was the continuing sale of Iranian oil to Israel. Indeed, one of the reasons behind Nasser's blockade of the Gulf of Aqaba in the build-up to the Six Day War was the Egyptian objection to the continuing flow of oil from Iran to the Israeli port of Eilat. Furthermore, Nasser took the step of calling upon the governments of Jordan and Saudi Arabia to announce to the Iranian government that oil could no longer be transported to Israel through the Gulf of Aqaba, as a consequence of the blockade.[126] Initially, the Iranian decision to sell oil to Israel was based on ameliorating Iran's financial hardship. However, Tehran was also keen to challenge the *status quo* of the major oil companies. For the period 1959–71, Israel's oil imports increased from 30,000 barrels a day in 1959, to 106,284 barrels a day in 1971. It has been estimated that possibly 80–90 per cent of these imports originated in Iran, which would mean that, in 1959, Israel was importing approximately 24–27,000 barrels of Iranian crude oil a day and in 1971, approximately 85–95,000 barrels a day.[127]

In 1972, both US President, Richard Nixon and Henry Kissinger flew to Tehran, in essence, to underline the importance of Iran as a regional superpower and to furnish the Iranians with the ability to purchase regional superpower status. To this end, the Shah was granted massive US financial and military aid and, between the years 1945 and 1972, Iran spent approximately US$1.2 billion on imported arms and, in the aftermath of the 'Nixon Doctrine,'[128] Iranian arms sales rocketed to approximately US$18 billion for the period 1972–78, most of the purchases being funded by oil revenues.[129]

The following year, the Iranian delegation to the UN voiced its criticism of Israel through Representative Hoveyda, 'the refusal of Israel to commit itself to withdraw from territories of Egypt, Jordan and Syria is an obstacle for meaningful dialogue to start. This negative attitude of Israel seems to us all the more unjustified as the Government of Egypt has shown courage and goodwill in responding to Ambassador Jarring's questionnaire'.[130] Hoveyda was keen to show that Israel's concerns over

Arab rejection were baseless. To this end, he stated that 'We have often heard Representatives of Israel alarmingly recalling the so-called Khartoum resolution of September 1967 epitomising it rhetorically in the phrase, "no recognition, no negotiation, no peace with Israel".' This attitude, according to the Iranian Representative, dramatised 'an intransigence which is now a relic from the past, it brings into focus a contrast which is very much relevant to the situation today'.[131]

Hoveyda took it upon himself to emphasise the readiness of Egypt, in particular, to reach agreement with Israel. He noted, 'from what we learn from Egypt's reply to Ambassador Jarring's questionnaire on February 1971, it has moved to accepting in principle to acknowledge the sovereignty of Israel and to make peace with Israel'. In addition, Hoveyda agreed with the Israeli Representative that 'peace is not an abstract concept, but that it must be built and preserved by those who aspire to live in peace together', but then retorted with, 'But is it not also a truism that peace cannot be built while the seeds of dissension still remain?' And that 'Is it not also a truism that claims to security, no matter how justified and understandable, cannot be hinged on the insecurity of others?[132]

As can be seen, the Iranian delegation was behaving with a semblance of impartiality over the Arab-Israeli conflict, though Nasser deemed Iran's behaviour unacceptable enough to sever ties. The rapid growth in trade between Israel and Iran, symbolised by the joint oil pipeline, revealed the strategic dimension of the Policy of the Periphery and caused concern in those states opposed to it. The military co-operation caused reverberations around the Middle East, and Israel, with the Shah announcing that Iran had never revoked its recognition of the Jewish state, even under Mossadeq, had achieved a major diplomatic success. Furthermore, both countries had agreed to arm the Kurds in northern Iraq and Mossad had offices in Iran. Indeed, the relationship between Israel and Iran was burgeoning and ripe for further development. The subsequent decade, however, would produce major domestic and international events that would alter the direction of the Policy of the Periphery.

CHAPTER 3

IRAN AND ISRAEL, 1973–82: FROM CONSOLIDATION TO REVOLUTION

The Yom Kippur War

On 6 October 1973, the combined forces of Egypt and Syria attacked Israeli positions in the Sinai and along the Golan Heights. The surprise nature of the attack allowed the Arab forces to make significant gains during the first two days. However, the Israeli army mounted an effective counter-attack and, by the time the UN cease-fire was initiated on 22 October, the Syrians were routed, the Egyptian army defeated and the conflict threatened to spark a Third World War, with the US taking the unparalleled step of issuing a nuclear alert. The eventual cease-fire agreement saw Israeli forces withdraw from the western side of the Suez, while the Egyptians maintained their forces on the eastern bank.[1]

Iranian sympathies with the Arab states during the Yom Kippur War were less ambivalent than those expressed in the Six Day War. Indeed, Sobhani has suggested that the Iranian authorities were aware of the approximate date of the Egyptian attack in the Sinai, and were privy to a number of Egyptian battle plans. Tehran, apparently, did not pass on this information to Israel.[2] During the war, Iran sent pilots and aircraft to Saudi Arabia and permitted the over-flight of Soviet cargo aircraft for the replenishment of Arab military stock. Furthermore, both Egypt and Syria were the recipients of Iranian medical supplies and facilities, while the Shah refused to allow Jewish volunteers from Australia to use Tehran as a transit point to Israel.[3] Moreover, after the outbreak of the war, the Shah agreed to an Iraqi request for the resumption of friendship between the two countries, thus allowing Iraq to withdraw three battalions from its border with Iran and divert them to the war effort.[4]

Though this episode was ostensibly damaging for the Policy of the Periphery, in a candid interview, the Shah noted that it had not been his intention to enter the war on the side of the Arabs. Rather, he had said, 'Iran was ready to intervene in order to assist in the implementation of Resolution 242'. In addition, he found no paradox in Iran's support for the Arabs, whilst maintaining an economic relationship with Israel. The Shah also believed that closing Israel's economic office in Tehran would be 'of no benefit'. Moreover, he said that Iran's relationship with Israel existed because Israel existed and he was curious as to why the Arab world did not 'demand that their friends among the great powers' sever ties with Israel, as demanded from Iran.[5] However, after taking into account this proactive involvement in the war, it remains true that, for Iran, the overriding issue was how to obtain the optimum balance of power between Israel and the Arab world in the aftermath of the war, in order to check Soviet influence in the region.[6]

The British Foreign Office believed that the Iranians had 'emerged well' from the war, though the 'element of hypocrisy is not particularly attractive'. Moreover, it was reported back to London that Iranian Foreign Minister, Khalatbari, told the British ambassador in Tehran that Iran's relations with the Arabs had survived the war and had even come out favourably.[7] Whitehall noted that Iran disagreed with the Israeli policy of retaining occupied territory, but found both sides to blame for the recourse to war over communication. Also, the Iranian Finance Minister revealed to the British that Iran would not support the reduction in oil production by the Arab countries, or the oil boycott directed against those Western nations perceived to have been pro-Israel in the war, but neither would it raise its own output. However,

Tehran was willing to agree to the price increase declared at the Gulf Organisation of Petroleum Exporting Countries (OPEC)[8] meeting.[9]

For Iran, it appeared that the war had aided in linking the politics of Arabia to those of the Persian Gulf. The implication was clear; in the future, knock-on effects emanating from the Arab-Israeli conflict could directly affect Iran.[10] The nightmare scenario for Tehran was either a further war between the Arabs and the Israelis, resulting in another Arab defeat; renewed polarisation of the region and the ensuing penetration by the USSR, or a growth in popularity and power of radical elements in the Arab world.

The Shah believed that the Yom Kippur War had shown that the Arabs could fight and that Israel was no longer invincible. Furthermore, in the aftermath of the war, he apparently thought that the Arab states should terminate the oil embargo, intended to punish the West for its perceived support of Israel, until it was clear whether efforts to achieve peace would bear fruit.[11] In the wake of US Secretary of State, Henry Kissinger's failed shuttle diplomacy, the Shah revealed that he blamed Israel for the lack of progress in the Arab-Israeli peace process, though did not deny Tehran a peace-keeping role of sorts, sending the 132nd Rifle Battalion of the Iranian army to join the UN forces on the Golan Heights in September 1975, and contributing a naval unit to the UNEF.[12]

Two weeks prior to the outbreak of war, Iranian UN Representative, Khalatbari, spoke of a 'world-wide disenchantment [with Israel] over the retention of Arab lands'. He continued, 'We heard the embittered world opinion voiced by Representatives of so many nations, including my own, clearly rejecting the retention of occupied territories by Israel'. After taking into account the possibility that the Iranian government knew of the impending Arab attack on Israel, Khalatbari's comments assume an added significance. He stated that 'negotiations amongst the parties can only be undertaken if there is a reasonable guarantee for the withdrawal of Israel from the occupied Arab territories' and 'a just solution for the problem of Palestinian-Arab refugees'.[13] Some weeks later, Iranian Representative, Hoveyda, spoke of the latest outbreak of fighting in the Middle East as proof that the 'Arab people would not accept the verdict of force, no matter what the price of defence might be'. He noted that the failure to bring peace to the region was 'directly linked to the refusal to redress the tremendous injustice suffered by the Palestinian refugees'.[14]

In addition, the Shah revealed there would be no peace in the region as long as the rights of the Palestinians were not fulfilled and, in 1974, stated that Israel's refusal to talk to the PLO would make peace negotiations more difficult. In the same year, at the UN, Representative Khalatbari, stated, 'I do not intend to stress the serious potential consequences of the intransigent policies pursued by Israel, nor do I need to emphasise the adverse effects of such policies'. He also revealed that, 'as was demonstrated by the war last October, the physical security of Israel can by no means be guaranteed by the occupation of Arab lands'.[15] In addition, Iran supported, along with the Arab bloc, Ethiopia and Turkey, UN Resolution 3210 (XXIX) of 14 October 1974, inviting the PLO to participate in discussions involving the Israel-Palestine conflict.[16] Indeed, speaking of the Palestinians, Hoveyda stated,

> Today, for the first time, the problem is now being put in its proper perspective: in other words, the legitimate, inalienable rights of the Palestinian people, as a distinct entity-and no longer as a mass of refugees living off international assistance.[17]

Moreover, Iran voted in favour, along with the Arab bloc, Ethiopia and Turkey, of UNGA Resolutions 3236 (XXIX) and 3237 (XXIX): the former codifying the inalienable rights of the Palestinian people, and the latter granting UN observer status to the PLO.[18]

In an interview given in 1975, the Shah noted that Iran had followed a policy of 'my enemy's enemy is my friend' *vis-à-vis* its relationship with Israel. He also said that the situation in the Middle East had changed and he envisaged a new equilibrium in the area, one that could eventually become integrated into an Islamic framework.[19] After President Sadat visited Tehran in 1976, the Shah purportedly stated that the Palestinians were a reality that could no longer be neglected and that they should have a territory in which to express their statehood. This said, it is interesting to note the Shah's realist attitude towards Israel did not prevent Iran from voting in favour of UNGA resolution 3379, determining Zionism a form of racism and racial discrimination. The resolution was sponsored by the Arab bloc and saw Britain, Israel and the US among those states opposing it; while Turkey and Iran supported it and Ethiopia abstained.[20]

Although ostensibly supporting the notion of Palestinian statehood, Iran was keen to discern between the various Palestinian factions. The Shah stated that Iran was capable of discriminating between the justness of the Palestinian question and the wrongdoing directed against Iran by some Palestinians.[21] Indeed, the Shah was concerned about radical Palestinian elements that aided in the training and support of his opponents. For example, in 1976, a letter from George Habash, the leader of the Popular Front for the Liberation of Palestine, to Hamid Ashraf, the head of a left-wing militant group in Iran, was captured in one of the group's buildings.[22]

This did not prevent Representative Khalatbari from harshly criticising Israel at the UN. Indeed, he noted, 'no one can harbour the illusion that a lasting peace will return to the area until such time as Israel withdraws from the Arab territories occupied by force.' Speaking of his country, the Representative added, 'we commend the renewal of the mandate of the United Nations Emergency Force and the acceptance by Syria of the mandate of the United Nations Disengagement Observer Force'.[23] Furthermore, speaking of the conflict in Lebanon, Khalatbari opined, 'yet another distressing situation has emerged in the Middle East. No respectable nation, especially States enjoying close and historical ties with Lebanon, can ignore the tragedy that has befallen this land ... peace must be returned before it is put beyond reach'.[24] Moreover, the issue of Palestinian refugees was unequivocally voiced by Iranian Representative Fard, when he noted that the Palestinians, 'have been subjected to gross injustice and unmitigated human suffering. They have been expelled from their homes, deprived of their inalienable human rights and property and forced to live a precarious existence'.[25]

These sentiments were echoed some two months later when Iranian Representative, Mokri, revealed that, 'a just and lasting peace in the Middle East calls for the ... withdrawal of Israeli armed forces from territories occupied in June 1967 and the recognition of the inherent right of the Palestinian people to self-determination and statehood'. He also noted that, 'effective participation by the Palestinian Representatives in peace negotiations is an essential element in resolving the Middle East dispute'.[26]

Whether the aforementioned statements were made cynically, in order to maintain a pan-Islamic narrative by Iran and to cover up the problem of Iran's relationship with the Palestinians, or whether they were sincere, the Shah saw Menachem Begin, Israel's right-wing prime minister who came to power in 1977, as potentially damaging to the Arab-Israeli peace process. The concern was that Begin would demand a higher level of commitment from the Palestinians than had previously been required by Israeli governments and, subsequently, the peace process would falter. As a consequence, the Shah threatened to reduce Iranian co-operation with Israel, if Israel were unreceptive during any future attempts at reconciliation.

This was a serious threat and was treated accordingly in Jerusalem. Foreign Minister Moshe Dayan was duly sent to Tehran following Begin's election, in order both to allay the fears of the Shah and to convince him that peace negotiations would not be hindered by the election of the Begin government. Meanwhile, at the UN, Khalatbari, stated that, 'recent moves by Israel in imposing its laws on the inhabitants of the West Bank and authorising new Jewish settlements in the occupied Arab lands have created new obstacles on the road to peace'.[27] In addition, Iran voted in favour of UNGA Resolution, A/Res 32/5, on Israeli actions in the West Bank and Gaza and requesting that Israel cease such actions.[28]

Though the regime in Tehran differentiated between the Palestinian people and those Palestinians engaged in terrorist activities against Iran, the Shah succeeded in limiting hostility between his regime and the PLO by supporting both its role as the sole legitimate Representative of the Palestinian people and its participation in the Arab-Israeli peace process. He did not, however, grant the organisation permission to open offices in Iran.[29]

Concurrently, at the UN, the Shah's Representatives maintained their harsh criticism of Israel. Representative Ehsassi, in particular, spoke of instances when Israeli police, or military units had entered Palestinian students' dorms and had detained students for extended periods, without charge, or without due process of law.[30] Moreover, during Begin's visit to Tehran in February 1978, the Shah took the opportunity to explain that President Sadat, in taking the decision to make unilateral peace with Israel, had placed himself in a position of danger in the Muslim Middle East and that it would be a grave mistake for Israel not to take the matter seriously.[31]

The fear of regional instability also made Iran alter its relationship with Iraq. By 1974, the Kurds in Iraq were being crushed by the Soviet-aided Iraqi war machine and, for Iran, the only way to ensure the continuance of the Kurdish rebellion was to introduce Iranian ground forces. This was more than the Shah was prepared to consider and, coupled with the belief that regional stability was vital in order to protect Iran's oil shipping lanes, Tehran decided to turn to the new regime in Iraq, under the leadership of Saddam Hussein, and negotiate a deal. Thus, on 5 March 1975, the Shah signed an agreement with Hussein at an OPEC meeting in Algiers. Under the terms of the agreement, Iran would end its support for the Kurdish rebellion and, in return, Iraq would cease its support for anti-Iranian elements operating in the Persian Gulf.[32]

The Algiers agreement came as a surprise to both the US and Israel. Upon returning from the meeting, the Shah ordered the Kurdish border closed and informed Israel, by way of its Mossad chief, only after the fact. For Israel, it was becoming clear that ties between the two countries were not only becoming a liability for the Iranians, but that an avenue of Iranian-Arab dialogue, hitherto closed, was now opening. Moreover, in practical terms, with the closure of the Iran-Iraq border, Israel would lose access to areas of Iraq. The Shah was quick in his attempts to placate the Israelis, revealing his belief that Iraq would eventually attack Iran and that Iran was merely buying time with the Algiers agreement.[33]

The following year saw a memorable event in the history of the pro-Israel lobby in the US. A highly respected member of the US Republican party, Senator Jacob Javits, supported arms sales to Iran, due to its firm support for Israel. Javits believed that Israel had precious few allies, especially in the Middle East, thus Iran's support was of paramount importance. Javits blocked US aid to Saudi Arabia, while fighting for military aid for Iran. Three meetings of the sub-committee on foreign assistance of the Senate Committee of Foreign Relations, held in September 1976, saw Javits co-sponsor a resolution reducing the number of Sidewinder and Maverick missiles requested by Saudi Arabia from 2,000 and 1,500 to 850 and 650, respectively.[34]

Indeed, despite differences between the governments of Begin and the Shah, military co-operation between Iran and Israel continued to flourish and arguably reached its zenith in 1977, when Jerusalem and Tehran signed a joint oil-for-arms agreement, worth US$1billion. The assistance Israel was able to offer Iran was more beneficial than a conventional arms procurement programme with a larger power, as it was less publicised, did not appear to be fuelling the arms race and the improvements Israel could make to existing Iranian weapons aided in making the Iranian armed forces more battle ready.[35] The joint development of a missile system was a particular attraction. In 1977, both countries were working on a project known as Operation Flower. The fruits of this project were to be a missile system capable of delivering a non-conventional strike against a threat emanating from the immediate area. For the Iranians, the missile system would offer a solution to the threat posed by Iraqi SCUD missiles, which had been supplied by the USSR. To this end, Iran showed its eagerness to take part in the project by shipping approximately £260 million of oil to Israel. For Israel, apart from the inherent value of an additional missile system, the development would allow it to fine-tune the software on its already existing Jericho missile and allow it access to Iran's long-range missile testing facilities.[36]

Moreover, in July 1978, General Hassan Toufanian, the Shah's vice minister for war, visited Tel Aviv, where he was involved in a series of talks with Israeli Foreign Minister, Moshe Dayan and Minister of Defence, Ezer Weizmann. In these meetings, Toufanian commented on the usefulness of a mutual missile project and suggested that Iran and Israel work together in order to safeguard Anwar Sadat and King Hussein of Jordan, two moderate and pro-Western leaders.[37]

The Shah, in addition, believed that arms procurement and Iranian industrialisation went hand-in-hand and, to this end, decided to manufacture Iranian versions of Israeli 120mm mortars and 155mm self-propelled guns in Iran. A site was chosen for the factory, south of Isfahan, and contracts were drawn up for the production of 60, 81, 120 and 160mm mortars and 155mm self-propelled guns. Also considered was the possibility of Iran exporting surplus weapons to Pakistan, in an attempt to neutralise India's military superiority.[38]

However, since the end of 1976, the level of social revolt in Iran against the Shah had been so great that preparations were being made for his abdication. The economy, after being overstretched, was placed under the control of Jamshid Amuzegar, a former Minister of the Interior, whom the Shah appointed prime minister, but the measures he took to combat inflation served only to worsen the situation. As a result, unemployment rose, particularly affecting the newly arrived rural immigrants and reductions in benefits and payments to members of the *ulama* aided in aggravating the dire social situation. In 1977, there was a crystallisation of newly politicised and emboldened elements of Iranian society, who began to campaign for greater human rights and democracy in Iran.[39] In addition, in January, 1978, the newspaper, *Ettela'at*, published a highly critical article on Khomeini, entitled 'Black and Red Imperialism'. Full of personal insults towards Khomeini, it resulted in mass demonstration and bloodshed. Eventually, the forces ranged against the Shah's regime comprised the religious, liberals and leftists. In February 1979, opposition forces took control of Tehran and the Shah fled into exile.[40] Israel was particularly concerned about the outcome of these events. As a US report stated,

> Like the rest of us, Israelis have watched with awful fascination Iran's progression to the lower depths. They believe the friendly and staunchly pro-West regime of the Shah has crumbled beyond repair and await with foreboding its successor. Few doubt that the next government, whoever its leader ... will terminate most, if not all, aspects of the carefully constructed and close Israeli-Iranian relationship.[41]

Israel, Iran and Khomeini

With the establishment of an Islamic Republic in Iran in 1979, the country became a theocracy under the rule of Ayatollah Ruhollah Khomeini. On 18 February 1979, the new regime severed ties with Israel. The only other country to receive such treatment was Egypt,[42] whose ties with Iran were broken as punishment for its peace treaty with Israel. Indeed, the Iranian revolutionary leaders concluded that Israel could never be compromised with, and neither could any third party doing so with the Jewish state.[43] The time of the severance was not random; the announcement was made a matter of hours after Yasser Arafat had met the Iranian cabinet.[44] The new Iranian revolutionary mantra dictated that Israel was the 'Lesser Satan', while the US occupied the position of 'Great Satan'. In addition, slogans calling for Israel to be annihilated became integrated into much of the rhetoric of the revolutionary propaganda.

This new Iranian doctrine was immediately apparent at the UN. Representative Shemirani was quick to reveal the essential difference between the regime of the new Islamic Republic and that of the Shah. He stated that 'this meeting marks the first opportunity for the Provisional Revolutionary and Islamic Government of Iran to address itself to vital issues confronting this world Organization'. He then decried 'the illegal Israeli occupation and colonization of Jerusalem and other Arab and Palestinian territories'. Eager to emphasise the Islamic Republic's religious credentials, Shemirani noted that 'This fact is especially true in the case of the world's 800 million Muslims, or nearly a third of the planet's population'.[45]

The Representative of the Islamic Republic believed that, 'the existing situation in Jerusalem and other occupied territories points quite clearly to a calculated and systematic process of desecration, emasculation and exploitation of shrines, legacies and peoples of these lands by their Israeli occupiers'. The symbolism of Jerusalem, again, was of particular importance and he noted that, 'The occupied Holy City of Jerusalem has quite accurately been described as a city having been reduced to a tiny enclave, a ghetto, by Israeli colonization'.[46]

Given its fervent Islamic nature, it is no surprise that the new Iranian delegation focused much of its efforts on what it viewed as Israel's intent to alter the status and physical characteristics of Jerusalem. As revealed in Shemirani's statement, 'Israel has proceeded to deface and demolish Islamic sites and shrines, with the Al Aqsa Mosque and its adjacent structures representing primary cases in point'. The Palestinian issue also became a more perceptible and vocalised tenet of Iranian foreign policy. Indeed, later in the same speech, the Representative explained that the inalienable rights of the Palestinian people,

Is now one of the main pillar (sic) of Iran's foreign policy consideration. This policy is not only predicated on the religious and cultural affinity Iranians have always had for their Palestinian brothers, but is also a natural product of the successful Iranian revolution, whose main objectives were the elimination of oppression, colonization and imperialism.[47]

The change of regime in Iran saw the replacement of Western orientated, secular politicians, with religious, conservative clerics, who saw the US and Israel as the main enemies of the new Islamic Republic. However, there were elements in both Iran and Israel who believed that the new political reality in Iran would not necessarily have an adverse effect on the ties between the two countries, as, they believed, the mutual interests of Jerusalem and Tehran transcended the nature of temporary political regimes. This point was brought in to sharp relief with the outbreak of the Iran-Iraq war in September 1980.

Saddam Hussein had attempted to take advantage of the turmoil that had engulfed Iran in the immediate aftermath of the revolution and had launched a large-scale military assault. Initially, the Iraqi army was successful and the Iranian regime turned to Israel for help.[48] Indeed, for Israeli policy makers, the war was testament to the efficacy of the Policy of the Periphery; Iran, by forcing Iraq to commit entire legions around the *Shatt al-Arab*, had neutralised a potential threat to Israel from the Arab eastern front.[49]

The arrival of the new regime in Tehran also conveyed an essential change in the Iranian leadership's attitude to the Arab-Israeli conflict.

Whereas previously it had been a geo-political struggle, now it was seen as a religious crusade. The relationship with those radical Palestinian groups shunned by the Shah, now changed under Khomeini and the same groups were proactively courted. Initially, Yasser Arafat had not acknowledged a Palestinian role in aiding the anti-Shah organisations, but now implied one and expected to be rewarded. Furthermore, on his visit to Tehran, which began on 17 February 1979, Arafat recited the Khomeini slogan of 'Today Iran, Tomorrow Palestine'.[50]

In particular, these Palestinian groups' activity in southern Lebanon became a focus of Iranian interest, as a nexus between potential Iranian military confrontation with Israel and concern for the plight of the Lebanese people began to crystallise. Iranian UN Representative Shemirani, noted that, 'Israeli intrigue, incursion into and general involvement in the domestic affairs of Lebanon and its violation of its sovereignty have on numerous occasions been the subject of reports and resolutions emanating from the Council'.[51] Furthermore, he opined the, 'Israeli invasion of Lebanese territory and the subsequent loss of inno-cent civilian life and destruction of property caused by those vicious attacks, have served once again to "drive the point home" regarding Israel's expansionist, belligerent and self-serving motives'.[52]

Reports have mentioned that the turmoil surrounding the departure of the Shah and the inauguration of Khomeini cost Israel some US$225 million in both 1978 and 1979.[53] However, in 1980, it was discovered that Israel was selling weapons to the Khomeini regime.[54] For ele-ments of the Ministry of Defence in Jerusalem, it appeared paradoxical to sell weapons to Tehran, whose armies pledged to liberate Jerusalem, after conquering Baghdad. A partial explanation of the Israeli behav-iour is rooted in the fact that Persian Jews had been treated well under the Pahlavi dynasty; the approximately 90,000 strong community had its own schools, synagogues and social institutions.[55] Moreover, many Iranian Jews prospered as merchants, lawyers, pharmacists and doctors and the 600 members of the Tehran Association of Jewish Physicians, *inter alia*, obtained a position of some standing.[56]

This changed, however, when the Shah fled Iran. The new regime affected immediate change in the relationship between Israel and Iran, with Jerusalem withdrawing its diplomatic staff before any harm could befall it. Whilst the Israeli diplomats were preparing to leave, many Iranian Jews were also making plans to abandon their long-time homes, though many others, instead, chose to demonstrate openly their loyalty to Iran. In March 1979, thousands of Jews marched from the Saadi Synagogue to the Ayatollah's offices, in order both to express support for the Ayatollah and to condemn what some saw as Israeli propaganda, designed to lure them away from Iran to Israel.[57]

Israel was made the scapegoat for many former perceived injustices. Foremost amongst these was the capture and control of Arab lands. In addition, Israel was blamed for anti-Iranian policies in Washington and its good relations with the Shah were a source of criticism. Indeed, Khomeini had stated in 1963 that Israel intended to expropriate the wealth of the Iranian people, that its goal was to 'suppress and exploit' and that it was supported 'by all the imperialists'.[58] This was an important rhetoric, as the success of the revolution depended partially on the success of its image in the international community, particularly in the non-aligned and Islamic world and amongst the rejectionist states in the region. To this end, Iran used Israel as a focus for its desire to consolidate its position in the Middle East, to castigate those Arab leaders who had negotiated with Israel and to support those elements fighting it.[59]

Prior to his return to Iran, Khomeini had stated that Iranian Jews would not be harmed, and on his return, he reiterated to Iranian Jewry that the Islamic revolution would not be detrimental to their well being. He declared that, although Iran would have no political relations with Israel, Iranian Jewry would be allowed to live and worship in a more conducive environment than that afforded to them under the Shah's regime.[60] In this way, Khomeini distinguished between Judaism and Israel/Zionism, as the Shah's regime had distinguished between Islam and Arabism at the UN.

In Tehran, Jewish centres of activity flourished and the city's Jewish hospital was highly respected.[61] However, in April 1979, Habib Elghanian, the President of Iran's Jewish community, was executed, as were a number of other Jewish leaders in the ensuing months.[62] In addition, on 7 August, the public prosecutor general of the Islamic revolutionary courts declared that opposition newspaper, *Ayandegan,* had been established with the aid of SAVAK, the CIA and Israel and that the aim of the paper was to undermine the Islamic revolution. As a result, the *Ayandegan* head office was occupied by armed members of the Islamic Revolutionary Guard, its printing machines closed down and thirteen members of its editorial board arrested and imprisoned.[63]

At the UN, Iranian Representative Yazdi stated that it was the first time 'since the *coup* engineered in Iran by the Central Intelligence Agency in 1953 that the Iranian delegation to the United Nations has represented the true preference of the Iranian people'. This was swiftly followed by a historical overview of the preceding quarter of a century, 'It is an undeniable fact that during the past 25 years, the Shah of Iran was a puppet of imperialism and zionism'. He went on to explain that, 'while the Iranians felt a deep sense of solidarity with the people of Palestine and their sole and legitimate Representatives, the PLO, the Iranian delegation voted with the Zionists, whose repression of the Palestinians and the Lebanese has become comparable to Nazi criminal acts'.[64]

For Jerusalem, it appeared clear that the new regime's animosity to Israel was being translated into hatred for Iran's Jews and, after the removal of the Israeli diplomatic representation in Iran, there was little Israel could do to influence the situation. Iranian Jews had been pro-Shah, pro-US and were pro-Israel, or so thought many Iranians, and the animosity existing between the Shi'a community of Iran and those Iranians of the Baha'i faith, who were seen as pro-Western, and who the Shi'a saw as heretics due to their belief that Muhammad was not the final prophet, was swiftly applied to the Jews, as many Jews had been in business with Iranian Baha'i. For the Iranian Jews, the situation was unclear: on one hand, Islamic Law allowed for, and protected, the 'people of the book', but slogans appearing in public, particularly in the months leading up to the revolution, calling for death to the Jews and the Baha'i, fuelled their anxiety.[65]

The Israeli concern was that excessive pressure on Iran to cease its persecution of Persian Jewry may enflame an already sensitive situation, whilst doing nothing may invite further attacks. The solution came in November 1979 with the decision of the US to place an arms embargo on Iran, following the seizure of the US embassy in Tehran. For Israel, this was an ideal juncture both to continue the Policy of the Periphery and to alleviate the predicament of the Iranian Jews. To this end, an agreement was reached between Tehran and Jerusalem, seeing Iran receive spare parts for its US manufactured weapons from Israel, whilst Israel was given assurances that Iranian Jews would be allowed to leave Iran.[66] This said, the new regime in Tehran was unflinching in its public opposition to Israel at the UN and, the following month, supported UN Resolution A/Res 34/136, concerning permanent sovereignty over natural resources in the occupied Arab territories.[67]

Regarding the logistics of the arms deals, in July 1981, Yaakov Nimrodi, Israel's former Military *Attaché* to Tehran, signed a US$135.8 million contract with Iran, which included forty 155mm field guns, 68 Hawk missiles, M-48 tanks, some 50 Lance missiles and 3,730 Copperhead laser-guided 155mm artillery shells.[68] The following year saw Ariel Sharon, then Israeli Defence Minister, discuss the possibility of selling arms to the Islamic Republic to the tune of approximately US$27 billion.[69]

The Iranian rhetoric at the UN, however, remained vociferous. Taking the context of the 1978 Litani Operation, when the IDF entered Lebanon up to the Litani River, and alleged Israeli responses to transgressions of the cease-fire agreement of 24 July 1981, Iranian Representative, Moussavi, pledged to fight with 'everything in our power against the Zionist aggression against the territories of our brother nations of Syria, Palestine and Lebanon'. He also emphasised Khomeini's distinction between Judaism and Zionism, 'There is no racial prejudice or animosity towards the Jewish people in revolutionary Iran. In our opinion, however, Zionism is a political movement rooted in racism and expansionism', which carries out 'Nazi-type crimes'.[70]

The 1982 Lebanon War

During the 9th Emergency Special Session of UNGA, convened from 29 January – 5 February 1982 to discuss Israeli actions on the Golan Heights, the Iranian delegation had ample opportunity to express the foreign policy tenets of the first Islamic Republic and they were not found wanting. Representative Velayati chose this juncture to attack both Israel and the US. Speaking in Persian, he stated,

> The catastrophe is, in brief, the Zionist aggression supported by imperialism, the occupation of the Islamic territory of the Palestinians, the continued expansion of the Zionist non-entity and its further encroachment on more and more of the Arab world in an effort to fulfil the illusionary promise of a territory extending from the Euphrates to the Nile.[71]

Talking of the US, Velayati exclaimed,

> In propagating the political cancer of Israel in the heart of the Islamic and Arab world and in giving support to the loathed regime of the buried Shah, that symbol of global arrogance - the Great Satan - has ultimately no intention other than that of shackling the rising and freedom-seeking nations of the world.

Returning to Israel, he opined,

> The annexation of the Golan Heights is only one part of the episode, and certainly not the last one. So long as expansion from the Euphrates to the Nile is the dream of the racist Zionists, so long as the merciless tradition of reliance on force and savagery constitutes the principal linchpin of the policy of the Zionists and of their imperialist supporters, headed by America, providing for all their needs from bread to bombers, this tragedy will continue.[72]

Certainly, since the removal of the Shah, Iran had become a forerunner amongst the Muslim rejectionist states. This was evident at a later stage in the same speech, when Velayati stated that the US 'is trying to achieve its Satanic goals by a show of its military strength. It is in this context that all the truth-loving forces of the world have expressed their firm opposition to the two Camp David agreements'.

The Representative believed that it was military action by the Arab world that was the most 'realistic approach of the Moslem Arab nations to deterring the Zionist aggression, and not the submissiveness ... that turned the great victory of 1973 into a humiliating defeat by welcoming and following ... the Satanic policy of Zionist Henry Kissinger'. Furthermore, he added, with Sadat's acceptance of the Camp David accords, Sadat had 'turned his back on the Islamic community, as well as on his own nation, and recorded his name as a traitor in the history of Islam'.[73]

Eager to emphasise the international context of the conflict in the Middle East and to parade Iran's Islamic empathy, the Representative, talking of Israel, stated,

> This aggressive regime, having come to an agreement with Egypt ... is trying to annex some other Islamic lands on the pretext of the strategic importance of the Golan Heights ... and also to increase its pressure on the Arab Steadfastness Front, at the head of which stands the heroic nation of Syria.

Moreover, he announced that the US was using 'the territory of Palestine' as 'a base for the American Government and a centre for the implementation of its satanic conspiracies. It is from there that America is exercising its intervention in other countries'. Velayati also believed that the US was behind the Iran-Iraq war, proposing that, 'To prevent active participation by the Moslem forces of Iran on the Palestinian front, America urged the Iraqi regime to attack Iran's borders in the south and the west'.[74]

In fact, the Iran-Iraq war sporadically succeeded in diverting Iranian rhetoric over the Arab-Israeli conflict in general, and towards Israel in particular. A prime example was a speech made by Iranian Representative Rajaie-Khorassani, who believed that criticism by Iraq of Israel's annexation of the Golan Heights was 'a statement of self-condemnation, because Iraqis have already occupied a part of our land'. The Iranian Representative then detailed Iraqi ignorance of Iranian political institutions.[75]

This mini-hiatus in Iranian criticism of Israel was brief; Rajaie-Khorassani stated the following month that, 'The Council is meeting today to discuss the question of the murderous policies of the Zionist non-entity in occupied Palestine, a matter that is by now well known even to the American public, which is usually deliberately kept ignorant'. Then he turned to the UNSC,

> For more than a third of a century the Council has been dealing with the question of Palestine without any concrete results. During these long, tedious years of Palestinian suffering and deprivation many officers have come to office in the United Nations ... and reached the age of retirement. Nonetheless the Palestinian problem is not yet settled.[76]

This was the opening salvo in an explicit attack on the UNSC from the Iranian delegation, led by Rajaie-Khorassani. Speaking of the PLO Representative, he announced, 'What generosity on the part of the Council, to which the Palestinians are indebted for more than 30 years of insecurity so far ... It is too slow a procedure'. The Representative offered an explanation as to the speed of the UNSC in acting upon the Palestinian issue and suggested that, 'the Council must have been very busy and must have had enough reliable evidence to ignore the problem of the Palestinians all through those good years'.[77]

Returning to Israel, he implicated the UNSC in the actions of the 'Zionist agent of imperialism', which had 'been gradually encroaching and occupying further pieces and places in every direction, the Golan Heights being the most recent'. Also, 'The Zionist usurper and its supporters in the Council had better keep in mind that expansionist aggression and security are contradictory and incompatible'. He then attacked the principles of the UN in general,

> When democracy is so much upheld in this part of the world, why should some members of the Council without any superiority in terms of virtue or wisdom enjoy the privilege of veto..? The law of the jungle, as Imam Khomeini has said, at least applies to the jungle itself, but democracy, which is the holy norm of the United Nations, does not apply even to its own organs.[78]

For Rajaie-Khorassani, the situation facing the Middle East in general
and the Palestinian cause, in particular, were the issues upon which the
credibility of the UNSC ultimately rested. This point was highlighted
by his assertion that, 'If, after a third of a century of United Nations
involvement in the debate over Palestine, the matter is resolved by the
sacrifices of the Palestinian people on the scene of the struggle, that
would then be the end of any credibility this system of collective security may have left'. In fact, he revealed,

> The achievement of any success by the United Nations, because
> of the special aspect of the Council, has been so minimal that it
> has already brought disillusionment to hundreds of millions of
> people all over the world. The confidence of the oppressed in the
> United Nations is almost completely gone.[79]

On 11 April 1982, Allan Goodman, an immigrant from the US, killed
two people and wounded nine others at the Temple Mount in Jerusalem.
The Iranian condemnation of the incident took the form of a statement
by Rajaie-Khorassani, who eulogised the 'large number of innocent
people, including children and persons of various ages' that had been
'murdered in a very sacred place'. The Representative used the incident
to reveal a litany of alleged Israeli actions, 'The racist forces occupying
Al-Quds have during the past 15 years demonstrated not only that they
are incapable of safeguarding the Islamic sanctuaries but that, on the
contrary, they are determined gradually to destroy them'.[80]

During this speech, he also alluded to possible anti-democratic
behaviour as a response to the attack. He suggested that, 'the potenti-
alities of all Muslim nations should be mobilized to establish Islamic
control over the Islamic shrines and sanctuaries in Al-Quds as well as
over the Islamic and Arab territories under occupation'. Furthermore,
he publicly called for martyrs to the cause. The UNSC heard of sacrifices that Muslims would have to endure. In particular military sacri-
fice 'on the part of all those Mojahedin of Sabilillah, who are all over
the Muslim world and are ready to accept martyrdom for the sake of
Islam ... In these circumstances this seems to be, as we believe, the
only practical way to achieve justice'.

Moreover, Rajaie-Khorassani confessed to the UNSC that, 'a prophetic tradition tells us: he who is martyred in defence of his dignity or property is a shahid — or a martyr. That is to say, when a Muslim achieves martyrdom in defence of Al-Quds he is a shahid. Muslims are therefore determined to defend it and go to paradise'. In the meantime, he spoke of 'The waves of human oceans ... rolling against the oppressive racists and the high tide is going to drown the imperialist Powers which are supporting the enemy'.[81]

Interestingly, the Representative drew a distinction between 'foreign subjects' and the 'native Jews of Palestine', recalling the distinction made by Khomeini between Jews and Israel/Zionism. To facilitate a solution to the problem of Palestine, he suggested that, 'Foreign subjects who under the fake claim of dual nationality have moved to Palestine to kill innocent local people must return to their countries of origin where street murder does not yield national demonstrations and protests'. However, he claimed,

> My delegation does not wish any discrimination or injustice for the native Jews of Palestine. Those Jews, like the Christians and Muslims, must have full freedom to administer their sanctuaries, to preach and practise their faith ... as well as the chance to participate in the administration of the country without any discrimination.[82]

On 6 June 1982, the IDF launched 'Operation Peace for Galilee' and the invasion of southern Lebanon. Israeli Prime Minister, Menachem Begin, ordered the operation as, at the time, more than 15,000 PLO fighters were based throughout southern Lebanon, and were using it as a base to shell northern Israel. In addition, earlier the same month, Palestinian gunmen had attempted to assassinate Israel's ambassador to Great Britain, Shlomo Argov.[83]

The attack on Argov was planned by an Iraqi named Nawal al-Rosan, who was found to be a colonel in Iraqi intelligence. This has led some to believe that the assassination attempt was an Iraqi ploy to entice an Israeli invasion of Lebanon in response, thereby facilitating a possible cease-fire between Iran and Iraq, thus enabling both countries to concentrate on their common enemy: Israel.[84] On the second day of the invasion, a high ranking Iranian delegation arrived in Damascus in order to co-ordinate a jihad against Israel and soon afterwards, several hundred Iranian combatants reached Damascus, on their way to Lebanon to confront the IDF.[85] On 10 June, with the Israelis on the outskirts of Beirut, the ruling Revolutionary Command Council issued a statement revealing that Iraq was ready for an immediate cease-fire and would accept a UN verdict on responsibility for the war.[86]

The Israeli invasion furnished the Iranians with an opportunity to confront the IDF and to export the tenets of the Islamic Republic further. It was also an opportunity to challenge both the forces of Zionism and their US patrons. Israel now found itself fighting with the Shi'a in the south. The Shi'a had, until this point, maintained a hesitant relationship with Israel, though it is arguable that Iranian association with the Shias in Lebanon predated the Iranian revolution.[87] Khomeini saw the Israeli invasion as a US inspired plot to draw Iranian attention from its war with Iraq and he berated the Arab world for doing nothing to help the Palestinians. To this end, the Iranian military began drawing up plans to engage the IDF in Lebanon.

The Iranian delegation at the UN encapsulated Tehran's attitude towards the Israeli invasion of Lebanon. Representative Velayati stated, 'we have in mind the most recent crime against humanity of American Imperialism and occupier Zionism committed in the Islamic world ... thousands of children and innocent ... old women and men have been drenched in blood in ... Sabra and Shatila ... by a group of ... Zionist terrorists'.[88] To elucidate his point, he opined that, 'This is not the first crime committed by Israel, nor will it be the last'.[89] The wrath of the Islamic Republic's new regime, however, was not reserved solely for Israel; the Representative noted that, 'As we have frequently stated, we can be sure that the Israeli criminals will not content themselves with the massacre of innocent people', rather they would also 'establish the influence of world devouring America'.[90]

What the Iranians had not presumed, however, was that the Iranian revolution may have been a significant catalyst in Israel's decision to invade Lebanon in the first place. Indeed, post-revolutionary Iran was no longer an ally of the US and, as Ramazani suggests, Israel saw a chance to invade Lebanon because it had the capability to do so without severely damaging its ties with the US; because Israel's strategic value to the US had increased dramatically after the demise of the Shah, and the Iran-Iraq war provided a distraction. In addition, Israel was aware of the US concern over the Soviet invasion of Afghanistan in 1979 and its commitment to defend the Gulf oil supplies.[91] Thus, the invasion drew little sustained criticism in Washington. However, the Iranian delegation at the UN made no attempt to hide its forces' intervention in the fighting. Velayati revealed that Iran had 'entered on the scene of the war against the savage attack by Israel on Lebanon ... and dispatched our forces to the scene of battle'. He also noted that Iran was the only 'non-front line country that embarked on such action'.[92]

Thus, the largely halcyon days of the Shah's Iran and Israel were over. Although the new regime in Tehran had allowed the immigration of Iranian Jews via Pakistan and had turned to Israel for aid during the Iran-Iraq War after Israel had stepped in to replace a withdrawing US, Israel was now facing Iranian fighters in southern Lebanon. The Policy of the Periphery had indeed initially transcended the temporal nature of political regimes, but would eventually falter, as the Islamic Republic began to promote regional instability. Velayati's statement surely revealed the beginnings of contemporary Iran's involvement in the Arab-Israeli conflict. Eventually, Iran would use proxies, such as Hezbollah, to target Israeli military and civilian targets. The effective use of regional proxies by Iran would also become apparent, with the rise in influence of Hamas as a political force in the occupied territories. The spirit of Israeli-Iranian co-operation was over.

CHAPTER 4

TURKEY AND ISRAEL, 1956–72: ALIGNMENT AND AMBIVALENCE

The Turkish approach to Israel in the post-Suez War period was, in many ways, similar to those of both Ethiopia and Iran. Initially, Turkish UN Representative Selim Sarper, was unwilling to vote in favour of the draft proposal submitted by the US, A/3256, later to become UNGA Resolution ES-997, pressing for a cease-fire and withdrawal to behind the armistice lines. Sarper stated that although his delegation realised 'the importance and extreme gravity of the situation [in Egypt] ... if the Assembly presses for a vote tonight ... I shall find myself in considerable difficulty in regard to voting'.[1] Moreover, he pressed the Assembly not to vote on the draft proposal 'at least during the next two or three hours.'[2] However, Turkey voted in favour of all draft proposals insisting on the withdrawal of non-indigenous forces from Egypt, but in the vote over A/3290 (UNGA Resolution ES-1000), establishing a UN Emergency Command Force to secure and supervise a cessation of hostilities at the Suez Canal zone, it chose to abstain.[3] The behaviour of the Turkish diplomat and, in particular, the Turkish abstention over such a draft resolution revealed the Turkish desire, not to take an overtly proactive stance on the war, for fear of endangering its relations with either Israel, or the Arab world.[4]

Turkish involvement in the Suez War debates at the UN was limited. Sarper returned to the issue on 7 November, when he explained that Turkey believed 'it is in nobody's interest to create a vacuum ... even of a temporary nature. It is with this understanding that we shall lend our support to the nineteen-Power draft resolution' (A/3309).[5] Turkey also supported the draft resolution presented by Argentina, Burma, Ceylon, Denmark, Ecuador, Ethiopia and Sweden (A/3308) 'in its present form'.[6] This was the furthest the Turkish Representative was prepared to go in involving his country in the Suez campaign at any level, preferring instead to make a lengthy statement concerning the Soviet invasion of Hungary, for example, on 4 November.[7]

Turkish-Israeli relations were subject to significant strains in the immediate aftermath of the war. Due to concentrated Arab pressure, Ankara downgraded its mission to Israel and recalled its minister, Sevket Istinyeli. At the fore of this pressure was Nasser, who reportedly stated that 'after struggling successfully to end 70 years of British rule and 400 years of Ottoman domination, we will not be again shepherded by the Turks'.[8] Nasser continued with his invective and accused Iraqi Prime Minister, Nuri al-Said, of having allied himself with the Menderes government in Turkey, the Israelis, the British and the French, in order to depose him. This anti-Israel stance was enforced by the President of Pakistan, Iskandar Mirza, who urged Menderes to break all ties with Israel, economic and political, because of its actions in Egypt.[9]

As a result of this pressure and due to the fact that the US condemned the tri-partite action, on 26 November 1956, Ankara issued a statement 'The Turkish government has decided to recall its Minister in Tel Aviv, who will not return ... until a just and final solution of the Palestine question has been achieved'.[10] Under the terms of diplomatic reciprocity, Jerusalem recalled its minister in Ankara and the heads of both missions were lowered to the rank of *chargé d'affaires*.[11] In fact, it was reported on 4 December, that Turkey had granted the *chargé d'affaires* in Israel, Rifat Ayandar, the personal rank of minister, and in January 1961, Israel announced that its *chargé d'affaires*, Moshe Sasson, had been awarded the same rank.[12] Thus, by 1961, diplomatic relations between the two countries had been restored to pre-Suez levels.

The change in the relationship was greeted with some disquiet in Turkey. Though the issue was scarcely reported in the media, the Turkish opposition attempted to question the government's actions in the Assembly.[13] In addition, there was resentment within the Israeli Foreign Ministry over the subsequent posting of Minister Istinyeli to Rio de Janeiro, while the former Israeli minister to Ankara, Maurice Fischer, remained ambassador, *in absentia,* to Ankara and would, it was hoped, eventually be returned to his post.[14] This point, however, was not clear from the statements made at the UN by Turkish Representative Esin, who noted that 'the outstanding achievement in the Middle East has been the attainment of full independence and sovereignty by the Arab countries of the region'. Speaking of Syria, Esin revealed that 'We, in Turkey, have affection and respect for the people of Syria with whom, as with all Arab nations, we are linked by cultural, religious and historic ties'. The diplomat believed a strong Syria to be 'an additional guarantee of our own security'.[15]

The break in relations between Israel and Turkey and the subsequent statements made at the UN by Turkish diplomats surely impacted on the viability of the Policy of the Periphery. Primarily, the Turks, in moving away from Israel, saw themselves as further cementing their relationship with Washington, after the US administration had castigated Israel for its involvement in the Suez War. In addition, Ankara succeeded in throwing a sop to the rising Arab nationalism that was virulent in the aftermath of the war.

The recalling of their minister was, for the Turks, a successful compromise in the face of Arab propaganda. Although the term *chargé d'affaires* implied a scaling down of relations between Ankara and Jerusalem, the reality was that the head of the delegation was usually a seasoned diplomat of ambassadorial rank, with a full team supporting him.[16] Moreover, it was made clear by Ankara that the withdrawal of the Turkish minister was done in order both to save the Baghdad Pact and aid Iraq and was not an anti-Israel act *per se.*[17] This episode revealed the Turkish desire to placate the Israelis and safeguard the relationship between the two countries and was similar to the actions of the Shah in allaying Jerusalem's fears after Iran had signed the Algiers Agreement.

The *coup* in Iraq in 1958, though, helped the administration in Ankara to overcome its reticence in further developing ties with Israel. As a result of the *coup*, the Israeli envoy in Ankara was called to the Turkish Foreign Ministry and subsequently relayed to Jerusalem that the Turks were taking action parallel to that of Israel and that the Turks would be pleased to see full co-ordination of mutual political actions.[18] It was at this point that Ben-Gurion informed US President Eisenhower of the Policy of the Periphery. Ben-Gurion stated that although 'it is a vital necessity for us, as well as a source of perceptible strength to the West in this part of the world,' the Policy of the Periphery would need both US support and the knowledge in the other countries involved that the US was favourably disposed towards it.[19] Eisenhower's initial response was lukewarm, but a further letter from US Secretary of State, John Foster Dulles, was more positive, urging Ben-Gurion to press ahead with his plan.[20]

On 29 August, Ben-Gurion met with Turkish Prime Minister Menderes and laid the foundations of the Israel-Turkey alliance. Although the meeting probably defined the framework for ties between Ankara and Jerusalem, there is very little documented evidence from the Turkish side. The Turkish view of the meeting was that it had indeed forged an understanding between the two countries; Sezai Orkunt, head of Turkish military intelligence between 1964 and 1966, admitted that there had been an agreement, and that no more than ten military and civilian officials knew about it.[21]

The same year saw the Israeli delegation to Turkey asked to persuade its government to reduce the level of Turkish debt to Israel by some 30–40 per cent. If this was not done, a Turkish official explained, Turkey may find it difficult to continue trading with Israel. At the time, Turkey owed Israel approximately US$2 million. The figure had been higher, but Israel had reduced the amount by purchasing cotton and low-grade wheat from Turkey. Also mentioned was Turkey's desire for bilateral quotas to be fixed. Both these statements caused some anger in Jerusalem, the latter due to Israel's desire for flexible buying power.[22] However, as time passed, the incident became less pressing and, the following year, Israel Radio announced that Turkey had granted import permits for US$4 million worth of Israeli goods, including cars and antibiotics.[23]

The same year saw the Turkish delegation at the UN become more focused on the issue of Palestinian refugees. Indeed, Representative Zorlu stated that 'the solution of all litigious questions between our Arab brothers and Israel ... would cause our profound satisfaction'.[24] At the Special Committee, Turkish Representative Menemencioglu noted that UNRWA would be in a position to remedy some of its most pressing problems, such as the registration of refugees and the case of the Azazma Bedouin and the frontier villagers in Jordan. His concern emanated from the Turkish people having close 'cultural, social and religious ties with their Arab neighbours and had every sympathy with the Palestinian refugees'.[25]

In March 1960, Turkey and Israel signed a new trade agreement in Ankara, covering an annual volume of approximately US$16 million. Israel was to import mainly agricultural products and Turkey, manufactured goods. Trade figures for that year show Israel exporting approximately US$8.9 million worth of goods and importing approximately US$7.7 million worth.[26] Two months after this agreement was signed, in May 1960, there was a *coup* in Turkey and the Democratic Party government was ousted. Almost immediately, the new government began the search for additional sources of support, as they felt the US aid they were receiving was inadequate.

On 2 January 1961, the agreement was extended for a further year and the annual commercial exchange was fixed at US$12.5 million for Israeli exports to Turkey and US$13.5 million for Turkish exports to Israel. The new figures seemed more realistic, as those for the initial agreement had not been achieved.[27] In fact, 1961 saw Israel exporting US$7.3 million worth of goods to Turkey and importing Turkish goods to the value of US$6 million. In addition, several notable Turks visited Israel in the same year: Brigadier-General Nuri Teoman, Governor and Mayor of Ankara and Seyfi Demirsoy, head of the General Confederation of Turkish Workers' Syndicates, the first official visit of a Representative of the Turkish labour movement.[28]

During these years, however, there were occasional sources of tension in the bi-lateral ties. In September 1959, an Israeli fishing vessel, *Snunnit*, was seized and its crew of five detained by the Turkish coastguard, accused of illegally fishing in Turkish waters. On 6 March

1960, the crew was sentenced to a year's imprisonment and the ship confiscated. A re-trial was ordered and the sentence was increased to five years' imprisonment and three years' exile in Turkey. Jerusalem was aghast at the seemingly disproportionate punishment, given the relationship between the two countries. However, on 22 November, the crew was released under the terms of a general amnesty and the ship was returned to Israel in 1961.[29]

The same year saw Turkey become an elected member of the UNSC.[30] On 11 April, the UNSC voted on draft resolution S/4777,[31] which was adopted by a majority decision and became UNSC Resolution 162. This resolution called for Israel to refrain from holding a military parade planned for 20 April in Jerusalem. On the day before the vote, Turkish Representative, Turgut Menemencioglu, briefly stated 'the only interest which my Government has in any question affecting the Middle East, of which we ourselves form a part, can be no other than the common interest of peace and security in justice and equity'.[32] He then went on to say that the decision taken by the Mixed Armistice Commission[33] on 20 March, was binding.[34] The Turkish desire for justice to prevail in the Middle East was evident in Representative Eldem's claim that the problem of the Palestinian refugees had deteriorated and become more complex in the previous thirteen years. He ventured that Turkish concern over the issue was based in both historical solidarity and sympathy emanating from their own experience.[35]

This theme had been enunciated at length by Representative Sarper some two months earlier. He stated that 'The sentiments of the Turkish people towards all their Arab neighbours stem from brotherly ties strengthened by common cultural and social bonds'.[36] Sarper spoke in such terms in the aftermath of the UAR severing its diplomatic ties with Turkey, due to its recognition of Syria's newly acquired independence. To this end, Sarper detailed his country's centrality to both Turkish and Arab histories and interests. In particular, he stressed the importance of the Turkish relationship with Syria, 'Turkey has a common frontier of over 400 miles with Syria', which contains 'trade routes, transit connexions, communications and other links of common interests'. Moreover, he noted that 'along this frontier there are

Turks who possess farms on the Syrian side, and Syrians who own land on the Turkish side' and that 'by mutual agreement they are allowed to cross over the frontier to earn their daily bread'. Indeed, Sarper expressed both confusion that the position of the Turkish government 'could be misinterpreted as though it were against anyone' and regret over the severance of relations.[37]

In an attempt to counter further Arab perception of Turkish militaristic motives and to blur the dimensions of the Policy of the Periphery, Sarper articulated the 'importance [to Turkey] to the maintenance of brotherly relations and friendly co-operation with all the Arab countries' and that, despite the fact that relations had been broken, 'the Turkish people will always continue to maintain most sincere feelings of friendship and good will towards the people of the United Arab Republic'. He added, 'we are desirous of seeing a close and brotherly co-operation among all the Arab peoples as an important prerequisite for peace and stability in our region' and that 'the form in which such co-operation may manifest itself is a matter which can only be decided by the various Arab countries themselves'.[38] These statements belied the rapid development of the Policy of the Periphery.

In 1964, concomitantly and in pursuance of the military aspect of the Turkish-Israeli alliance, General Cemal Tural, who would later become Turkey's Chief of Staff, visited Israel. Furthermore, the head of Israeli Military Intelligence, Meir Amit, along with other members of the Israeli intelligence community, visited a secret US military base at Erzurum, Turkey, at the invitation of Turkish officials and unbeknownst to the US. In the same year, moreover, Turkey hosted Uzi Narkiss, then head of the Israeli military academy.[39] Whilst the diplomatic stance of Turkey was one designed to placate the Arab world, the timing of the visit revealed the Turkish desire both to lessen its fear that NATO would not come to its aid were it attacked by Warsaw Pact countries, and to reduce its dependence on US graciousness. Furthermore, it was aware that it required support in the UN for its policy over Cyprus. Indeed, the fact that the US was not informed of the visit to the base revealed a certain disdain on the part of Ankara towards the US administration.

Turkey, Israel and Cyprus

In June 1964, US President, Lyndon B. Johnson, sent a dispatch to the Turkish government, stating that the US would not allow Turkey to invade Cyprus[40] and implied that NATO may not come to its aid were Turkey to provoke subsequent Soviet intervention.[41] The incident, coming after the Cuban missile crisis, served to weaken Turkey's pro-Western attitude and further emphasised its need of support over the Cyprus issue at the UN.[42] The stance taken by the Johnson administration had indeed exposed the limitations of Turkey's potential relationship with the US and seemingly demonstrated its seclusion in the developing world, in spite of its Western-orientated foreign policy.[43]

Turkey began to make overtures to the USSR,[44] creating concern that the anti-Soviet fear drawing Israel and Turkey together was becoming less relevant. These overtures culminated in March 1967, with Turkey and the USSR signing the most significant industrial co-operation agreement that Turkey had hitherto negotiated with any state. The deal saw the USSR agree to construct several industrial plants in Turkey, including a steel mill, an aluminium smelter and an oil refinery. Moreover, by the end of the decade, Turkey was receiving more economic aid from the USSR, *per annum,* than any other country.[45] For Israel, this negative scenario was emphasised by the development of the Palestinian problem and the realisation that the Arab world was about to become a vital factor in Israeli-Turkish relations.[46]

In fact, the Arab world quickly identified the Cyprus issue as a potential tool in its confrontation with Israel. To this end, the Arab states attempted to seduce Turkey by promising diplomatic support at the UN on its Cyprus policy, in return for Turkey's rejection of ties with Israel. However, the Arab overtures were not successful. Essentially, the Turkish government objected to external forces attempting to influence its foreign policy, thus turning the matter into one of a nationalist nature.[47]

However, 1964 saw a number of episodes which seriously threatened the longevity of the Turkish-Israeli relationship. The first occurred as a result of Turkey's bombing of Greek-Cypriot positions in Cyprus.[48] After the bombing, the Greek-Cypriot authorities issued a letter to international heads of state, condemning the attack in the strongest possible terms, maintaining that it was unprovoked. Then Israeli President, Zalman Shazar, with the blessing of his prime minister, Levi Eshkol, sent a reply in which he expressed sorrow at the Turkish action and raised the issue of a potential aid package. The Turkish reaction to this offer was one of irritation and surprise. Indeed, Prime Minister Inonu sent a message to Eshkol, in which he claimed that the Israeli offer was a show of support for Makarios. Turkey's anger and shock was compounded by the fact that Makarios, concomitantly, was strengthening Cypriot ties with Israel's adversary, Egypt.[49]

In addition, Turkey felt unable to aid its own nationals on the island, whom they saw as suffering at the hands of the Greek-Cypriot authorities.[50] For the Turks, it again appeared that continuing loyalty to the West did not guarantee their national security and Ankara now began looking to the developing world, particularly the Arab states, for potential support.[51] For Israel, a dilemma existed: on the one hand, it was loathe to jeopardise its relations with Turkey and went to great lengths to assert this to the Turkish government whilst, on the other, it was keenly aware of the debt it owed to Cyprus for aiding Jewish immigration to Palestine during the days of the British Mandate.[52]

At the UN, as if to reflect its government's disenchantment, the Turkish delegation was once again talking of the 'painful problem of Palestine' and the Palestinian refugees. Representative Erkin noted that the refugees numbered some 1,250,000 and that 'these unfortunate people, far from their land and from their homes, lead a precarious existence in camps and barracks, dependent on international charity and the hospitality of the host countries' and that the situation 'cannot continue indefinitely'.[53] Moreover, the Turkish delegation was keen to see the introduction of various measures to alleviate the plight of the Palestinian refugees. Indeed, Representative Turel highlighted the success of the UN High Commissioner for Refugees in fund-raising drives and drew special attention to the sale of gramophone records, suggesting that the same initiatives be used to aid the Palestinian refugees.[54]

Although not directly affecting Turkey's policy towards Israel, these statements marked the beginning of the process which culminated in the ostensible freezing of ties between the two countries. In November 1966, Israeli Minister of Housing and Development, Yosef Almogi, made an official visit to Turkey, the first for an Israeli minister. The Turks were keen to keep the visit a secret and did not fly the Israeli flag, nor did they allow Almogi to visit Ataturk's mausoleum.[55] The final official event preceding the freezing of ties was the inclusion of the names of a Rabbi, and the chairman of the anti-Defamation League of B'nai Brith, in a letter published in the *New York Times*, which articulated a growing concern over the future of the Ecumenical Patriarchate of Constantinople and the Greek Orthodox Church in Istanbul. The shock felt in Ankara was ensured by the majority of the signatories being bishops and other clergy, many from the Armenian and Greek Orthodox communities. The Turks took a particularly dim view of this episode, as they believed their treatment of the Jews in the past had been good and, as such, Jews should not have expressed this view on 27 April 1966, the Turkish director of military intelligence, Sezai Orkunt, delivered a message to Israel's Military *Attaché* in Ankara, Baruch Gilboa, who informed Jerusalem of the freezing of relations.[56]

Though the above episode was undoubtedly painful for Turkey, there can be little doubt that it was a pretext for the freeze. Indeed, after the *New York Times* incident, Prime Minister Eshkol suggested that Israel place a counter-letter, in order to placate the Turks. However, Gilboa revealed that such an act would be pointless, as Orkunt had admitted personally that the real reason for the freeze was Turkey's pro-Arab policy. This was followed, on 17 May 1966, by a meeting between Israeli Foreign Minister, Abba Eban, and Turkish Foreign Minister, Sabri Caglayangil. During the meeting, Eban stated that there was no need for Turkey to be overly concerned about possible Arab reaction to their countries' relationship, but, despite this, Caglayangil insisted that the most personal contacts between the countries should be halted temporarily.[57] It is at this point that the relationship reached its nadir. However, it must be noted that overt contact continued and Turkey continued to allow the IAF access to its airspace for their flights to and from Iran. In addition, in the aftermath of the Adapazari earthquake in the north-west of Turkey in the summer of 1967, Israel reacted faster than the Turkish government, and dispatched 300 units of plasma to aid those who had been injured.[58]

Turkey, then, found itself on the horns of a dilemma: after overcoming Arab pressure to abandon its ties with Israel in the aftermath of the Suez War and although strongly opposed to permanently renouncing these ties, it nevertheless saw the importance of the numbers game at the UN, where the solitary voice of Israel would seemingly be of little help. The Arab-Israeli war of June 1967, though, would serve to sharpen Ankara's political stance towards Jerusalem.

Turkey at the UNGA and the Six Day War

With his government surely impressed at the speed and scope of the Israeli victory in the Six Day War, Turkish Representative Ihsan Sabri Caglayangil, adopted a more supportive approach towards Israel. On 22 June 1967, he stated that 'If this forum is used only for invective and sterile polemics ... we shall not only have worsened the situation but we shall have dealt a mortal blow to the prestige and moral influence of the United Nations'.[59] Moreover, analogous to the Iranian perspective, the Representative believed that the war might have been avoidable, stating 'the events leading up to the crisis ... showed clearly enough that the Middle East had embarked on a perilous and tragic course ... the international community did not use all the pacific means available to it to prevent the outbreak of an armed conflict'.[60]

Caglayangil then noted Turkey's geographical proximity to the warring countries, thus attempting to emphasise his country as a regional player, though not an Arab state. 'We deeply deplore this situation in a region whose destinies are so closely linked with ours. It has always been Turkey's policy to promote good relations with all its neighbours and other countries in the region'.[61] This apparent show of impartiality was then tempered 'we have many historical and cultural ties with the Arab countries in particular', based on a 'profound affinity'. As if to highlight the point, the Representative later asked to 'take this opportunity to express our profound sympathy and friendship towards the people of the Arab countries and our firm hope that they will soon emerge from this perilous and painful stage of their history'.[62]

Continuing with this theme, Caglayangil revealed later the same year that

> 'with regard to the Arab countries, we rejoice to see that they are acting in a constructive spirit which leaves the door open to an improvement in the situation' and that 'the Arab countries have given proof of goodwill, realism and flexibility, and if that spirit could be reciprocated it would undoubtedly serve to bring an end to the political deadlock'.[63]

Using this language, Caglayangil succeeded in emphasising the non-Arab nature of Turkey. In addition, implicit through these speeches was the Turkish perception of Israeli intransigence which, in not being overtly expressed, allowed both the Israeli and Arab sides to interpret the Turkish stance to their advantage, thus not endangering the potential strengthening of the Policy of the Periphery.[64]

It is within this framework that Turkey voted in favour of draft resolution A/L 522/Rev.3,[65] but abstained in the vote over all four paragraphs of draft resolution A/L 519, thus showing that, like Iran, Turkey did not believe that Israel should compensate the UAR and was unafraid of challenging the position taken by the Arab Member States, which voted in favour of the draft resolution.[66] In addition, Turkey voted against the hard-line Albanian draft resolution, A/L 521, while the Arab states voted in favour.[67] Turkey then abstained in the vote over draft resolution A/L 523 Add.1, while the Arab states voted against and voted in favour of draft resolution A/L 526 Add.1–3 (2252) which it co-sponsored, calling for aid to the Palestinian refugees.[68] Turkey also abstained in the vote over draft resolution A/L 529/Rev.1 (2256), while it is unclear how it voted over draft resolution A/L 530.[69]

The issue of refugees had been raised by Caglayangil previously 'we have always advocated a just and fair settlement that would end the tragic plight of over a million refugees who for twenty years have been leading a precarious and miserable existence and who are now afflicted by fresh suffering and misfortune'.[70] Caglayangil, later the same year, revealed that 'Turkey has always felt sympathy for those Arab refugees',[71] but also revealed that 'Israel has always maintained that its desire was to live in peace with its neighbours in respect for independence and its territorial integrity'. However, for the diplomat, it was unclear how Israel could 'reconcile that expressed wish with its refusal to withdraw from the territories it has occupied, with the unilateral measures it has adopted in Jerusalem'. Caglayangil, though, believed that 'the Arab countries ... are acting in a constructive spirit which leaves the door open to an improvement in the situation'. The same Arab countries, opined the diplomat 'are being reproached for wanting simply to return to the conditions which prevailed before 5 June 1967'.[72]

Representative Eren revealed that a film had been shown to the Special Political Committee after its 587th meeting, and had demonstrated the urgency of the Palestinian cause. He added that the Turkish government had made regular financial contributions to UNRWA and, by 1967, had increased its annual participation by 25 per cent. Moreover, it had augmented its financial aid with a programme of scholarships for refugees and had provided the equivalent of US$611,000, in response to UNGA resolution 2252 (ES-V). The Representative also criticised those countries deemed unsupportive of UNRWA. Eren could not believe that the subsistence of approximately one million people could be left to the vagaries of international charity.[73]

Turkey then voted in favour of UNGA Resolution 2443 (XXIII),[74] establishing the 'inalienable rights' of these refugees and voted for draft resolutions A/SPC/L 166[75] and add.1, A/SPC/L 198[76] and A/SPC/L 231,[77] all dealing with the rights of the Palestinian refugees. Continuing in the same vein, Turkey voted in favour, along with the Arab states of draft resolution A/L 602.rev.2 and add.1 (2628), codifying respect for the rights of the Palestinians.[78] Finally, within this context, Turkey voted in favour,[79] along with the majority of Arab states, for draft resolution A/L 650 rev.1 (2799), calling for, *inter alia*, the renewal of the work of the Special Representative; and the assistance and promotion of agreement to reach a peace settlement.

Turkey, like Iran, was keen to both internationalise a solution to the Arab-Israeli conflict and emphasise its affinity to the Holy City of Jerusalem. As such, it co-sponsored and voted in favour of draft resolution A/L 527/Rev.1 (2253) and A/L 528/Rev.2 (2254), which condemned the alteration of the status of Jerusalem.[80] In addition, Caglayangil insisted that the government of Israel 'should ... not ... create a *fait accompli* in Jerusalem' and revealed that he 'would at this point remind it of the Turkish people's close interest in the Holy Places in that city'.[81] In order to express his government's position on the matter, the Representative chose language of a non-specific nature, suggesting that the Turkish people were interested in the Holy Places of all the religions in Jerusalem, thereby placing no greater significance on Islam than on other faiths.[82]

The Turkish concern over Jerusalem also manifested itself in a speech made by Caglayangil some two years later, when he claimed that 'the burning of the Al Aqsa mosque has added a very critical element to an already alarming situation. This sacrilegious act has plunged the Moslems of the world into a state of great emotion and deep sorrow.' He continued 'it is difficult to absolve the country occupying the Arab part of Jerusalem of responsibility for an act committed in a place under its military jurisdiction'.[83] The latter part of this statement is particularly interesting as, unlike his Iranian counterpart, the Turkish Representative was quick to attribute some blame for the arson to Israel. In fact, an Australian, non-Jew carried out the act.[84] Dennis Michael Rohan was a follower of an evangelical sect known as the Church of God and admitted to the crime, claiming that it would hasten the coming of the Messiah. The Turkish statement, however, was little more than a political concession in order to placate the Muslim members of the UN after an attack on a symbol of such significance to the Muslim world.

In September 1969, Turkey was an observer at the first Islamic summit conference held in Rabat, Morocco. The summit was convened to discuss both the fire in the Al Aqsa Mosque and the status of Jerusalem, after the Israeli capture of the city during the Six Day War. The Turkish government made clear that the summit was political rather than religious in nature, as participation in a religious summit would be anathema to Turkish secularism.[85] For the Turks, it was clear that the fire and the status of Jerusalem would be the sole subjects for discussion. In addition, the Turkish delegation at the conference stated that its government would not move beyond criticism of Israel to actual censure, and would discuss the Palestinian issue on humanitarian grounds only for the duration of the conference.[86] This latter point was a central issue at the summit, with the majority of the Arab states applying heavy pressure on Turkey to sever its ties with Israel. The Turks condemned what they deemed as external interference in their foreign policy and did not break contact with Israel.[87]

Concomitantly, the Turkish UN delegation, not differing in essence with other nations in its concern for the plight of the Palestinian refugees, accepted the report of the Commissioner-General of UNRWA, which revealed that food rations for the refugees could not be cut further, as they were receiving 1,500 calories per day in the summer and 1,600 calories per day in the winter. The concern for Turkey and for UNRWA was that any further cuts would jeopardise the very existence of the refugees. The Turkish belief was that the Special Political Committee could not allow the next generation of refugees to experience the hardships of its parents. Representative Eren, in his role as Chairman of the Working Group on the financing of UNRWA, noted that there were approximately 250,000 children in UNRWA schools, whose future education hung in the balance. The diplomat also outlined the UNRWA budget for food, education, health services and shelter, which in 1971, stood at US$47 million.[88]

Turkish association with Jerusalem, in particular and to Islam in general, was re-emphasised the following year. Keen to show that the continuing military actions in the area had far-reaching effects, Turkish UN Representative, Umit Haluk Bayulken, stated that 'first and foremost, geographic proximity dictates our daily anxiety'.[89] Bayulken then detailed the cause of the Turkish apprehension 'our skies reverberate with the whistle of the jets and the thunder of the guns in the neighbouring lands to the south'.[90] He also noted that 'the Turks have been in the forefront of Islam for a thousand years',[91] thus continuing the Turkish affiliation with Islam, but then admitted that 'the region graced by the three prophets was blessed with the peace of peoples of different faiths living in mutual acceptance and in mutual trust.' [92]

The Turkish government, at this time, was experiencing a period of turmoil.[93] Members of the Turkish armed forces were attempting

to warn the government that elements within the military were planning a *coup*, which was called off when one of the protagonists turned
whistleblower.[94] The resulting tension saw a civilian government assem-
bled, which soon faced tough opposition from radical elements based
in the country's universities. Consequently, in March, 1971, the army
intervened and implemented martial law in a number of provinces,
as well as shutting down several leftist and rightist organisations and
newspapers.[95] When Israeli Consul to Turkey, Efraim Elrom, was
kidnapped on 17 May 1971, Turkish security forces reacted by arrest-
ing intellectuals around the country. Eventually, the number of those
arrested was in the hundreds, with many of the Turkish political and
cultural elite amongst them. Elrom was found dead later the same
month and his kidnappers arrested.[96] The Turkish Liberation Army
claimed responsibility.[97]

The following year, Representative Olcay returned the attention of
the Special Political Committee to the plight of the Palestinians. He
told the committee that only around half the registered refugees had
received full food rations, which were not sufficient to be called an
adequate daily diet and that approximately 375,000 infants and children received no rations at all, due to budgetary limitation.[98] Moreover,
any reduction in the health services would jeopardise the health of
the children, a scenario exacerbated by the fact that UNRWA, whilst
providing schooling for approximately 250,000 children, could only
award 687 scholarships for higher education. The Turkish concern was
that any reduction in this aid would jeopardise the children's future
and that the negative effects of the Israeli military actions in Gaza
had not been eliminated. The Working Group reported that approximately US$5 million was required to finance the minimal services of
UNRWA.[99]

Ostensible even-handedness was a central tenet of Turkish diplomacy at the UN throughout this period. Indeed, at one of the final
UNGA sessions of 1972, Turkish Representative Olcay revealed that
'during the course of this century the Middle East has become one
of the most tormented parts of the world. Unfortunately, owing to
unavoidable circumstances its rich resources, which should have been
devoted to the welfare and progress of its people ... remain largely

allotted to military purposes'.[100] But also that 'this summer marked the fifth anniversary of the tragic war of 1967, which shook the Middle East for the third time in two decades and resulted in the occupation of territories of Egypt, Jordan and Syria.'[101]

This was the essence of Turkish policy towards the Middle East during this period of volatility; a policy sometimes ambivalent towards context and not averse to contradiction but, nevertheless, ensuring that the warring parties would, intermittently, feel placated. In addition, the Turkish refusal to vote uniformly with the Arab bloc at the UN displays, what Efraim Inbar has described, as Turkish diplomacy's preference not to be perceived as partisan in Middle East conflicts, lest it should entangle itself in regional political and military quagmires.[102]

Even with the stance of the Turkish government over the Palestinian refugees and the burning of the Al Aqsa Mosque, the Policy of the Periphery was holding fast, underpinned as it was by financial and military dimensions. Indeed, from initially recalling its minister in the wake of the Suez War, Turkey went on to reject Arab demands to sever its ties with Israel, even though the reward was potential Arab diplomatic support at the UN over its stance on Cyprus. Representative Olcay attempted to crystallise the central characteristic of the UN with the words 'Our deliberations on various issues indicate clearly that we all agree on at least one point: that war brings no lasting solution to our differences and that it only sows the seeds of hatred and injustice, thus leading to more tears and bloodshed'. He continued, 'The problem of the Middle East is no exception to this rule and no other region requires the application of mankind's common will for peace more urgently than the Middle East'. Finally and portentously, he noted 'To our regret, we are even witnessing an increase in violence, sometimes taking the shape of full-scale military operations in the area'.[103] With that, the region went to war.

CHAPTER 5

TURKEY AND ISRAEL, 1973–82: REJECTION AND REALIGNMENT

The Yom Kippur War

Eight days prior to the outbreak of the Yom Kippur War, Turkish UN Representative Bayulken was prescient in his statement concerning the delicate situation in the Middle East. He noted that 'This unhappy and stagnant situation of no war, no peace should not be viewed only in the light of its negative effects on the search for a solution ... it carries in itself the seeds of violence' and, the diplomat added 'it must be recalled that peace means a lot more than ... the lack of war ... ' Furthermore, he stated that 'no amount of rhetoric should be able to supply with a cloak of legitimacy any attempt at gaining territory or political prestige by the use of force or by means of forcible *faits accomplis* ... and the delaying of the evacuation of territories'.[1]

By October 1973, relations between Turkey and Israel had reached an *impasse*. Indeed, as a result of Arab pressure, Turkey had allowed the USSR to over-fly its airspace in order to re-supply the Arab armies during the war and, concomitantly, refused the US use of its airbases, thus hampering the re-supply of the IDF. Although the reason behind the Turkish decision was probably its dependence on the oil supplied by the OPEC countries,[2] Turkey benefited from these gestures and, consequently, was not subject to the 1973 Arab oil embargo, though it did have to pay high prices in order to import oil from its neighbours.[3] The OPEC countries' decision to raise the price of oil in 1973–74 in the aftermath of the war had three major effects on Turkey: it became an increasingly vocal member of the Islamic Conference of Nations; it proactively pursued stronger ties with Member States of OPEC and the Turkish position towards the Arab-Israeli conflict transformed to one of a pro-Arab nature.

Although not readily admitted by the Turkish government, the then Turkish Prime Minister, Bulent Ecevit, stated that his country's position was one of positive neutrality,[4] but it became clear, particularly at the UN, that Turkey was supporting the Arab world in its stance against Israel. However, Representative Turan Gunes described Turkish foreign policy as 'based ... on pacifism' and that the 'Turkish nation not only does not support oppression but indeed is always on the side of the oppressed'[5]

Nowhere was this developing pro-Arab sentiment more apparent than the draft resolutions of 1974, calling for the PLO to participate in all relevant discussions on the Middle East. In fact, the Turkish adoption of the Palestinian issue at the UN was unequivocal. In the same year, the Turkish delegation at the UN was instructed to recognise the PLO as the representative body of the Palestinian people. To this end, Representative Olcay stated,

> The plight of the Palestinian people ... can be well understood by us Turks, for obvious reasons. Turkey's active participation in the efforts made for nearly two decades to find ways and means of alleviating, if only partially, the sufferings of a part of the Palestinian people is not a coincidence.[6]

This served as a preamble for the diplomat, who then stated 'We therefore respect the decision of the Arab States which recognised the PLO as the sole Representative of all the Arab people of Palestine and entrusted it with Palestinian national authority'. In addition, Olcay took issue with those opposing the Palestinian cause. He expressed the Turkish government's strong 'disagreement with those who claim that the Assembly had no right to invite the Representatives of the PLO to express their views on behalf of the Palestinian people'.[7]

In the aftermath of the Yom Kippur War, came the perception in Turkey, as in Iran, that Israel was not invincible and that the Arab armies, learning from their destruction in the Six Day War, could now fight. Consequently, the Turkish embrace of the PLO seemed irreversible. This was highlighted by Olcay's statement that Turkey had

> Listened carefully to the statement made by Mr Yasser Arafat, the Chairman of the PLO, the national Representative of the people of Palestine. We consider that he gave a convincing expose of his people's plight resulting from the injustice it has been made to suffer for a quarter of a century.

Finally, Olcay opined that,

> No useful purpose other than continued tension and conflict in the area can be served by refusing to negotiate with the PLO, which is unquestionably the sole legitimate representative of the Arab people of Palestine, for the purpose of the negotiations is obviously to return what lawfully belongs to the people of Palestine.[8]

Indeed, Olcay seemed to champion the Palestinian cause. Some two weeks after the aforementioned speech, the diplomat noted that the UNGA was, for the first time in twenty-six years, considering the question of Palestine in its proper perspective, as a political problem. He also felt that, as UNWRA was in financial deficit, it was pointless to hope for miracles and it was immoral to make the fate of hundreds of thousands of Palestinians dependent on such miracles.[9] He was clear in his opinion that those countries that had not donated to the UNWRA coffers were required to do so, as were those countries whose contributions had not been sufficient. In fact, he believed there was a need for all countries to contribute to UNWRA, even if only symbolically. He also made it clear that while said contributions could serve to alleviate the suffering of the Palestinian people, they would not, in themselves, deliver a lasting peace to the region.[10]

Turkey not only supported nearly all statements and proposals supporting the Palestinians, but also refused to recall the conditions stated in UNSC Resolution 242, guaranteeing the 'termination of all claims or states of belligerency and respect for and acknowledgement of the sovereignty, territorial integrity and political independence of every State in the area and their right to live in peace within secure and recognized boundaries free from threats or acts of force'.[11]

Then, in November 1975, Turkey voted in favour, along with Iran, of UNGA resolution 3379 (XXX), equating Zionism with racism.[12] For Israel, this was the most disturbing resolution passed against it and would serve as a yardstick, against which many countries would be measured by Israeli governments. Thus, according to Israel, in doing so, Turkey had libelled the Jewish state. However, the relationship between the two countries had developed to such a stage that the Turks were unable and unwilling to turn their backs on Israel entirely. To demonstrate this, Turkey was adopting an anti-Israel stance in the public arena of the UN, but at the same time, it also began purchasing arms from Israel. Thus, in 1975, Turkey purchased Israeli made Shafrir air-to-air missiles, Hetz anti-tank shells and Uzi submachine guns and ammunition.[13]

To veil this, there came a Turkish championing of the Palestinian cause at the UN. Representative Caglayangil stated that, 'we have always maintained that Israel should withdraw from all the territories it has been occupying since 1967,' but also added that 'a settlement should allow all countries of the region to protect their independence, their sovereignty and the security of their borders'. In addition, he noted,

> During recent years we have supported all efforts to ensure rec-
> ognition of the political rights of the Palestinians because we are
> and continue to be convinced that this question is at the very
> heart of a broader problem-that of establishing a just and lasting
> peace in the Middle East.

Finally, the diplomat revealed the Turkish diplomatic stance,

> We have supported General Assembly resolutions reaffirming
> the inalienable rights of the Palestinians in Palestine-their rights

to self-determination, national independence and sovereignty and requesting that the Palestine Liberation Organisation should be invited to participate on an equal footing with the other parties in all deliberations and conferences on the Middle East.[14]

The issue of UNWRA was again raised by Representative Akiman in the same year. He made the case that the Palestinian problem was both political and humanitarian and that it was not possible to separate the two aspects. In relation to the funding of the organisation, he noted that the Palestinians had been receiving the minimum in basic services and that any reduction or cessation of such services was unthinkable. Thanking those countries that had given voluntarily and those who had made extra contributions, Akiman suggested that the framework for UNWRA funding be altered, making it more stable. The diplomat revealed that, even if the expected monies were donated in 1977, UNWRA would still face a deficit of US$25 million. At this juncture, he again called on those Member States that had not made a donation to do so and urged others to donate more.[15]

Some two weeks later, Representative Turkmen, gave the UNGA a brief survey of the positive ties between the Turks and the Arabs, in order to facilitate his explanation of Turkey's support for the Palestinians. He noted that 'The Ottoman governments never acceded to demands for a change in the demographic composition of Palestine. In 1947, Turkey voted against resolution 181 (II), calling for the partition of Palestine'. The diplomat noted that the Turkish government had always attempted an even-handed approach to the situation in the Middle East and it was 'on the basis of these considerations that we became a member of the Committee on the Exercise of the Inalienable Rights of the Palestinian People'.[16]

Turkmen then informed the Israeli delegation of the Turkish belief that 'peace, coexistence and understanding with the Arab countries will contribute more effectively to the security and well-being of the people of Israel than the retention of the territories it has occupied since the 1967 war'. In addition, he believed that 'the participation of the Palestinians in any future multilateral negotiation has inevitably become a prerequisite for a meaningful and constructive search for an over-all settlement'. Finally, the diplomat enunciated the report of the Committee on the Exercise of the Inalienable Rights of the Palestinian People and the recommendations of the Chairman of the Committee, Gauci of Malta, namely the 'return of the refugees in two phases and lay down the prerequisites for the exercise of the rights of the Palestinian people to self-determination, national independence and sovereignty'.[17]

Turkey's reaction to Egyptian leader, Anwar Sadat's historic decision to go to Jerusalem in November 1977, was, ostensibly, positive. However, in spite of its pro-Arab leaning during the war, Turkey was, at the time, suffering economically from the rise in oil prices, after the 1973 crisis and although Ankara had been keen to see Sadat take a more pragmatic line regarding the Arab-Israeli peace process, many Arab states vehemently opposed such an accommodating move and condemned Sadat's visit to Jerusalem vociferously. Oil producing countries, such as Libya and Iraq were foremost amongst these countries' ranks.[18] To this end, Turkey was forced to maintain a diplomatic and political aloofness, for the sake of self-preservation. This was perceptible in the words of Turkish Representative Turkmen, less than a week after Sadat stepped off his aircraft in Tel Aviv. Although not celebrating the visit, Turkey had a 'constant belief that an over-all solution of the problem of the Middle East should imply respect for the sovereignty, territorial integrity and independence of all States in the region-including, of course, Israel'.[19]

As part of the Turkish delegation's efforts to internationalise the Arab-Israeli peace process, Representative Akiman celebrated UN resolution 32/40B. This marked an International Day of Solidarity with the Palestinian People which, 'we commemorated only a few days ago at a solemn meeting of the Committee. This occasion provided another opportunity of focusing the attention of the international community on the inalienable rights of the Palestinian people and giving the widest possible publicity to the facts relating to those rights'.[20]

The following year, the Turkish delegation, through Representative Eralp, expressed concern over 'fresh news about the increasing number of Israeli settlements, demolition of houses and buildings, expropriation of land and property belonging to the Arab people, and measures calculated to change the institutional organisation of the Holy Places.[21] Furthermore, he informed the UNSC that, according to 'many reports and news items ... such practices are being concentrated in and around the Holy City of Jerusalem, which is sacred to the Moslem world'. The diplomat opined that 'The international community as a whole and the Muslim people in particular cannot remain indifferent to those developments.'[22]

A Unified Jerusalem and the 1980 Turkish *Coup*

On 30 July 1980, the Israeli Knesset passed the Jerusalem Law which, *inter alia*, stated that Jerusalem, complete and united, is the capital of Israel, the seat of the President of the State, the Knesset, the Government and the Supreme Court.[23] On 2 December 1980, the Turkish Foreign Ministry announced, at the Islamic Conference in Taif, Saudi Arabia, that it was to limit its relations with Israel and withdraw all diplomatic personnel within three months, except for a secretary, who would continue with the title of *chargé d'affaires*.[24] This was a curious development indeed. The initial decision was taken by Ankara on 26 November 1980; however, it did not come into effect until February 1981. The official reason given for Turkey's actions was Israeli intransigence over the Middle East conflict, and particularly, its attitude and behaviour towards Jerusalem. Turkish concern over Jerusalem featured strongly at the UN. Indeed, Representative Eralp noted,

> For centuries, Turkey was part of a large 'commonwealth', which included the whole of the Middle East ... Furthermore, our membership in the Conciliation Commission for Palestine, our membership in the Islamic Conference and our membership in the Committee on the Exercise of the Inalienable Rights of the Palestinian People constitute additional reasons for our not being able to remain silent over the fate of Al Quds.[25]

Eralp was intent on emphasising Turkey's Islamic credentials at the meeting. He presented the UNSC with a brief survey of Islamic benevolence over the holy places of Jerusalem, to emphasise that Israel had no reason to act unilaterally over the status of the city. Indeed, he noted,

> The Church of the Holy Sepulchre in the Old City of Jerusalem ... is frequented by several different denominations of Christians which were often at loggerheads ... To avoid conflicts ... the keys ... were entrusted for generations to an Ottoman Moslem who would open the church in the morning and lock it up at night.[26]

The Israeli behaviour towards Jerusalem, according to Eralp, was not an isolated incident; far from it. In fact, 'the recent bill ... has really been the culmination of the numerous previous unilateral measures taken by Israel in Jerusalem itself as well as other occupied Arab territories'. The diplomat opined that 'The earlier examples of the sacrilege committed against the Al Aqsa Mosque ... and several other measures to demolish the Holy Places of Islam in Palestine cannot be seen as isolated incidents but constitute an integral part of the Israeli plan permanently to occupy Al Quds'.[27]

The Turkish delegation used the Jerusalem Law to launch another attack on perceived Israeli aggression in the Middle East. Turkmen, some three months after the passing of the law, revealed that,

> We are particularly alarmed by recent developments which reflect Israel's intransigence. Israel persists in its policy of establishing settlements in the occupied Arab territories in total disregard of repeated United Nations resolutions and of world public opinion.

This statement, no doubt, was inspired by the 'widespread indignation' that Israel had provoked by 'proclaiming Al Quds as the indivisible and eternal capital of Israel'. The diplomat believed that said Israeli action was 'arbitrary and unilateral' and 'totally incompatible with the principles of international law'.[28]

On the point of Jerusalem, again, he revealed that Turkey 'feels a very strong commitment to Al Quds Al Sharif on historical, spiritual and moral grounds. Al Quds has special significance to all the three monotheistic religions. It has been an Arab and Islamic city for centuries; it will have to remain so'. Furthermore, alluding to the decision taken by the Turkish government to remove most of its diplomatic staff from, and limit its relations with Israel, the diplomat expressed 'satisfaction that since the adoption of Security Council resolution 478 (1980), all embassies located in Al Quds have moved out. The whole world has now been duly alerted to the potential dangers involved in the present course of Israeli policy'.[29]

Representative Kirca stated, some two months later that,

When Israel also realizes the true dimensions of the Palestinian issue and associates itself with the international consensus that is already emerging on the question of the achievement of Palestinian national rights, we shall come closer to the solution of the whole question than we have so far.

He continued, 'According to reports, some Knesset members are even considering a bill to annex the Golan Heights', and added, 'the mayors of Hebron and Halhoul in the occupied Arab territories and the Sharia Judge of Hebron were expelled last May, and those two mayors are now being detained by the Israeli authorities'.[30]

Turkey eventually closed its consulate in Jerusalem in 1980, though this move was of symbolic importance only, as, according to Turkish legal commentators, the main Turkish delegation had always been based in Tel Aviv and the decision to close did little, other than hamper interaction.[31] The Turkish concern over the Jerusalem Law was such that, even before it became law, Turkish Prime Minister Demirel had condemned it and called for political action to counter it. Necmettin Erbakan's[32] party presented the Turkish parliament with a motion calling for the severance of diplomatic ties with Israel and for the expression of no confidence in then Turkish Foreign Minister Hayrettin Erkman, whom Erbakan deemed, politically, too Western-orientated and pro-Israeli.[33]

Demirel, in addressing a delegation of Representatives from 13 Islamic countries and the PLO, who had come to praise him for his stand on Israel, stated that Israel's actions were contrary to international law and that Turkey was opposed to 'gaining territory by the use of force'. He also mentioned the sanctity of Jerusalem and that it 'should never be in Israeli hands'.[34] This statement, however, may be attributed to the fact that, at the time, Demirel's government was dependent on the support of the pro-Islamic National Salvation Party and, as such, was useful as a concession to these elements.[35] When this factor is added to the virtual financial bankruptcy facing Turkey at the time and the appearance of new statesmen as a result of the 1980 *coup*, it becomes clear that the Turkish behaviour was a tool for further strengthening ties with the Arab world, in order to alleviate Turkey's financial predicament. Indeed, the economy was experiencing severe shortages of hard currency and the revenue generated by its exports was not sufficient to pay for its oil, the price of which had reached new heights after the fall of the Shah. In 1980, Turkey's exports totalled approximately US\$2.2 billion, while its oil imports cost approximately US\$3.5 billion.[36]

Necmettin Erbakan had been arrested on 6 September 1980, six days before the military *coup*, at a rally called in order to demonstrate against the Jerusalem Law. Erbakan made a speech at the rally and called on the Turkish government to sever ties with Israel and for all Muslims to 'liberate Jerusalem'. The rhetoric did not cease there and Erbakan demanded that Turkey be released from the western influences that it was labouring under. Demonstrators carried banners with Islamic statements, some demanding the reintroduction of Sharia law and a number of individuals burned the Israeli, US and USSR flags. An added, menacing facet of this rally was the rumour in the Turkish Jewish community, numbering some 20,000 people, that there had been a banner calling for the Jews to be put to death.[37]

This fear was allayed by General Kenan Evren, who stated that Turkey was a nation for all its citizens and that no sector of Turkish society could be criticised for its religious beliefs.[38] It was at this point that the Turkish diplomatic position on the Middle East began to change once more. The initial cause for this was the inability of the Arab world and the PLO to adopt and support Turkey's stance on Cyprus. There was no recognition from Turkey's Muslim allies, either at the UN, or the OIC, of the Turkish Cypriots' demand for a national identity, or their desire for self-determination. In fact, many Arab countries, as well as the PLO, saw the Greek Cypriot government as the Representative of the Cypriot people as a whole.[39]

The eventual lifting of the US arms embargo in 1978, which had been in place since the Turkish invasion of Cyprus in 1974, had been welcomed by Turkey, but the forthcoming US aid was spent in areas deemed of greater importance than the economy, such as the military.[40] Due to its financial turmoil, Turkey was forced to turn to the Arab countries and plead for oil at a reduced price and attempt to increase its exports, particularly within the Middle East. These efforts saw Turkey's exports rise from US$2.3 billion in 1978 to US$5.7 billion in 1982.[41] In 1980, the Turkish government purchased approximately 5 million tons of oil from Iraq, 3.4 million tons from Iran, 2 million tons from Libya and 1 million tons from Saudi Arabia. Saudi Arabia also furnished Turkey with an extra 2 million tons of oil and economic assistance, totalling approximately US$75 million.[42] In addition, in 1981, Turkish imports from Israel totalled US$22.2 million, while its exports to Israel totalled US$14.5 million.[43]

Furthermore, the decision to downgrade Turkey's relations with Israel was taken on the day that then Turkish Foreign Minister, Ilter Turkmen, returned to Turkey, following a trip to Saudi Arabia, with a Saudi Arabian cheque for US$250 million.[44] The downgrading resulted in severe criticism from the US. Indeed, a bipartisan group of 69 senators delivered a letter to Turkish Ambassador to the US, Sukru Elekdag, on 21 January 1981, in which he was told to relay to his government the apprehensions of the senators regarding the Turkish downgrading of ties with Israel. The senators believed that such an action would only serve to embolden extremist elements in the Middle East and potentially jeopardise the Camp David peace process.[45]

Turkey, the year after closing its consulate in Jerusalem, continued a pro-Arab stance *vis-à-vis* Israel. This is evident from a speech made by Representative Turkmen, who noted that,

There must be a fundamental change in the present policies of the Government of Israel. In the course of the past year it has become all the more evident that Israeli policies based on aggression, intransigence and arrogance constitute the principal source of tension and instability in the Middle East.[46]

The diplomat did not limit himself to generalisations, rather he spoke of the Israeli attack on the Iraqi nuclear reactor at Osirak,

> Israel has escalated and widened its attacks in recent months. The premeditated aggression against the nuclear reactor in Iraq and the indiscriminate bombing of Lebanon demonstrate that Israel recognises no limits to its policy bent on domination.[47]

Some three months later, the Turkish delegation expressed its concern over the Israeli decision, taken on 14 December 1981, to annex the Golan Heights.[48] The following day, Kirca noted that,

> Israel is now bent on creating yet another *fait accompli* with respect to the Golan Heights in Syria. The decision of Israel to apply Israeli laws and administration to the Golan Heights is tantamount to the annexation of that portion of Syrian territory under occupation.

The diplomat continued,

> Such Israeli legislation and its implementation would ... be in flagrant violation of all the relevant United Nations resolutions ... the Geneva Convention relative to the Protection of Civilian Persons in Time of War ... as well as ... the Agreement on Disengagement between Israeli and Syrian forces, signed on 31 May 1974.[49]

Turkish displeasure at the Israeli action was placed within Turkey's perception of the region and the international arena by Kirca when he opined that 'Israel, by its Golan Heights decision, proves once again that it prefers to pursue a path of arrogance, short-sighted opportunism and complete disregard for the legitimate interests of its neighbours'. Furthermore, the Turkish delegation believed 'Israel's fait accompli with respect to the Golan Heights is fraught with extreme danger and portends the most serious and highly destabilising repercussions in a volatile and fragile region'.[50]

Turkey and the Lebanon War

The Turkish political and military elites had a clear interest in ending the pre-Israeli invasion *status quo* in Lebanon, which had allowed groups of international fighters to train openly. In the wake of the Israeli invasion, information was relayed from Jerusalem to the Turkish government, revealing the existence of Turkish militant groups operating in the country, as well as the presence of elements of the Armenian Secret Army for the Liberation of Armenia, an organisation dedicated to the murder of Turkish diplomats abroad and to the creation of an independent Armenian state in eastern Turkey. Those Turks that were not required to stand trial in Israel were offered to the Turkish government for extradition.[51]

The Turkish diplomatic stance at the UN prior to the war, however, was far from supportive of Israel. At the Ninth Emergency Special Session of UNGA, the Turkish delegation was critical of Israeli actions. Representative Kirca, noted that,

> we are deeply disturbed by Israel's intransigence, arrogance and imperviousness. Israel's latest act of practically annexing the Syrian territory of the Golan Heights has introduced a new and serious variable of regression into the Middle East situation.[52]

Turkey, however, abstained, with Iran and Ethiopia voting in favour, over UN Resolution ES-9/1, which called for, *inter alia*, all Member States to cease forthwith, individually and collectively, all dealings with Israel in order to totally isolate it in all fields.[53]

The Turkish explanation for their abstention came from Kirca, who revealed that 'We abstained not because we disagree in any way with the condemnation of Israel for this act and with the call to take appropriate measures against it', but rather because 'we feel that the resolution just adopted contains certain elements which do not enhance its fundamental political force. Moreover, some of them are not useful in the search for a just, lasting and comprehensive settlement in the Middle East'.[54]

In fact, Kirca noted at the UNSC, 'Following Israeli actions purporting to change the status of Jerusalem and the Syrian Golan Heights, Israel now appears to have turned its attention to the West Bank and the Gaza Strip'. Lest this were to appear ambiguous, he continued,

We are confident that Israel's decision to disband the Al-Bireh elected Municipal Council and to replace it by direct Israeli rule, and the further decision to dismiss the Palestinian mayors of Nablus and Ramallah, as well as Israel's ruthless oppression of the Palestinian people, will also be condemned by the Council.[55]

He then emphasised Turkish historical benevolence towards the Jews, 'Turks during the Ottoman Empire contributed to a large extent to saving Mediterranean Jews from the ... Inquisition' and 'Turks have also deeply deplored and condemned the Nazi persecution of the Jewish people. It is ... for us an extremely sad spectacle now to observe the same people ... trying to suppress the freedom and basic rights of another people in its homeland'. Furthermore, the diplomat explained, 'The Arab and Muslim character of the Palestinian homeland was preserved and safeguarded entirely intact to the limits of its strength ... by the same Ottoman Empire even in its period of decline'.[56]

The Turkish condemnation of the attack on the Temple Mount on 11 April was quick in coming. Kirca stated that a 'sacrilegious crime was committed last Sunday in Jerusalem against one of the holiest sanctuaries of mankind'. Furthermore, he added, 'Most deplorably, it is not the first time that such criminal profanity has been perpetrated against the Holy Places in the City'. Although admitting that the government of Israel had condemned the attack, the diplomat continued 'The issue ... is not whether the Israeli soldier involved in the incident is insane and whether he acted alone ... Israel cannot be absolved of its obligations towards the Holy Places in Jerusalem'. Moreover, he stated that in the view of the Turkish delegation 'to argue that the deplorable situation is the product of the lunacy of a single, deranged person and to condemn the crime within that framework is not credible, nor is it sufficient to dispose finally of the issue'.[57]

Turkey's refusal to blame Israel outright resulted in the Turkish government clashing with the PLO leadership publicly, particularly in the Turkish media. A prime example of this occurred in August 1982, when Foreign Minister Turkmen revealed in an interview with the left-of-centre Turkish newspaper, *Cumhuriyet,* that the PLO had misunderstood Turkey's sensitivity to terrorism, but also stated that Turkey's support for the Palestinian cause would not be lessened, despite differences with Arafat's organisation. Turkmen elaborated further at a meeting of Islamic foreign ministers in Nigeria, some days after the interview. At this forum, he stated that it was the duty of the Muslim world to prevent Lebanon from becoming a safe haven for elements operating against Turkey and Turkish interests. Israel did not escape the foreign minister's comments, though, and he criticised Israeli behaviour towards the Palestinians and the Lebanese.[58]

Overall, the Turkish approach at the UN to the war in Lebanon was belligerent towards Israel. Turkmen noted that 'The whole world is stunned by the massacre of innocent men, women and children in the refugee camps of west Beirut. That outrage against humanity has compounded the tragedy unfolding in Lebanon since the Israelis invaded that country in early June'. Furthermore, 'The responsibility of Israel in the mass killings of the Sabra and Shatila camps is irrefutable. Israel has shown that it is not encumbered by any moral scruples in the pursuit of its political ambitions in the Middle East'.[59]

Turkmen also noted that the Turkish public was deeply affected by the situation in Lebanon by revealing that,

The aggression against Lebanon, the ruthless Israeli actions, the staggering human losses and the suffering and material damage inflicted upon the Lebanese and Palestinian peoples have been followed with abhorrence and revulsion by Turkish public opinion.

He singled Israel out by stating that 'the withdrawal of foreign forces from Lebanon is of paramount necessity and every effort should be exerted to prevent dilatory tactics by Israel' and that 'It is now up to Israel … to alter its perception of security for itself as consisting of continuous confrontation with its neighbours'.[60]

Israel's neighbours were also the topic of Representative Akin's appearance at the Special Political Committee, which took place the following month. He expressed concern at the conditions of the civilian population in the occupied territories, which had deteriorated drastically, he felt, as a result of Israel's policies of 'annexation, illegal settlement and endless and increasingly brutal repression'. He also spoke of the Palestinian Arabs being 'systematically deprived of their lands and means of livelihood' due to Israel's 'repressive policy in the occupied territories', with the 'apparent aim of destroying the Palestinian cause and the Palestinian struggle for national liberation'.[61]

It was not only the Palestinian Arabs who were suffering, apparently. Representative Gokce noted that,

> The year 1982 has been marked by momentous and tragic events in the Middle East. The invasion of Lebanon by Israel has highlighted in a compelling manner the imperative character and added to the urgency of some of the long-standing realities about the Arab-Israeli conflict.

He continued, 'The Arab Palestinian and Lebanese peoples have paid a terrible price, and their suffering will for ever weigh on the conscience of mankind. Their supreme sacrifices will not be redeemed, however, until the Arab Palestinians are given their homeland and that of the Lebanese people is restored to them'.[62]

The diplomat was clear over which party was to blame for the instability in the region,

> If the current possibility of a settlement in the region is to have any real chance at all, Israel must shoulder its prime responsibility. Israel must ponder the future and realize that force cannot for ever serve as the exclusive instrument of security and recognition … that the Arab Palestinian people are entitled to a homeland and a State of their own; that Israel cannot liquidate

the Arab Palestinian cause through its illegal policies of occupation, annexation, repression and settlements.[63]

This was followed by a statement from Kirca explaining that his delegation had voted in favour of draft resolution A/37/L.52, concerning the massacre of Palestinian civilians in the Sabra and Shatila refugee camps. However, he noted that, 'my delegation is not certain whether the General Assembly, given the information available to it, is in a position to make an exact determination about the nature of those events'. This did not prevent him from expressing,

> Deep indignation and shock at this horrible crime perpetrated against innocent men, women and children. The victims of this appalling massacre were defenceless people who were living in those camps not out of choice but because they were forced to do so by the reality of not having their own homeland.[64]

The Turkish government, much like the Iranian government under the Shah, distinguished between the Palestinian cause and the actions of the PLO. This was primarily because of the apparent nexus between anti-Turkish militant organisations and the PLO. Additionally, from the Turkish perspective, the PLO had close connections with Greece, a fact underlined by the PLO's adoption of the Greek position on Cyprus and by Greece allowing the PLO to openly operate within its borders. Indeed, when Papandreou came to power in 1981, he entered into an era of rhetorical attacks against Israel; invited the PLO to upgrade its diplomatic status in the country and, in December of the same year, Arafat arrived to witness Papandreou grant the PLO the same *de facto* recognition that Israel had. Papandreou also turned his sights on the US and demanded that US military bases in Greece not be used to attack, what Greece deemed to be, friendly countries. Concomitantly, Papandreou continued to develop Greek ties with the Arab world.[65]

In the immediate aftermath of the Lebanon War, the intelligence services of both Israel and Turkey entered a new phase of co-operation, particularly in the field of anti-terrorism strategies. However, the Turkish government was embarrassed by a leak to a popular

Istanbul daily newspaper, *Gunes,* which revealed, on the front page, that a number of Turkish security personnel had been dispatched to Israel, in order to verify possible links between the PLO and Turkish and Armenian terror organisations. The paper denied that this was the purpose of the visit, but did not deny that Israel had supplied the information to Turkey.[66]

In 1975, as Turkey voted for UNGA resolution 3379 (**XXX**) equating Zionism with racism, it was buying large amounts of military hardware from Israel. Moreover, after closing its consulate in Jerusalem in 1980, Ankara was happy to receive the intelligence fruits of the Israeli invasion of Lebanon, detailing anti-Turkish organisations.

The military dimension of the relationship would prove to be the future of the alliance, and aided Turkey in overcoming internal and external pressure, often the result of its ties with Israel. Indeed, this aspect of the Policy of the Periphery would develop, reaching its apogee from 1996–1999, when the Ankara-Jerusalem relationship was second only to that between Washington and Jerusalem.

CHAPTER 6

ETHIOPIA AND ISRAEL, 1956–72: FROM PARTNER TO PARIAH

The reaction of Ethiopia to the Suez War was complex, with the Selassie regime ever wary of jeopardising its ties with Jerusalem. Certainly, at the UN, Ethiopia expressed its concern over the hostilities, through Representative Yilma Deressa. On 1 November 1956, at the UNGA Emergency Special Session, Deressa, referring to the Suez crisis, stated 'this is a sad and grave moment in the history of the United Nations. Two great nations which hold permanent seats in the Security Council, and Israel, have launched armed attacks against the territorial integrity of Egypt.'[1] Deressa further elaborated that Israeli forces had 'penetrated deeply' into Egypt and that Egyptian cities were 'subject to bombardment' by aircraft from Britain and France. Although noting that Britain, France and Israel had 'grievances' against Egypt, the Representative was adamant that the UN Charter prohibited such use of force.[2]

Deressa explained his country's opposition to this aggression by drawing an analogy between the Suez War and the loss of Ethiopian independence to Italy in 1935. He explained that Ethiopia 'sacrificed millions of its sons and daughters' in its ultimately futile struggle against the ensuing, albeit temporary, loss of independence. Using this as a context, Deressa was compelled to add Ethiopia's voice in support of the 'rule of law' in such a 'dark hour … for the people of Egypt.'[3]

Ethiopia supported all UNGA resolutions pertaining to an immediate end to hostilities, the withdrawal of non-indigenous forces and the establishment of UNEF. Deressa stipulated that the emergency force should have 'limited functions' and that it should 'secure the cessation of hostilities in accordance with all the terms of resolution 997 (ES-1),'[4] and that the emergency force should not 'take over the functions which the Franco-British forces had set out to accomplish'.[5] It is worthy of note that in this relatively short statement, Deressa mentioned three times that Ethiopia had co-sponsored draft resolution A/3308, revealing a desire on the part of his country to be seen taking a stance against the Franco-British-Israeli venture, which prevented verbal condemnation from the Arab states.

This approach was further promulgated by Deressa approximately a month after the outbreak of hostilities. On 29 November 1956, he once more emphasised the importance of territorial integrity and that, within this context, Egypt had 'the clear right to nationalise the Universal Suez Canal Company'.[6] This statement offered seemingly unequivocal support for Egypt, something the diplomat had been unable to demonstrate at the outbreak of hostilities. Intriguingly, in the following paragraph, Deressa revealed the importance of the closure of the Suez Canal for the region and for Ethiopia in particular. He stated that 'it can well be questioned whether the national economy of any Member of the United Nations ... stands to lose more than the national economy of Ethiopia.'[7] The concern over the future of the canal, Ethiopia's vital aperture to the trade routes of the Red Sea, was indeed a central motivation both behind the Ethiopian desire to maintain ties with Israel and behind Israel's desire to see Ethiopia prevail against the Eritrean rebels.

Finally, at the same session, Deressa addressed Ethiopian concerns over Palestine, which he felt should 'not be forgotten in our preoccupation with the Suez question'.[8] He also desired 'to draw attention ... to the miseries of the Arab refugees and to the urgent necessity for avoiding any further prolongation of their hardships'.[9] In essence, the diplomat said little of import throughout the debates over the Suez crisis, preferring instead to follow a diplomatic path which allowed his country to retain its relationship with Israel and maintain its position within the African-Asian group at the UN.

In May 1958, civil war broke out in Lebanon between Christian and pro-Nasser, Muslim factions, which were attempting to move Lebanon into Egypt's sphere of influence. Furthermore, in July of the same year, Jordan was threatened by pro-Nasserist subversion and Iraq witnessed a military *coup*. At once, the Western strongholds in the Middle East were threatened, leading to military intervention by both the US and Britain.

In addition, these years saw the culmination of a process of Arab unity which manifested itself in the establishment of the UAR and an escalation in Ethiopia's conflict in Somalia over the future of the Ogaden desert. This coincided with an escalation in the ferocity of the *Shifta*[10] tribes in Eritrea and Nasser's intervention in Yemen. This regional tension was further exacerbated by Nasser's active support for the Somalis, who would gain independence in 1960, in their aspiration of a Greater Somalia, including the Ogaden and the province of Harar.[11] Indeed, the Somalis had long championed their claims on Ogaden by insisting that the area was populated with nomadic Somalis. This, coupled with the Somali belief of unity of people through language, religion and ethnicity, meant that the area came to be seen politically as part of Somalia.[12] Moreover, Egyptian involvement in post-independence Somalia was substantial, leading Emperor Haile Selassie to proclaim 'The Somalis would not have dreamt of such an idea without being incited by Nasser'.[13]

The confluence of interests for both Israel and Ethiopia is clear. Israel could foresee the results of the Suez War being effectively undone were Nasser to succeed in his desire for regime change in Yemen, thereby ensuring that the Red Sea would be surrounded by pro-Nasserist elements, who could, in turn, attempt to deny Israel access to this sea route.[14] This was very much in accordance with Selassie's fear of a resurgent Egypt. Indeed, the emperor revealed in 1957 that Colonel Nasser 'is trying to stir up the large Muslim minority with the aim of dismembering this Christian Kingdom'.[15]

The combined effect of these events created a sense of foreboding in Ethiopia, and the belief in the need for arms and military advice was heightened.[16] Moreover, Ethiopia needed development projects that would both improve its standard of living and aid in boosting the popularity of Selassie. However, in the year until September 1958, exports from Ethiopia to Israel totalled approximately £618,000, with approximately £83,000 moving in the opposite direction, and Israel was successfully operating a meat canning factory at Asmara.[17] Though this was indeed a sound basis for the underpinning of ties, it belied the depth of the eventual relationship between Jerusalem and Addis Ababa.

The British government was aware that Israel was attempting to deepen its penetration of Ethiopia, both through agriculture and by obtaining concessions and partnerships with Ethiopian landowners. In 1958, *Solel Boneh* submitted the lowest bid for a road building project, costing more than £1.5 million.[18] However, Ethiopia's relations with Israel at this time were described as a 'balancing act' by the British Embassy in Addis Ababa. Indeed, in December 1957, Ethiopia had rejected a call from Saudi Arabia to participate in the blockade of Israel, and in 1959, it had relations with three Member States of the Arab League: Egypt, Sudan and Saudi Arabia, but would not allow anything more than an Israeli Consulate-General in Ethiopia. On the other hand, the British Embassy in Addis Ababa revealed that the Empress of Ethiopia 'when spending last Easter in Arab Jerusalem, also visited the Israeli part of the city', and that the Emperor had apparently informed the Saudis in 1957 that 'sooner or later he would feel compelled to regularise his relations with Israel'.[19]

A clear example of the mutual interest and trust that the two countries began to share during this time was revealed by Israel's role in saving Haile Selassie during a failed *coup* in December 1960. Selassie was in Brazil when Addis Ababa was taken by rebels, led by the commander of the Imperial Bodyguard. Israeli Prime Minister, David Ben-Gurion, and Foreign Minister, Golda Meir, ensured that Selassie was able to communicate with loyal followers on the ground throughout the episode, most notably Abiy Ababa, then regent in Eritrea, and soon to be regent, Asrate Kassa, who led the successful counter-*coup*.[20]

However, Israeli help for Selassie was not automatic. In fact, a number of rebels in Addis Ababa were on good terms with the Israeli delegation in Monrovia, where the Emperor had stopped on his journey back from Brazil.[21] Ben-Gurion, though, decided to act in favour of Selassie and thereafter sea links between Eilat and Asmara were developed, with Israel creating observation posts along the Ethiopian Red Sea coast, to monitor Arab and Soviet shipping. Moreover, Selassie allowed Israeli advisers to cross the border into Sudan and initiate ties with the Christian guerrillas who were fighting the Sudanese government.[22]

This year, 1960, proved to be a watershed for relations between the two countries.[23] In April, it was reported that the UAR demanded that Israel be excluded from an Ethiopian Red Cross bazaar, on the grounds that it was involved in political gamesmanship. The Ethiopian authorities rejected the demand.[24] On 19 April, Abebe Aragai, Chairman of the Ethiopian Council of Ministers and Minister of Defence, and Ras Imeru Haile Selassie, cousin of the Emperor, arrived in Israel, accompanied by the Ethiopian Ambassadors to the US and Greece, Ras Michel Imeru and Lij Araia. The visit, although described as part of an Easter pilgrimage, nevertheless included a meeting with the Israeli Prime Minister.[25] In August, as a result of its reluctance to bow to Arab demands, a discussion was held about Ethiopia's ties with Israel, at the Economic Boycott against Israel Conference in Tripoli. In addition, it was widely reported in the Israeli press that the UAR co-operated with intelligence networks both in Ethiopia and Eritrea and was actively inciting elements of the population against ties with the Jewish state.[26]

Israeli co-operation with Ethiopia at this stage included two Israeli doctors, who were managing the hospital at Massawa (a port city on the Red Sea), two members of *Egged*, the Israeli transport co-operative, who had been invited to the country to aid in the planning of public transport and vehicle maintenance, and an Israeli expert who advised the Ministries of Commerce, Industry and Agriculture; while a course in agriculture was run for Ethiopian students at the Ruppin Institute in Israel.[27] The Israeli fishing company, *Yotvat,* also began operating in the Red Sea, employing fishermen from both Israel and Ethiopia, thereby allowing the shipment of frozen fish to Eilat. The following year, this company expanded to six trawlers, a refrigeration ship and a fishmeal plant in Massawa.[28] In addition, the Israeli co-owners of an Israeli-Ethiopian meat processing factory, Incode, signed a contract with the Ethiopian government for the lease of land for farming.[29]

Moreover, Moshe Dayan, then Israeli Minister of Agriculture, flew to Addis Ababa on 16 September, where he was greeted by Haile Selassie. Upon his return, Dayan revealed that Israeli co-operation with Ethiopia would be developed in several ways, including the despatch of Israeli advisors to various Ethiopian ministries; the involvement of Israeli experts in water drilling, medical services and engineering and the joint construction of projects in arid areas. Dayan also noted that the number of Israeli experts in Ethiopia would shortly exceed those in any other country.[30] Both 1960 and 1961 saw exports from Israel to Ethiopia reach approximately US$1 million and Ethiopian imports to Israel reach approximately US$1.8 million in 1960 and US$1.7 million in 1961, respectively.[31]

In September 1961, after the dismemberment of the UAR, Ben-Gurion felt able to ask for the establishment of formal diplomatic relations between Israel and Ethiopia.[32] Israel opened an embassy in Addis Ababa, while Selassie preferred Ethiopia to maintain a lower profile and opened only a consulate in Jerusalem, demanding the Israeli officers in charge of training Ethiopian troops not wear Israeli uniforms or insignia on state and special occasions.[33] This was a clear example of the ambivalence that Selassie was attempting to create: Ethiopia would ostensibly temper its ties with Israel, but would not abandon them in order to appease Arab feeling. This was reinforced when Abd al-Haliq Hassunah, then Secretary-General of the Arab League, urged Member States of the League to make a united stand against Ethiopia for her *de jure* recognition of Israel on 24 October 1961, and stated that any county which aligned itself with Israel was, in effect, adhering to an anti-Arab policy.[34] Furthermore, it was reported that Arab countries were contacting Ethiopia, in an attempt to pressure it to decrease its ties with Israel.[35]

Throughout the period 1961–64, *Egged* provided the General Ethiopian Transport Share Company, Ethiopia's major bus company, with both its general and technical manager.[36] This was the fruit of the visit in 1960 by the two members of *Egged*. The two men had been received by the Emperor and the company underwent a large scale modernisation drive, which succeeded in reversing its previous course towards bankruptcy and, in 1964, the company was able to report pre-tax net profits of approximately 550,000 Ethiopian dollars (approximately USD$220,000) and a healthy return on capital shares.[37] In addition, the bus service on inter-urban routes also improved and 1964 saw the company carry approximately 22 million passengers in Addis Ababa alone, compared with 12 million in 1961.[38]

Ethiopia also received the largest programme of Israeli academic assistance. This began with the inauguration of a professor from the Technion (the Israeli Institute of Technology) as Dean of the College of Engineering at Haile Selassie I University, in 1959. From that time, many Israelis taught at the university.[39] Indeed, in 1963, there were no fewer than 14 Israelis on campus, including the Deans of the Faculties of Science, Engineering and Social Sciences. However, from the 1960s, the number of Israelis at the university began to fall as Ethiopians, with proactive encouragement from their Israeli counterparts, began to fill the faculty positions.[40]

The decline of Israel's relationship with Ethiopia commences with the civil war in Eritrea. Asrate Kassa, the regent of Eritrea, appointed in 1964, championed close ties with Israel, due to his fear of pan-Arabism and the potential spread of political Islam throughout the Horn of Africa.[41] The mutual interests of Ethiopia and Israel on this issue were encapsulated in *The Washington Post* thus: 'At stake, Ethiopians feel, is the survival of their traditionally threatened Christian island in a hostile Muslim sea ... In this they are joined and even encouraged by Israel which sees the Eritrean problem and pressures on the Empire as part of its own battle with Egypt and Islam.'[42]

To this end, Kassa enlisted the help of Israeli experts in counter-terrorism, in order to train his own police force and commando units. In fact, Kassa formed a force known as '101',[43] likely to have been modelled on its Israeli namesake. These soldiers, mostly Christian Eritreans, wore different uniforms from the rest of the army, carried different weapons and, at the end of the 1960s, the unit comprised some nine well-trained companies.[44] The influence of Israeli advisors on the US trained and supplied 2nd Division of the Ethiopian army, however, was minimal. There was an attempt to merge the two forces, in order to temper the behaviour of the regular soldiers and co-ordinate the fight against the separatists, but to no avail and the Israelis witnessed the

Ethiopian army play directly into the hands of the separatists through its brutal behaviour in Eritrea.[45]

Indeed, Israel was concerned that the Ethiopian army was unable to deal effectively with the situation in Eritrea; the army was perceived by at least one figure in the Israeli military to be competent only in the killing of civilians and the disaffecting of the Eritrean people.[46] This was due mainly to the fact that corruption at officer level was rife, with many officers monopolising the food and equipment of their companies, leaving those patrolling inside Eritrea with few supplies. These factors had a detrimental effect on the soldiers, who tended to behave like occupying forces and engaged in both violence and terror towards the Eritreans.[47] As Kassa's influence lessened, his rival, Prime Minister Habta-Wald Akilu, who was opposed to Ethiopia's relationship with Israel, seeing it as an unnecessary provocation of the Arabs,[48] decided to solve the Eritrean problem by placating the Arab allies of Eritrea and by eradicating rebel organisations through violence.[49]

The nature of the bilateral ties between Israel and Ethiopia at this point facilitated a moderate Ethiopian stance at the UN, enabling Ethiopia to cement its place within the African-Asian group. Throughout the period immediately prior to the Six Day War, the Ethiopian delegation continued a stance based on equidistance between the belligerent sides. Talking of the Arab-Israeli conflict, Representative Makonnen suggested a 'two-phased and double-pronged approach to the problem'. The first phase would consist of 'restraining the principal parties and all other countries from taking action that could only aggravate the situation. This can only be done in the form of an appropriate appeal formulated in language that will not be susceptible to interpretation by any party as prejudicing some of its claims'. This sentence serves to encapsulate the Ethiopian stance towards Israel at the UN. Indeed, as if to highlight further the Ethiopian desire to maintain strong links with both belligerent parties, Makonnen noted that 'If we ... in an attempt to formulate an appeal at this stage introduce elements and controversial concepts ... then I submit we shall not be advancing our work, nor shall we be advancing the cause of peace'.[50]

Makonnen emphasised the Ethiopian position of apparent objectivity and tolerance when he stated that 'I should like to associate myself ... with the remarks made by the Representative of France: his call for restraint, his call for time, his call for the continuation of the intensive consultations that we are carrying out and which are well under way'.[51] The diplomat, like his peer Representatives of Iran and Turkey at the UN, also revealed disappointment, tempered with belief in the eventual triumph of diplomacy and the UNSC. He noted that 'My delegation shares the feeling of disappointment expressed by many other delegations that the United Nations has not been able so far to make any headway in the urgent task of building permanent peace in the Middle East'. However, Makonnen opined 'it is never too late to try again and again, ever prompted by the conviction that the cause of peace is too vital to be abandoned'.[52]

Ethiopia at the UNSC and the Six Day War

On 6 June 1967, then president of the UNSC Hans Tabor of Denmark, presented draft resolution S/7935, calling on all parties to observe an immediate cease-fire. More specifically 'the Security Council calls upon the Governments concerned to take forthwith as a first step all measures for an immediate cease-fire and for a cessation of all military activities in the area'.[53] Ethiopia voted in favour of the draft resolution, which was adopted unanimously and became UNSC Resolution 233.[54]

At the same meeting, Makonnen, representing Ethiopia, the sole representative of the Policy of the Periphery states to sit on the UNSC during the war, strove to explain his country's position on UNSC Resolution 233.[55] He stated that 'all signs indicate that we are faced with a ferocious war in this troubled area. Scarcely two days have passed since hostilities broke out, but we see that this war is indeed a total war involving all the Arab States and Israel'.[56] Moreover, he believed that the war would 'no doubt bring about untold damage and suffering to all peoples involved and much devastation ... to the many historic and holy shrines'.[57]

It is evident from the above statement that the Ethiopian government was keen to appear politically impartial, as it had during the Suez War, in order not to jeopardise its diplomatic relations with either

Israel, or the Arab world. As a result, Makonnen announced that 'the immediate objective of the Council must be to return the present situation of military conflict to a situation and position from which a fair and just settlement of issues can be obtained.'[58] In the same speech, the diplomat re-iterated his country's ostensible neutrality 'as the Representative of a country that is a neighbour ... of the Middle East ... my country and people have been closely associated with all the peoples of this area and have lived with them in friendly coexistence ... throughout a long and glorious history.'[59]

Clearly concerned by the destruction of both their Arab clients' forces and their own military equipment during the war, the following day, 7 June 1967, the USSR sponsored draft resolution S/7940. The draft resolution demanded that all parties cease firing at 20.00 GMT and was accepted unanimously, thus becoming UNSC Resolution 234.[60] This was followed on 9 June, by the president of the UNSC presenting draft resolution S/7960,[61] demanding, *inter alia*, 'hostilities should cease forthwith'. The draft resolution was adopted unanimously and became UNSC Resolution 235.[62]

Ethiopia voted in favour of these three cease-fire resolutions and thus perpetuated its position of neutrality in the conflict. This palpably changed, however, on 10 June, when UN representatives of the UAR and Jordan launched a verbal tirade against Israeli military actions. Mohammad Awad El-Kony of the UAR stated that 'the Israelis are ... repeating the same policy which they learned from the Nazis, namely the persecution of the population of the invaded lands of Jordan, and the expulsion of those people from their homes'. Moreover, he termed Israel's actions as 'treacherous aggression ... an aggression which in essence reflects a denial of morality and a crumbling of human values'.[63] In addition, Mohammad El-Farra of Jordan, although not mentioning Israel specifically, nevertheless stated that 'it is necessary to look at the experience of 1948, when they had a specific and well-planned campaign to terrorize the area and to make room for immigrants. I am putting before the Council the question of a well-planned formula which started working this morning'.[64]

In an apparent defence of Israel, Makonnen suggested that 'the information we have been receiving from United Nations personnel in the area of conflict has understandably been sketchy ... in the confirmation of certain specific facts and events.' He elaborated that 'it may also be due to limitations imposed by the situation and the circumstances prevailing at present in the area'.[65] Having said this, however, Makonnen did criticize Israel by citing a UNTSO message, detailing a reported attack by the IAF close to Damascus and Damascus airport.[66] He explained that 'my delegation cannot remain silent in the face of this highly dangerous development', and, as such, it 'joins ... in condemning the air attacks over Damascus'.[67] However, it was at this point that the diplomat ceased in his condemnation of the reported raids and retreated somewhat from his aggressive approach. He urged the UNSC to 'call on all parties to adhere strictly to the cease-fire resolutions of the Council' and stated that 'my delegation joins ... in appealing to all concerned to adopt humane attitudes towards civilian populations and prisoners of war ... The parties concerned should realize that ... the day will soon come for them to live together again.'[68]

Then Israeli Ambassador to the UN, Gideon Rafael, denied that IAF combat aircraft were attacking Damascus and stated that UN observers had seen smoke rising from Israeli settlements, thus implying a Syrian attack on Israel. However, when the sighting of IAF combat aircraft over Damascus was corroborated by other reports, Jerusalem admitted that the aircraft were not attacking Damascus, rather they were providing covering fire for Israeli ground forces.[69] The Ethiopian stance, in this context, could indeed be interpreted as a consequence of a lack of specific data concerning the Israeli attacks. It is apparent, though, that the episode furnished the Ethiopian delegation with a pretext for their continued diplomatic neutrality, and avoided potential aggravation of Arab members of the UN.

The following day saw Hans Tabor, orally propose a draft resolution,[70] which was unanimously adopted and became UNSC Resolution 236, calling for 'the prompt return to the cease-fire positions of any troops which may have moved forward subsequent to 16.30 hours GMT on 10 June 1967'.[71]

On 14 June 1967, Representative Makonnen, in response to remarks allegedly made by figures in the Israeli defence community, stated

We cannot but be disturbed and dismayed by recent statements reported to have been made by high-ranking Israeli officials, expressing unwillingness to accept United Nations participation in the settlement of outstanding disputes and stating the untenable contention that Israel has the right arbitrarily to decide the disposition of territories of sovereign States now under Israel's military control ... we therefore urge Israel to abandon stands which are not compatible with the principles and practices of the United Nations Charter.[72]

The final resolution adopted during the war was draft resolution S/7968 and Revs.1–3,[73] which was co-sponsored by Ethiopia. It was adopted unanimously and became UNSC Resolution 237, calling for the government of Israel 'to ensure the safety, welfare and security of the inhabitants of the areas where military operations have taken place and to facilitate the return of those inhabitants who have fled the areas since the outbreak of hostilities'.[74]

On 25 October of the same year, the UNSC met to discuss a draft resolution,[75] which was presented by new president, Senjin Tsuruoka of Japan. The draft resolution was adopted unanimously and became UNSC Resolution 240, demanding 'the Member States concerned to cease immediately all prohibited military activities in the area, and to co-operate fully and promptly with the United Nations Truce Supervision Organisation'.[76]

The following month saw another resolution to be passed on the Six Day War, a resolution which was to become a cornerstone for future negotiations. On 22 November 1967, Britain, through its ambassador to the UN, Lord Caradon, proposed draft resolution S/8247,[77] which was unanimously adopted and became UNSC Resolution 242.[78] The resolution called for, *inter alia*, the 'withdrawal of Israel armed forces from territories occupied in the recent conflict; termination of all claims or states of belligerency and respect for and acknowledgement of the sovereignty, territorial integrity and political independence of every State in the area and their right to live in peace within secure and recognized boundaries free from threats or acts of force'.

Moreover, it affirmed the necessity of 'guaranteeing freedom of navigation through international waterways in the area; for achieving a just settlement of the refugee problem' and 'for guaranteeing the territorial inviolability and political independence of every State in the area, through measures including the establishment of demilitarized zones'. Finally, it requested the Secretary-General to 'designate a Special Representative to proceed to the Middle East to establish and maintain contacts with the States concerned in order to promote agreement and assist efforts to achieve a peaceful and accepted settlement'.[79]

To give a semblance of political context to UNSC Resolution 242, one need look no further than comments made by Caradon himself,

We left the Assembly with nothing achieved. Worse still we had shown up the gulf which existed not only between the Arab Governments and the Government of Israel but also between the two super powers. It seemed that the Middle East was doomed to ... another conflict on a far wider scale.[80]

Caradon further highlighted the 'gulf' between the super powers thus,

The Russians seem to have made all the mistakes they could. Having themselves called the emergency session and demanded condemnation of Israel and unconditional Israeli withdrawal, their resolution was voted down clause by clause ... Thus, having led the Arabs into battle and having with them sustained a resounding defeat, they then showed that they were ready to abandon them.[81]

Prior to the vote, at the same meeting, Makonnen revealed his desire that 'due emphasis be put on the inadmissibility of acquisition of territory by war and hence on the imperative requirement that *all* [author's italics] Israel armed forces be withdrawn from *the* [author's italics] territories occupied as a result of military conflict'.[82] It is precisely because of its deliberate phrasing that UNSC Resolution 242 was, and continues to be, interpreted in varying ways, often in order to serve different parties' interests.

Indeed, in the ten days before the vote, it was the desire of the Arab delegations to include the definite article, as they believed that a sentence reading withdrawal of Israeli armed forces from *the* territories occupied in the recent conflict would mean complete withdrawal, whereas, omitting the definite article could imply a partial withdrawal, or withdrawal from only a percentage of the territory under Israeli jurisdiction.[83] The Norwegian, General Odd Bull, then Head of UNTSO, offered his own interpretation of the resolution, when he stated that the linking of 'withdrawal of Israel armed forces,' to the preambular, 'the inadmissibility of the acquisition of territory by war', left 'no room for argument'.[84]

Caradon too saw the phrasing of UNSC Resolution 242 as unambiguous, but was diametrically opposed to Odd Bull in his conclusion. Caradon revealed that,

> Much play has been made of the fact that we did not say 'the' territories or 'all the' territories. But that was deliberate. I myself knew very well the 1967 boundaries and if we had put in the 'the' or 'all the' that could only have meant that we wished to see the 1967 boundaries perpetuated in the form of a permanent frontier. This I was certainly not prepared to recommend.[85]

Indeed, Caradon went further in order to explain his position: 'what were the 1967 boundaries?' He asked, 'They were no more than the cease-fire borders decided nearly two decades previously. They were based on the accident of where exactly the Israeli and the Arab armies happened to be on that particular night'. Moreover, he stated 'knowing as I did the unsatisfactory nature of the 1967 line I was not prepared to use wording in the Resolution which would have made that line permanent'.[86] These contradictory statements concerning Resolution 242 served the Ethiopian desire to maintain an impartial stance over the war. Although Makonnen had enunciated his country's desire to see Israel withdraw from the territories it had captured, the wording of the resolution allowed him to vote in accordance with the Arab/Muslim bloc, whilst not forcing Israel to withdraw to the pre-war boundaries, though, for Ethiopia, this was more by accident than by design.

The following year, 1968, saw the UNSC continuing to adopt resolutions pertaining to the Six Day War. Makonnen preceded discussions of new draft resolutions on 21 March, with a speech condemning reports of IDF raids into Jordanian territory. It is likely that Makonnen was referring to the attack of the same day on a PLO base in the Jordanian village of Karameh, positioned approximately five miles north of the Allenby Bridge and eight miles south of the Damiya Bridge.[87] The operation was carried out by the IDF in response to an attack on an Israeli school bus, which killed two and wounded 28, on 18 March of the same year.[88]

Karameh had been almost entirely deserted by its civilian population, after leaflets were distributed by the IDF warning the inhabitants of the looming attack, but was re-populated by various elements of the PLO. The task of the IDF was threefold: to block a possible reaction from the Jordanian army, to capture Karameh and to prevent fighters in the town from being able to leave.[89] By 08.00 hours, Israeli forces had captured the town, and discovered that it was a larger base than previously thought.[90] Running concomitantly to this operation, was another IDF action against the PLO, south of the Dead Sea, in the Jordanian village of Safi, also in response to armed infiltrations into Israel.[91]

Speaking of the attacks, Makonnen stated 'it is with deep regret and with a sense of grave anxiety that we have learnt of the military reprisals that have been undertaken by the armed forces of Israel in Jordanian territory ... my delegation deplores this act' and 'the military reprisal that Israel has undertaken cannot even be justified ... as being measures undertaken to meet the need to avert terrorist activities'.[92] The Ethiopian stance here showed no semblance of context, but followed the previously outlined pattern of unpredictability in its reaction to reports of military engagements. This unpredictability allowed Ethiopia the fluidity to modify its diplomatic stance towards the interests of either, or both, the belligerent sides, depending on estimates of what served its best interests.

On 24 March 1968, the UNSC voted on a draft resolution that had been orally presented by a member of the Secretariat. The draft resolution was unanimously adopted and became UNSC Resolution 248,[93] condemning the Karameh raid, terming it a 'military action launched by Israel in flagrant violation of the United Nations Charter and the cease-fire resolutions', and deploring 'all violent incidents in violation of the cease-fire'.[94] Furthermore, the resolution called upon Israel to 'desist from acts or activities in contravention of resolution 237 (1967)'.[95]

On 2 April 1968, the Ethiopian stance seemed aimed at moderating the rhetoric of the UNSC, by neglecting to focus on Israel exclusively when talking of military actions. Indeed, Makonnen stated that 'the large-scale military operations ... in violation of the cease-fire that have been taking place of late in the Jordanian-Israeli sector, have increased the tension in the area'.[96]

On the 27 April, the UNSC met to discuss draft resolution S/8563, which was co-sponsored by India, Pakistan and Senegal.[97] This draft resolution was adopted unanimously and became UNSC Resolution 250,[98] calling on Israel to 'refrain from holding the military parade in Jerusalem which is contemplated for 2 May 1968', as it may 'aggravate tensions in the area and have an adverse effect on a peaceful settlement of the problems in the area'.[99] In addition to voting in favour of the draft resolution, Makonnen stated 'in this ... case of the intended military parade in Jerusalem we have an example of the kind of action that could risk creating a much feared exaggeration of the delicate and explosive situation ... we join the members of the Council in calling on the government of Israel ... to abandon its plans for a military parade in the Holy City of Jerusalem on 2 May 1968'.[100]

On 2 May, the UNSC passed an orally presented draft resolution, which Ethiopia supported, and which was adopted unanimously, becoming UNSC Resolution 251,[101] deploring 'the holding by Israel of the military parade in Jerusalem on 2 May 1968 in disregard of the unanimous decision adopted by the Council on 27 April 1968'. Jerusalem was also the focus of draft resolution S/8590/Rev.2, co-sponsored by Pakistan and Senegal.[102] The draft, which was adopted as UNSC Resolution 252, with Ethiopia voting in favour, did not have the support of either Canada or the US, both of whom abstained.[103] The resolution considered that all 'legislative and administrative measures

and actions taken by Israel, including expropriation of land and prop-
erties thereon, which tend to change the legal status of Jerusalem are
invalid and cannot change that status'.[104]

Whilst at the UN Ethiopia was adopting a harsh stand on Israeli
actions, the two countries were, meanwhile, conceiving of a joint venture which became known as the 'Coffee Project'. It enhanced co-
operation between them in the Red Sea, essentially using the port
of Assab as a joint naval base, and allowed Israel the use of ground
facilities, should the IAF be required to take action in the area.
Israel would also supply Ethiopia with an advanced radar system and
would construct a new mechanised infantry brigade for the Ethiopian
army.[105] This effort was also to involve Iran and the IDF Chief of Staff,
Lt General Tsur noted,

> Our interest is to prevent turning the Red Sea into an Arab-Soviet
> lake. We have been courting Ethiopia for years now, but lately
> they have become more responsive, for they are worried because of
> Eritrea. They lead us now to believe that we have a chance to sign a
> military and political alliance. Since we are very interested in deep-
> ening our presence in Ethiopia and turning it into our close military
> and political ally, we have to respond to Ethiopian demands.[106]

The same meeting saw Akilu Habte-Wold, then prime minister of
Ethiopia reveal,

> Ethiopia is interested in a strong Israel the same as Israel is inter-
> ested in a strong Ethiopia ... Ethiopia is a Christian island in a
> Muslim sea, and the Muslims make no distinction between reli-
> gious and political goals. Their aim is to destroy Ethiopia, and
> they criticize her for every step she takes together with Israel ...
> Recently the Egyptian delegate to the OAU told us they knew
> about every detail in the Ethio-Israeli context ... If they find out
> about the suggested project, about a joint base in Assab and the
> like, they will do everything to destroy Ethiopia.[107]

Some three months later, the UNSC voted on a draft resolution, orally
proposed by the Under Secretary-General for Political and Security

Council Affairs.[108] It was adopted unanimously and became UNSC Resolution 256, condemning the 'further military attacks launched by Israel in flagrant violation of the United Nations Charter and resolution 248 (1968)'.[109]

Makonnen, aware of his country's desire to maintain friendly ties with both Israel and the Arab world, revealed that 'It is not in the habit of Ethiopian Representatives to make themselves the self-appointed prophets of doom. On the contrary, those who have worked with us on many difficult international problems ... will surely testify that we rather tend to be incurable optimists'. However, he stated that 'we cannot hide our anxiety over the turn of events. Not only does there seem to be no progress in the main effort ... but even the fragile cease-fire ... seems threatened'.[110] To underline both Ethiopian concern and neutrality, Makonnen declared 'our sincere sympathies and condolences go out to the families of those who have fallen victims of this conflict on both sides ... we share the grief of those Israeli and United Arab Republic families who have lost their loved ones'. That said, the Ethiopian stance was unchanged, with the diplomat calling for 'all parties to exercise the utmost restraint; second, a renewed call ... for strict observance of the cease-fire resolutions of the Security Council; third, an urgent appeal to the parties to co-operate fully with the United Nations'.[111]

The UNSC was subsequently presented with a draft resolution by the president,[112] which was not accepted unanimously, Algeria abstained, becoming UNSC Resolution 258.[113] This resolution stated that the 'cease fire ordered by the Security Council in its resolutions must be rigorously respected'[114] and urged 'all the parties to extend their fullest co-operation to the Special Representative of the Secretary-General.'[115] The same month saw Pakistan and Senegal propose draft resolution S/8825 Rev.2,[116] which was adopted by a majority decision, with Canada, Denmark and the US abstaining, thus becoming UNSC Resolution 259.[117] It deplored 'the delay in the implementation of resolution 237 (1967) because of the conditions still being set by Israel for receiving a Special Representative of the Secretary-General'[118] and requested 'the Secretary-General urgently to dispatch a Special Representative to the Arab territories under military occupation by Israel'.[119] Interestingly, at the same meeting, before the vote, Makonnen made the following statement, revealing a more pro-Arab stance by Ethiopia.

> In sponsoring 237 (1967) our primary purpose was to ensure the safety, welfare and security of peoples who had been directly affected by the military conflict of June 1967 and more particularly, those people inhabiting the territories which came under Israeli military control ... resolution 237 and the present draft resolution here before us [S/8825/Rev.2] deal with the specific problem of the safety, welfare and security of Arab populations affected by the occupation that followed the war of June 1967, in those areas in particular that are under Israeli military occupation.[120]

In addition, Makonnen stated that 'It must be obvious to everyone that the cause of peace in the Middle East can in no way be served by military actions and counter-actions which can only intensify and perpetuate the military confrontation and conflict'. The central concern of his delegation at the time was that 'If a cycle of violence and counter-violence is allowed to continue, the chain of events will lead inevitably to the gradual escalation of the conflict, to such an extent that we shall have total war before we are aware of it'.[121] In this context, Makonnen believed, 'that by its unanimous resolution 242 (1967) of 22 November 1967 the Security Council has indeed initiated such a positive approach that goes to the roots of the problem in the Middle East'.[122]

On the final day of 1968, the Under-Secretary-General for Political and Security Council Affairs presented a draft resolution,[123] which was adopted unanimously,[124] thus becoming UNSC Resolution 262.[125] The resolution concerned an Israeli military attack on Beirut airport, and condemned Israel for its 'premeditated military action in violation of its obligations under the Charter and cease fire resolutions.' It also stated that 'such premeditated acts of violence endanger the maintenance of peace'[126] and issued a warning that 'if such acts were to be repeated, the Council would have to consider further steps to give effect to its decisions'.[127]

Although the Israeli attack was certainly 'premeditated', the Under-Secretary-General did not place it in context. The IDF operation came in response to an attack by Palestinian gunmen on an EL AL aircraft in Athens in December 1968, which killed one passenger and injured others. In reply, IDF commandos raided Beirut International Airport in the same month, destroying thirteen Middle East Airlines aircraft and injuring no one.[128]

The subtle change in approach by the Ethiopian delegation towards a more pro-Arab position was surely the result of many UN Member States turning their attention to the *denouement* of the Palestinian refugees' situation. Moreover, Makonnen was aware of the political capital Ethiopia stood to gain from the Arab-Muslim bloc if it adopted a harsher line towards Israel, particularly on the issue of Palestinian refugees. Furthermore, the regime in Addis Ababa was constantly observing its worsening conflict over Eritrea.

Ethiopia at the UNGA and the Six Day War

Upon realising the scale of the defeat inflicted upon its clients in the Six Day War, the USSR rushed to request an emergency special session of the UNGA, which was convened between the 17 June and 18 September 1967. At this forum, Ethiopia, having previously vowed not to 'participate in any separate vote on any separate paragraph,'[129] first voted on the non-aligned powers draft resolution A/L 522/Rev.3.[130] Ethiopia abstained, thereby again freeing itself from an explicit political stance. It found itself in a minority, with other African states such as Sierra Leone, South Africa, Central African Republic, Chad, Dahomey, Ivory Coast, Kenya, Niger and Rwanda. The US and Britain voted against the resolution, while the USSR, along with the Arab states, Iran and Turkey voted for the resolution,[131] which was rejected in accordance with Makonnen's speech on the same day,

> If my delegation shows any misgivings with regard to the draft resolution submitted by eighteen Member States and introduced by Yugoslavia, it is only because we have a preference for the kind of comprehensive approach outlined in the Latin American

draft and not because there is anything which we do not support in the substantive provisions of document A/L 522/Rev.3 and Corr.1.[132]

True to his word, Makonnen did not take part in any one of the four separate votes on USSR draft resolution A/L 519. Previously, he had stated that 'very much for the same reasons [for Ethiopia abstaining on the non-aligned draft resolution] we shall abstain on the two draft resolutions submitted, respectively, by the delegations of the Soviet Union and of the United States of America.'[133] Ethiopia also voted against Albanian draft resolution A/L 521.[134]

However, the more moderate, Latin American draft resolution A/L 523 Add.1 and 2,[135] found favour in Ethiopia's eyes and Makonnen duly voted for the resolution, which was also rejected.[136] Internationalising a solution to the burgeoning Arab-Israeli conflict was evident in draft resolution A/L 526 and Add.1–3,[137] which Ethiopia and Turkey co-sponsored, welcoming UNSC Resolution 237 and calling for humanitarian assistance to the refugees and contributions to UNRWA. Ethiopia voted in favour of the draft resolution, which was adopted with only Cuba and Syria abstaining,[138] and thus became UNGA Resolution 2252 (ES-V).[139]

Jerusalem featured again in the text of draft resolution A/L 527/Rev 1,[140] co-sponsored by Turkey and Iran, which considered as 'invalid Israel's measures to change the status of the city of Jerusalem' and called upon the government of Israel to 'rescind these measures'.[141] The 'measures' in question were conceived, in the first instance, as a direct result of Israel's rapid military success in the battle for Jerusalem during the war. The battle culminated in the unification of the Old City, under Israeli control.

In light of this new situation, the Israeli Knesset amended two already established laws which 'integrated Jerusalem in the administrative and municipal spheres'.[142] The draft resolution was duly adopted, with Ethiopia voting in favour,[143] thus becoming UNGA Resolution 2253 (ES-V). The US abstained in the vote, while Britain, the Arab states, Iran and Turkey voted for the resolution. The issue of Jerusalem, however, was not resolved with one resolution. Draft resolution A/L

528/Rev.2,[144] co-sponsored by, *inter alia*, Turkey and Iran, deplored Israel's 'failure to implement UNGA Resolution 2253 (ES-V)'[145] and re-iterated its call for Israel to desist in any attempts to alter the status of Jerusalem. Ethiopia voted, with the Arab states, in favour of the draft resolution,[146] which became UNGA Resolution 2254 (ES-V).[147]

The final Emergency Special Session draft proposals were A/L 529/Rev.1,[148] which became UNGA Resolution 2256 (ES-V), 'requesting the Secretary-General to forward the records of the 5th emergency special session to the Security Council'[149] and A/L 530 and Rev.1 (Russian only), which became UNGA Resolution 2257 (ES-V),[150] 'deciding to place on the agenda of the 22nd session the question of the situation in the Middle East.'[151] Ethiopia voted in favour of A/L 529/Rev.1, with the Arab states voting against,[152] but it is unclear how it voted over A/L 530.[153]

The essentially pragmatic tone of the Ethiopian Representatives at the UN continued after the dissolution of the Fifth Emergency Special Session. Indeed, on 7 October 1968, Ethiopian Representative, Ato Ketama Yifru, stated 'eventually a resolution of the problem of the Middle East will have to be based on the renunciation of any state of belligerency and any claim of rights arising from it and the acceptance by all of the existence of Israel as a sovereign State with rights which, like those of all other States, must be respected by all.'[154]

However, he later opined 'it cannot be too strongly emphasized that the withdrawal of Israeli troops from the territories they now occupy as the result of the June war is an obligation which has to be fulfilled'.[155] The theme of Israeli occupation was subsequently elaborated on further when Yifru revealed that 'foreign occupation of a territory cannot be tolerated without also generating resistance from the occupied people; the longer the occupation lasts the stronger will that resistance be'.[156]

Within this context, the Special Committee to Investigate Israeli Practices Affecting the Human Rights of the Population of the Occupied Territories was established on 19 December 1968,[157] after the adoption of UNGA Resolution 2443 (XXIII) and established a precedent; affirming the 'inalienable rights of all inhabitants who have left their homes as a result of the outbreak of hostilities in the Middle

East to return home, resume their normal life, recover their property and homes, and rejoin their families according to the provisions of the Universal Declaration of Human Rights'.[158] Ethiopia did not take part in the vote over the resolution, which the Arab states supported.[159] It did, however, vote in favour of draft resolution A/SPC/L.166 and add.1, co-sponsored by, *inter alia*, Turkey and Iran, calling for Israel 'to take immediate steps for the return of the inhabitants who fled the areas since the outbreak of hostilities'.[160] The Arab states voted in favour.[161]

Haile Selassie added a further ostensible note of neutrality to the Ethiopian position, when he personally addressed the UNGA on 23 October 1970, revealing his desire to see efforts to achieve peace in the Middle East continue until 'a lasting peace is established in accordance with the decision of the Security Council of 22 November 1967.'[162] This apparent even-handedness, however, may be questioned, as Ethiopia voted in favour, along with the Arab states,[163] of draft resolution A/L 602/Rev.2 and add.1, which was adopted and became UNGA Resolution 2628. The resolution codified the refugee problem following the Six Day War. It stated that the UNGA 'recognises that respect for the rights of the Palestinians is an indispensable element in the establishment of a just and lasting peace in the Middle East'.[164]

Ethiopia, though, chose to abstain in the vote over draft resolution A/SPC/L.198, which declared that 'respect for the inalienable rights of the people of Palestine is an indispensable element in the establishment of peace in the Middle East'.[165] The Arab states voted in favour.[166] Such a position was amplified by Ethiopian Representative Y. Tseghe, on 12 October 1971, when he revealed that the Assembly of Heads of State and Government of the Organisation of African Unity (OAU)[167] had formed a committee comprising ten heads of state (including Selassie) 'to seek ways and means of bringing about lasting peace to that cross-road of civilisations'.[168] Having said this, some two months later, Ethiopia abstained on the vote over draft resolution A/SPC/L.231, with the Arab states voting in favour,[169] which concerned the 'inalienable rights and the right of self-determination of the Palestinian Arab refugees'.[170]

Talking of the Middle East the following year, Ethiopian UN Representative Haile noted that 'one hostile action invites a counteraction more deadly and destructive than the act that provoked it' and, regarding a possible solution, 'the fulfilment by the parties concerned of all the obligations contained in resolution 242 (1967) must be vigorously pursued'.[171] Ethiopia, along with Iran, *inter alia*, then co-sponsored draft resolution A/L 650/Rev.1,[172] which was adopted, with the majority of the Arab states voting in favour,[173] and became UNGA Resolution 2799 (XXVI), calling for the renewal of the work of the Special Representative in order to reach a peace agreement 'as envisaged in the Special Representative's *aide-memoire*[174] of 8 February 1971', and called upon Israel to 'respond favourably' to the Special Representative's peace initiative. Moreover, all parties involved in the conflict were to co-operate with the Special Representative for 'guaranteeing freedom of navigation through international waterways in the area; achieving a just settlement of the refugee problem' and 'guaranteeing the territorial inviolability and political independence of every state in the area'.[175]

In Ethiopia, Kassa's influence began to fade as his political adversary, Prime Minister Habt-Wald Akilu came into the ascendancy. This was important for the relationship with Israel, as the prime minister favoured downgrading his country's ties with the Jewish state and, as already stated, placating the Arab sponsors of the Eritrean independence movement. Consequently, Israeli influence in Addis Ababa was challenged by the growing power of Arab and Muslim elements. This, however, did not mean that the Israeli connection was lost completely. Indeed, the two countries continued in their mutual support of the Anya-Aya rebels in the Sudan.[176]

Israeli concern over any potential downgrading of ties with Ethiopia was so great, however, that a senior member of the Israeli Foreign Ministry visited Ethiopia twice in 1972. During the meetings, Akilu emphasised that Ethiopia was merely pretending to side with the Arabs, and actually wanted an Israeli presence in the country. The Ethiopian fear was that, were the relationship not kept secret, the Arab world would concentrate its anger on Ethiopia. But Israeli concerns were underlined by Colonel Muammar Qaddafi of Libya paying Idi Amin to expel the Israeli diplomatic detail from Uganda in April.[177]

Ethiopia, then, facing conflict with both Eritrea and Somalia, had turned to Israel for help, particularly with military advice and hardware. For Israel, it was imperative that Ethiopia keep the Red Sea open to Israeli shipping and for this reason, *inter alia*, it sent its advisors to Ethiopia. This period of high level co-operation saw Israel open an embassy in Addis Ababa and saw both countries working on the 'Coffee Project'. However, Ethiopian internal politics contrived to jeopardise this element of the Policy of the Periphery. The following year, would see the start of a process that was to place the relationship between Israel and Ethiopia under enormous strain.

CHAPTER 7

ETHIOPIA AND ISRAEL, 1973–82: PRESSURE AND RESISTANCE

At the OAU meeting of May 1973 in Addis Ababa, Libya organised an Arab front against Ethiopia, designed to persuade it to sever ties with Israel, which it duly did on 23 October 1973.[1] In order to enforce their demands, the Arab members of the OAU had threatened to move its offices from Addis Ababa to an Arab capital city, were the demands not met.[2] In addition, the Algerian government assured the Ethiopians that it would attempt to persuade the Arab countries to cease in their support of the Eritrean Liberation Front, in return for Ethiopia's adoption of an anti-Israel position.[3]

Explanations for the breakdown of Israeli diplomacy in Africa in the aftermath of the Yom Kippur War are numerous. Some are based on the premise that Africa, as a whole, was cajoled into the move by economic and diplomatic pressure exerted by the Arab world, reaching its zenith during the war. Others place the ostracising of Israel in the context of the African world discovering a sense of communality with the Arab states. This explanation posits that the behaviour of the African states was a sign of their *en masse* conversion to the Arab political cause against Israel. In this framework, Israel came to be seen as an imperialist tool occupying Arab lands, which produced a negative reaction in the African world, with its history of both imperialism and colonisation. Others still include the African world succumbing to its concerns over the ever-increasing co-operation between Israel and apartheid South Africa.[4]

Many of Israel's critics have emphasised the ties between the Jewish state and South Africa under the apartheid regime, which, the critics believed, served to highlight the racist character of Zionism. Although the nature and scope of this relationship is too large to analyse here, it is worth noting that only in the wake of the Yom Kippur War did Israel change its attitude towards its relations with South Africa. Hitherto, Israel had been critical of South Africa for its apartheid regime and, in 1971, offered to contribute to the coffers of the OAU African Liberation Committee, in order to strengthen its position on Africa.[5]

In 1974, Israel appointed its first ambassador to South Africa. In 1975, the South African government opened its embassy in Tel Aviv and, in the same year, there were several meetings between diplomats of both countries to discuss future political and economic co-operation. This was a substantive change in outlook by the Israelis, as, prior to this, Israel had allowed its ministers to visit South Africa only in order to address Jewish matters. Indeed, one can witness the improvement in the relationship through the level of trade between the two countries: in 1973, Israel exported approximately US$12 million worth of goods to South Africa, whilst it imported goods to the value of US$27.5 million. In 1974, these figures rose to US$28.7 million and US$38.4 million respectively.[6]

The Yom Kippur War transformed Israel, which had until that point, the second largest diplomatic representation in Africa, after France, into a pariah state.[7] The breaking of ties between Israel and Ethiopia was accompanied by a statement by Ethiopian Foreign Minister, Minasse Haile, who said: 'Every Ethiopian knows your [the Israelis'] situation and every Ethiopian hopes for your victory, for we know you are right in your war with the Arabs. But we have to take care of our interests, and this calls upon us today to break the relations with you'. The minister added that it was not a 'popular move'... and that it ... 'will help us in the short run only'. Haile revealed that the break also involved the moderate Arab League states: Egypt, Morocco, Tunisia and Jordan, restraining radical ones: Syria, and Libya.[8]

Speaking of the severing of relations, Israeli Ambassador Aynor noted,

> The Ethiopian public was taken by surprise and reacted with amazement upon hearing this unexpected news. The roots of historical, religious and emotional ties between Christian Ethiopia and Israel are so deep and rich that they occasionally verge on the irrational. The cutting of relations while Israel is struggling for survival had a stunning effect on many, for on top of all that it had the smack of betrayal and a stab in the back ... It may be the case that some ... Muslims are happy about it, but there is no doubt that the overwhelming majority of Christian Ethiopians ... conceive the breaking of relations a matter of great shame and little benefit ... What was done is seen as an act of surrender to Arab blackmail, an act for which Ethiopia is soon to pay dearly.[9]

Concurrently, the Arab states moved to blockade the strait of *Bab al-Mandeb*, and, in so doing, achieved one of the very goals that the Ethiopian element of the Policy of the Periphery had been designed to prevent.[10]

While it is true that the threat made to relocate the OAU may have had an impact on the Ethiopian decision and that Selassie desired to steer his country's foreign policy towards the general parameters of those of the non-aligned states, the perceived Israeli occupation of Palestinian territories was becoming a source of discomfiture, even for those states not openly sympathetic to the Arab cause.[11] The decision by Selassie to break relations with Israel quickened his downfall, as the removal of the Israeli military advisors meant that there was no longer a point of contact between the Ethiopian officers' corps and the regular soldiers. Thus, discontent amongst the soldiers, which helped to create the catalyst for revolution, was not identified and dealt with. Moreover, many Ethiopians saw the move to expel the Israelis as a betrayal.[12]

During this time at the UN, the Ethiopian delegation was largely silent over the situation in the Middle East, but by September 1973, it began to adopt a more fatalistic character. Representative Haile stated that,

> We note that no progress has been achieved in the past year in the effort to bring peace ... the Middle East, where the task of finding a just and lasting solution to the problem continues to be stalemated ... violence and retribution continue to be perpetrated, as what has come to be described as 'the Arab-Israeli secret war' assumes new scope and dimensions with its inevitable hazards to those innocent bystanders who are unrelated in any way to the conflict in the Middle East.[13]

He continued to register disillusionment with the UN on this issue, 'On the diplomatic front, the recent broad review conducted by the Security Council of the situation in the Middle East has failed to yield any new direction ... in the important search for ... peace in the Middle East'.[14]

It was not until 4 October 1974, nearly a year after the outbreak of the Yom Kippur War, that Ethiopian Representative, Gabre-Selassie, spoke out. He stated that his government 'would particularly note the limited but significant agreements concluded in the Middle East'. Moreover, he stated that Ethiopia 'whole heartedly welcomed the troop disengagement agreements which have followed the cease-fire in the Middle East'. The Representative, however, expressed concern that 'what has been accomplished may be frustrated by the explosive potential of the present situation'.[15] Gabre-Selassie also served a warning to the international community, when he revealed that he had no desire to 'oversimplify the complexity of the problems ... [of the] Middle East' and that, given its proximity to the conflict 'Ethiopia has most acutely suffered from the long closure of the Suez Canal and will assist in every way possible efforts to reopen this vital artery of international commerce'.[16]

Prior to that, in September 1974, the Ethiopian revolution brought a Marxist cadre of army officers, known as the Derg, to power. The reasons behind the collapse of the Selassie regime are numerous, but include the adverse effects on the Ethiopian economy as a result of the closure of the Suez Canal in 1967, the oil embargo, and the ensuing high prices of oil in the wake of the Yom Kippur War.[17] The Derg did not restore relations with Israel and closed the sea passage between Massawa and Eilat.[18] However, the Arab states continued to support Eritrean rebel groups and the Israelis never revoked their aid to the Ethiopian government.[19] As a result, the new regime in Ethiopia turned to Jerusalem and invited a number of Israeli advisors to aid in Ethiopia's military training. This decision was taken by the new Ethiopian government in December 1975 and, by 1977, some 30 Israeli military advisors were engaged in the country.[20]

Due to their open support for the Eritrean separatists, the Arab states aided in transforming what had been a largely contained conflict into open warfare, during which time, the Derg expressed regret for Selassie's decision to sever ties with Israel.[21] In fact, the belief in Addis Ababa was that Ethiopia's neighbours were determined to destroy the Ethiopian regime, with the main protagonists being Sudan, Egypt and Saudi Arabia.[22] Although diplomatic ties were not renewed, and there was no discussion of the subject, this was, nevertheless, an important episode in the re-evaluation of the relationship between Israel and Ethiopia.

As a consequence of the Derg relationship with Jerusalem, Israel had, by 1975, developed a modest fleet of missile boats in the area, which was allegedly allowed to refuel at Ethiopian Red Sea islands, such as Halib and Fatima, and was designed to counter the Arab challenge to the Red Sea.[23] In return, and out of mutual regional concern, Israel agreed to supply ammunition and spare parts to the US manufactured weapons used by the Ethiopian armed forces.[24] In addition, Israel was actively engaged in creating new units within the Ethiopian army, specifically a number of Israeli officers began working with the new 5th division, which would see military action from 1976 onwards.[25]

This interaction between the two countries came at time when the Ethiopian position at the UN regarding the situation in the Middle East appeared to be more positive. Indeed, Representative Wodajo noted that

The momentum generated by the recently signed interim agreement between the Arab Republic of Egypt and the State of Israel

must be sustained with a view to ensuring the legitimate rights
and lasting interests of all the peoples in the region. I only wish
to express here my Government's appreciation to all concerned
for their statesmanship in achieving the recent agreement, which
we hope will be a signal beginning towards a final settlement of
the Middle East problem.[26]

This pragmatic approach led the Ethiopian delegation to abstain in
the vote over UN Resolution 3379 (**XXX**), equating Zionism with
racism.[27]

Furthermore in 1976, Representative Wodajo revealed that 'The
Middle East is one of those problem areas where, the longer we wait,
the more intractable a peaceful solution becomes. After so many
missed opportunities, time now seems to have imposed a limit on
a peaceful solution'. He added that, 'Although we may disagree on
the time-frame, there is no doubt that it is not one that can allow us
indulgently to proceed at the present pace'. He also stated that 'The
requirements for a peaceful solution are known and have often been
repeated here and in other international forums'. Finally, he opined
that, 'Israel must withdraw from all Arab territories that it has occupied since 1967' and that the PLO 'must take part in all negotiations
for peaceful settlements'.[28]

Keen to internationalise the conflict, Wodajo stated,

A world that refuses to accommodate changes that have taken
place will be hard put to bring about those far-reaching trans-
formations on the relations of States, especially between the rich
and the poor, the exploited and the exploiter, the weak and the
powerful. Thus, the urgency to solve some of the outstanding
problems, in addition to ensuring international peace and security, is directly linked with the effort to create a more secure and
prosperous world.[29]

The following month, Ethiopian Representative Bekele announced that
the Palestinian people are entitled to 'a homeland within the former
Mandated Territory of Palestine' which, he claimed was 'one of the

central requirements for a just solution to the Middle East problem'. This, though, was tempered by the admission that 'the problem as a whole has evolved to take on wider dimensions and newer ramifications, especially as a consequence of four wars'. For Bekele, this meant that 'an overall settlement ... requires apart from implementing the rights of the Palestinian people to a homeland, the recognition and existence of Israel as a Sovereign State'. The delegate emphasised his point by revealing that his government did not 'subscribe to any view that the State of Israel should be supplanted and denied existence'.[30]

These statements surely revealed both the tenuousness and importance of the bi-lateral ties that were proceeding concomitantly, particularly in the sphere of trade, between Israel and Ethiopia.[31] Bekele's statements did not reveal an inherent contradiction. On the contrary, the Ethiopian adoption of a two-state solution was the perfect compromise for the regime in Addis Ababa. There is little doubt that the Ethiopian delegation was influenced by the increase in trade figures and the Israeli military prowess revealed in July of the same year, when the IDF successfully rescued Jewish hostages held by German and Palestinian terrorists at Entebbe, Uganda.

On 24 February 1977, US President Jimmy Carter ended US military aid to Ethiopia as a protest against its human rights' violations. Somalia saw this as an opportunity to press home its claims to Eritrea and the more conservative Arab states became wary that Ethiopia may become a proxy for Soviet machinations in the region, with the USSR potentially filling the vacuum left by the US. As a result, they began to increase their support for the Eritrean movement.[32] The Israelis perceived this to be the opportunity that the USSR had been waiting for[33] and maintained a positive relationship with the Ethiopian government, as they continued to oppose Eritrean rebel groups and Arab and Muslim expansionism in the area.[34] Furthermore, with a desire to develop even stronger ties, the Israelis proactively developed additional arms deals with the new regime in Addis Ababa.

The timing of the deals was not random. The on-going border war between Ethiopia and Somalia intensified in July 1977, when the Western Somali Liberation Front attacked Ogaden and, by October, had gained control over much of the province.[35] However, the deals were rejected by Ethiopia when Moshe Dayan leaked details of them to the press in February 1978.[36] A furious Ethiopia expelled the Israelis, who would have to wait some four years to return. Concomitantly, the Ethiopian government changed its political stance and began to gravitate towards the USSR in its desperate search for weapons.

The Israeli reasoning behind aiding the Derg was set out by Moshe Dayan in the course of a meeting that took place between himself and King Hassan of Morocco, in September 1977. Dayan noted,

> The King asked me at one point whether Israel was involved in the war then going on in Ethiopia, and if so why? I told him that we were not involved in the war but only in aid to Ethiopia, towards whom we had moral obligations. Ethiopia had helped us in the past with port and air facilities when our ships and planes were in desperate straits. We would not refuse them now when they were in trouble and asked for arms. The King argued that times had changed, that Ethiopia would soon be left without any ports, and perhaps we would do better to try to get closer to the moderate wing of the liberation movement along the Red Sea coast. I told him there was no chance of that. The liberation movement was already affiliated to the Arab League and would not come to our assistance in time of need.[37]

The following year saw a thinly veiled attack on Israel at the UN by Ethiopian Representative Gedle Giorgis, who stated that 'The situation in the Middle East has continued to deteriorate as a result of the arrogant refusal by the forces of aggression, occupation and expansion to implement the relevant United Nations resolutions'. He continued, 'Repeated acts of aggression against the Arab Peoples have been paralleled only by newer and ever more insidious manoeuvres to procrastinate and further complicate a solution to the Middle East conflict'. Talking of possible peace initiatives, the delegate noted that there had been opportunities 'for reconvening the Geneva Peace Conference in which all parties to the conflict could be involved. However ... the world has witnessed the most dramatic surrender to the forces of aggression and expansion, as well as capitulation to imperialist domination'.[38]

Not content with this tirade, Gedle Giorgis stated that 'We are also convinced that no accord can be just and lasting unless it takes full cognizance of the rights of the Palestinian people to establish their own national homeland under the leadership of the Palestine Liberation Organisation ... , the sole spokesman and legitimate Representative of the Palestinian people'. In contrast to his wish that the hopes of the Geneva Conference could have been rekindled, the delegate revealed that 'In our view, the Camp David accord is nothing but a sophisticated imperialist plot designed to exacerbate further the already difficult and complex situation in the Middle East'.[39]

The following month, Ethiopian Representative, Ibrahim, chose to convey his country's new, hard-line approach towards Israel through the International Day of Solidarity with the Palestinian People. This was the perfect opportunity for the Ethiopian delegation to vent concerns over the continuing plight of the Palestinian refugees, without endangering its ties with Jerusalem. At the outset of his speech, Ibrahim asked permission to express his delegation's 'best wishes and to reaffirm to the people of Palestine Ethiopia's solidarity with them in their just struggle for the restoration of their inalienable rights'. Moreover, he stated that the observance of said day 'was a victory for the Palestinian People ... and this despite innumerable schemes calculated to erase the national identity of a people whose only crime is its steadfast opposition to the forces of occupation and aggression'.[40]

In addition to possibly accusing Israel of attempted genocide, the representative opined that 'The tragedy of the Palestinian people has been its historic misfortune as a victim of past imperialist Powers and contemporary expansionist conquerors'. Also, he noted 'From the days of the Ottoman Empire to the present, the people of Palestine have been subjected to successive waves of imperialist, colonialist and expansionist aggression'.[41]

Seemingly undeterred by the complexity of the Middle East conflict, Ibrahim noted that 'No matter how complex and intractable an issue it is made out to appear by some, the question of Palestine is first and foremost a question of the denial of justice to a people that has been uprooted and made a stranger in its own land'. The explanation for this refugee status was supplied by Ibrahim, 'the Israeli policy of expansionism, its intransigence and the machinations of imperialist as well as of some other States to confuse the real issue must be condemned as retrograde, constituting a threat to peace and security in the region'. Finally, the representative revealed that 'Relegated to the status of refugees for decades, the Palestinians have been denied their fundamental right to a homeland. Since the redressing of this gross injustice is the crux of the matter, it is evident that no half-hearted measures can ensure the fulfilment of Palestinian aspirations'.[42] With the voice of the Ethiopian delegation combining with those of other nations expressing concern over the welfare of the Palestinian people, Ethiopia ensured that its rhetoric against Israel was diluted in its veracity. This, at a time when Israel's exports to Ethiopia stood at approximately US$7.6 million.[43] Ethiopia was treading a very fine line between Israel and the Arab world.

Ethiopian Jewry

With the ascension to power of the Likud-led government of Menachem Begin in 1977, Jerusalem arranged an arms deal to Ethiopia, in exchange for Ethiopian Jews wishing to immigrate to Israel.[44] Although Ethiopian Jewry was not harshly treated and never faced systematic persecution, Ethiopian Jews were second-class citizens, and were confined to the rural areas of the country. With the Begin government, there appeared a new, religious factor in Israeli politics, with elements of the new government believing in the concept of Greater Israel. Begin and his government offered a renewed emphasis on Zionism and the nature of the Jewish state. This, coupled with the contextual backdrop of UN Resolution of 1975, equating Zionism with racism, were factors behind the new Israeli government's renewed interest in Ethiopia.

Interestingly, until the election of the Likud government, no Israeli minister had agreed to meet with Representatives of Ethiopian Jewry. Begin, however, reversed this. Taking the 1975 ruling by Sephardi Chief Rabbi, Ovadia Yosef that the Jews of Ethiopia were halachically Jewish and members of the lost tribe of Dan, he initiated a radical programme which would culminate in the transporting of many Ethiopian Jews to Israel clandestinely, known as Operation Moses.[45]

Meanwhile, Ethiopian UN Representative Gedle Giorgis, turned his attention towards the situation in the Middle East, and, in particular, the fragile attempts at peace between Israel and Egypt. 'The cleverly orchestrated manoeuvres and betrayals which we have witnessed of late have succeeded only in highlighting the fact that the question of the rights of the Palestinian people is at the core of the Middle East problem'.[46] Moreover, he opined that 'The Camp David agreements and the subsequent treaty between Egypt and Israel have not only ignored and circumvented this important and central issue but have also made Israel more arrogant and intransigent'. Portraying Egypt as a collaborator with Israel, the representative then explained that Israeli intentions had been 'amply demonstrated by the continued establishment of illegal settlements in occupied Arab territories and has increased Israeli aggression against the unity, sovereignty and territorial integrity of Lebanon'.[47]

Far from applauding the Israeli-Egyptian framework for peace, the Ethiopian stance was hostile. Indeed, Gedle Giorgis stated that the 'deals between Egypt and Israel have increased tension and conflict among the States of the region. For these reasons, socialist Ethiopia rejects these separate deals and maintains that there can be no lasting solution to the Middle East problem unless it is sought within the framework of the ... United Nations'. The diplomat then revealed that his country 'extends its full support to the just cause of the Palestinian people and the Arab States whose territories have long been occupied'.[48] This approach was not a surprise, as the Camp David Accords had, in bringing about peace between Israel and Egypt, lessened the strategic importance of Ethiopia.

The tone of the Ethiopian delegation did not soften when expressed by Representative Deressa, even though this year, 1979, saw Israel's exports to Ethiopia increase to approximately US$9.3 million.[49] He stated that 'The uprooting of the Palestinian people from their homeland, as well as the injustices they have been made to suffer as a result, is a most unfortunate, indeed tragic, situation, which continues to vex and haunt the conscience of all peace-loving people throughout the world'. As if to remove any doubt as to the identification of the aggressors, Deressa declared, 'this great human tragedy and injustice against the people of Palestine is being perpetuated in the name of a people that has itself suffered intolerance and oppression through-out the centuries.'[50] The actions of the Jewish state were viewed by the Ethiopian Representatives as nothing short of criminal. Indeed, Deressa asked rhetorically 'Why the Arab people of Palestine should be held responsible for the crimes committed by others, why they should be subjected to degradation, repression and wanton killings, why they should continue to be denied their inalienable rights ... is incomprehensible'.[51]

Not satisfied with such rhetoric, Deressa offered the Ethiopian view on a possible solution,

> In our view, it would be in the enlightened self-interest of Israel, and its imperialist collaborators therefore, to realise that under no circumstances can one wrong justify another ... that the ... expulsions, deportations, systematic repression and denial of the right of the Palestinian people to return to their homeland would only ... aggravate the very dangerous situation prevailing in the region.[52]

Again, attacking the Camp David agreements, Deressa opined that 'Any settlement in the region such as the Camp David scheme cannot ... be durable or, ... viable, since it fails to take full account of the Palestinian problem and has been undertaken with the exclusion of the Palestine Liberation Organisation and the other directly interested parties'. In fact, thought Deressa 'the separate deal only sacrifices the legitimate rights of the Palestinian people to the goals and objectives of international imperialism'.[53]

In 1980, Begin began to further develop Operation Moses, which ultimately led to some 10–15,000 Ethiopian Jews arriving in Israel between 1980 and 1984.[54] In 1981, the Jewish Organisation for Rehabilitation, which was operating in Ethiopia, was expelled by the authorities, after being blamed for encouraging Ethiopian Jews to leave the country, a far cry from 1977, when at least one planeload of Ethiopian Jews flew from Addis Ababa to Tel Aviv.[55]

There was not always consensus among world Jewry that the plight of Ethiopia's Jews warranted an exodus to Israel. Indeed, there existed a school of thought which favoured aiding the Jews of Ethiopia in the areas in which they lived, particularly the north-west region of Gondar. However, 1981 witnessed several incidents in the area of Waleka, where the local synagogue was closed for over a year and, in 1982, there were demonstrations throughout Israel by Ethiopian Jews, designed to highlight the disadvantages that their brethren in Ethiopia were facing. This hardship, though, was not borne out when foreign journalists visited the area in December 1982 and observed that the Falashas were living in satisfactory conditions. The journalists could not see any sign of persecution.[56]

As Israeli exports to Ethiopia plummeted from US$11.2 million in 1980, to US$3.2 million in 1981,[57] the Ethiopian stance at the UN became more vitriolic, revealing the political influence of trade on the relationship between the two countries. Representative Gedle-Giorgis condemned Israel's 'repeated acts of aggression against peaceful Lebanon'. He continued, 'The strategic alliance between the United States, Israel and South Africa is nothing but the consolidation of an imperialist-racist axis threatening the freedom and independence of the States of the region'.[58]

Lebanon also featured in the Representative's diatribe 'It is sad to note that repeated crimes are being committed against peaceful Lebanon by a neighbour that is armed to the teeth. A free and sovereign State has been subjected to naked aggression'. The diplomat believed he was in a unique position to comment on such matters 'As a victim of similar aggressions, both in the distant past and in recent years, my own country views these criminal acts with indignation'.[59]

Speaking of the Lebanon war, Representative Gedle-Giorgis stated,

Israel's recent invasion of Lebanon and the resulting loss of life and destruction of property have once again thrown the entire region into turmoil. The subsequent massacre in west Beirut of innocent people, after the withdrawal of Palestinian combatants under a guarantee of the safety of their families and other civilians, has shocked and angered the international community.

In no doubt as to whom was to blame for the attack, the envoy declared 'Ethiopia condemns in the strongest terms possible the genocide perpetrated against the Palestinian people ... In any event, Israel and its imperialist allies cannot escape responsibility for that shameless and inhuman episode'.[60]

With these words, Gedle-Giorgis encapsulated the final twist of the Ethio-Israeli relationship. The halcyon days of the 1960s were gone, never to return. The severance of ties in the wake of the Yom Kippur War and the rise to power of the Derg had not extinguished the Ethiopian dimension of the Policy of the Periphery; in fact, Ethiopian military vulnerability had allowed it to burgeon. With the outbreak of the Lebanon War, however, Ethiopia began to distance itself from Israel. Whilst Israel continues to symbolise the potential for development in Ethopia, it seems that Addis Ababa, along with Jerusalem, is unable, or unwilling, to promote the pluralism that would encourage both states to integrate more fully into the Middle East, without losing their unique identities.

CHAPTER 8

THE POLICY OF THE PERIPHERY

The UNGA partition plan of 29 November 1947 revealed very clearly the tensions that would come to characterise the relationships between Israel and Iran, Turkey and Ethiopia. It also revealed each of the countries' overriding national interests and showed that the UN, in many instances, could be used as a multilateral pressure valve, in order to fulfil regional and/or religious/ideological commitments that prevented open identification and co-operation with Israel.

For the Iranian delegation, the creation of the Jewish state signified not only an anti-democratic decision by the UN, but was also a danger to the Iranian perception of regional stability, tainted as it was by the fear of both further regional penetration by the USSR and the rise and spread of Nasserism. The Iranian delegation, though, at the outset was keen to show no partiality on the matter and explained that its decision to vote against partition was not based on any dislike of the Jews, but was due to its belief that the future of Palestine was better left to its inhabitants.

The ostensible impartiality shown by Iran during the vote was evidence of its desire to maintain cordial relations with the Arab world, whilst, concomitantly, functioning as an element of Israel's Policy of the Periphery. This could be seen both through the speeches of the Iranian delegation during the period of the vote, and by Iran, along with India and Yugoslavia, supporting federation. The Iranian position changed, however, after Israel's victory in the 1948 War of Independence, during which *Aliyah Bet* established links with its Iranian counterpart, SAVAK, links that had been facilitated by Iran's admiration for the IDF's military prowess during the fighting.

For Turkey, its initial position on the creation of the Jewish state was similar to that of Iran. Indeed, it voted against partition, as it too stated its opposition to the UN imposing a government on the people of Palestine. The Turkish UN delegation at the time, like that of Iran, went to great lengths to explain that it was torn between affection for the Jews and its Muslim heritage. Although Turkey opposed a permanent imposition of government on the people of Palestine, it did support a temporal trusteeship, in order to quell the bloodshed and resulting instability of the burgeoning Arab-Israeli conflict.

Turkey, like Iran, also saw the Israeli victory in 1948 as a catalyst for the development of the Policy of the Periphery. Indeed, in the aftermath of the war, Turkey assumed its position on the PCC, along with the US and France and did not represent the sentiments of the Arab/Muslim world, as was assumed it would. For Ankara, there was the added incentive that improved ties with Israel could encourage the West to view it in a more favourable light and offer it aid at a time when Turkey was keen to stem the rise of Arab radicalism and check the regional influence of the USSR. Indeed, Turkish recognition of Israel was carried out in the face of strong condemnation by the Arab states, many of whom accused Turkey of betraying the spirit of Islamic solidarity. For Turkey, Realpolitik was the decisive factor.

There is a similar thread running through the initial response of Ethiopia to the creation of Israel. Ethiopia was largely silent in the UN discussions over partition and abstained in the vote. The Ethiopian behaviour can be attributed to the government's desire not to aggravate its Muslim and Arab neighbours in an already hostile region, in which it was the sole Christian country. The Ethiopian approach to partition, like that of both Iran and Turkey was based on the belief that partition of a country should not be based along religious lines.

As partition was the only option available to those voting, Ethiopia chose to abstain. Ethiopia's geographical position also ensured that it would be potentially receptive to Israel's overtures, situated as it was on the Red Sea, with access to the richest trade routes in the world and aware that anything other than unfettered access to the seas could spell economic ruin.

For the three pillars of Israel's Policy of the Periphery, the confluence of interests was clear: they all had a natural instinct to protect the *status quo* of the region and, as a result, were reticent in voting for the creation of a new state in such contentious circumstances. For Iran and Turkey, in opposing the creation of Israel, the UN was not needed to placate the Arab/Muslim world. For Ethiopia, in abstaining in the vote over partition, the UN served as the perfect arena to allay the fears of the Arab world, via neutral statements on the matter, all the time aware that it was vital for Israel and the West as a buffer against Nasser's Egypt. Thus, the attitudes and positions of Iran, Turkey and Ethiopia, albeit hesitantly, combined to allow the fledgling alliance between themselves and Israel the first vital breaths of life in a harsh environment.

The Suez War of 1956 saw many of the attitudes adopted by Iran, Turkey and Ethiopia towards Israel after the War of Independence continue. In 1956, the Iranian delegation was reticent in condemning the tri-partite action against Egypt. Indeed, it was only after some deliberation that the Iranian delegation castigated both Britain and France for their involvement in the military campaign and then went on to vote for the withdrawal of Israeli forces from Egyptian territory. This was a diplomatic position of some safety for Iran as, whilst ensuring non-indigenous forces would leave Egyptian soil, it rejected calls to occupy its seat on UNEF, suggesting instead that Ceylon take its place; it mildly rebuked Britain and France and, in so doing, supported the position of the US, which was diametrically opposed to the military campaign. It is no coincidence that, after the Suez War, trade between Israel and Iran began to grow, with Israel becoming the largest consumer of Iranian oil in the region in 1957. The prowess of the IDF was proving also to Tehran that the Jewish state could be a formidable buffer to Nasserism.

For the Turkish delegation at the UN, the Suez War proved a considerable strain on the Policy of the Periphery. Although Turkey was reticent in criticising the belligerent parties, it voted for the withdrawal of non-indigenous forces from Egyptian territory. This position, again, ensured that no Turkish partiality was shown either to Israel, or the Arab world. However, Turkish Representative, Selim Sarper, made it clear through his speeches that the central Turkish concern in the aftermath of the fighting was the creation of a vacuum, likely it was feared, to be filled by the USSR; a position similar to that of the Iranian fear of the insidiousness of Nasserism.

In contrast to Iran, however, the Turkish government, in the face of coordinated Arab pressure, downgraded its relationship with Israel in the aftermath of the war. Indeed, the Turkish minister to Israel was recalled, a move reciprocated by Israel, and Nasser, who had spearheaded the attacks on Turkey for its recognition of, and relationship with, the Jewish state, claimed that the Turks would never again have the influence they once wielded through the Ottoman Empire. For the Policy of the Periphery, this was just the challenge to Nasserism that was desired; one that could potentially undermine Nasser's position as regional strongman and leader of the Arab world.

For Ethiopia, though, the post-1956 situation was more complex. Although critical of the actions of Britain and France, the Ethiopian delegation duly noted that both countries did indeed have grievances against Egypt. However, for the Selassie regime's representatives at the UN, the actions of Israel, Britain and France in Egypt were a grim reminder of Ethiopian loss of independence to Italy in 1935 and, as such, Ethiopia felt a certain sympathy toward the Egyptian people. To this end, Ethiopia supported all UN resolutions pertaining to the withdrawal of non-indigenous forces from Egypt and the establishment of UNEF.

The Ethiopian delegation also believed that the Egyptian government had merely exercised its right to nationalise the Suez Canal and, in so doing, distanced itself from the actions of Israel, Britain and France, whilst, *ipso facto*, supporting the position of the

US. For Ethiopia, which stood to lose a great deal from the closure of the Suez Canal to Ethiopian shipping, Egyptian territorial integrity was ostensibly the most important issue at the UN. National interest guided the Ethiopian delegation through this diplomatic minefield. It was at this juncture that both Israel and Ethiopia identified a significant mutual interest: protecting the integrity of the Red Sea and preventing it from becoming an Arab asset. The Policy of the Periphery had been created for just such an event.

The Iranian stance in the aftermath of the Six Day War mirrored, almost exactly, its stance after Suez. Iranian diplomat and Minister for Foreign Affairs, Ardeshir Zahedi, revealed Iranian disdain towards the UN for failing to prevent the war in the first instance. Indeed, he bemoaned the price in lives that had been exacted before the implementation of the UN cease-fire. Although voting in favour of IDF withdrawal to positions held prior to 5 June 1967, the Iranian delegation refused to vote for the Albanian draft resolution, calling for Israel to compensate the UAR and, in so doing, voted against the Arab-Muslim bloc at the UN.

Iranian admiration for the speed and efficiency of the Israeli victory in the Six Day War, as in the Suez War, served as a catalyst for the development of the Policy of the Periphery. However, in the wake of the Six Day War, Iran also began to differentiate between issues of Arab and Islamic natures at the UN, and began to adopt a more ambiguous voting pattern. This did not prevent Iran from revealing its concern for the Palestinian refugees, already unsettled for nearly two decades and now adversely affected by the Six Day War. This concern, though, by no means more significant than that voiced by many other UN Member States, was offset by the joint Israeli-Iranian oil pipeline project, created following the Six Day War, that reached from Eilat to Ashkelon.

The Turkish delegation, like that of Iran, was disillusioned with the failure of the UN to prevent the war and openly stated that events leading up to hostilities clearly showed that the region was heading for war, while the international community looked on. Turkey, like Iran voted in favour of IDF withdrawal to pre-5 June 1967 lines, but abstained over draft resolution A/L 519, thus eschewing the voting pattern of the Arab bloc. In so doing, Turkey ensured that, although not agreeing with Israel's actions, it did nothing to condemn the Jewish state outright, thereby facilitating the potential further development of the Policy of the Periphery.

Indeed, Turkish UN representative, Ihsan Sabri Caglayangil, ensured that the Arab bloc at the UN was mollified, and emphasised his country's ties with the Arab world, but also its desire to promote cordial ties with all its neighbours. Again, the Turkish desire for equilibrium between Israel and the Arab world is clear. Interestingly, it was some two years after the Six Day War that Turkey, at the first Islamic summit conference, held in September 1969, not only refused to discuss its ties with Israel, but saw any attempt by Member States of the summit conference to criticise it relationship with the Jewish state as unacceptable, outside interference. Surely, for the Turks, the Israeli victory in 1967 allowed them the confidence to take such a pro-Israel stance.

For Ethiopia, the Six Day War was the perfect opportunity to display its neutrality. At the UNSC, Ethiopian diplomat, Makonnen, stressed the horrific damage that would be done to all the peoples of the area and emphasised his country's ties with all states in the region. Ethiopia did, however, vote in favour of UN Resolution 242, and Makonnen emphasised his country's desire to include the definite article in the wording of the resolution, thereby requiring that Israel withdraw from *all* (author's italics) territories it had acquired during the war.

At the UNGA, however, Ethiopia abstained in the vote over draft resolution A/L 522/Rev.3, and voted against Albanian draft resolution, A/L 521. In so doing, it walked a tightrope between the Superpowers and showed Israel that it had understood the positive implications of Israel's military victory *vis-à-vis* the Policy of the Periphery, although Ethiopia would later vote against Israeli actions to alter the status of Jerusalem. It was at this juncture that Ethiopia, along with Iran, Turkey and many other UN Member States, focussed on the plight of the Palestinian refugees, an issue that would resurface in the wake of the Yom Kippur War.

Just as the Suez and Six Day Wars had persuaded Iran to pursue its relationship with Israel further, the Yom Kippur War initially caused it to do the opposite. Not only does it appear that the Iranian government knew of the impending Arab attack and did not inform Israel, but also that Tehran aided the Arab states during the war on a far greater scale than it aided Israel. The Shah believed that his country's actions during the war would not damage its relations with the Jewish state and, moreover, when pressured by the Arabs to sever ties with Israel completely, he demanded they ask the same of their allies amongst the great powers.

The British believed that the Iranian government blamed both the Arabs and the Israelis for the war and the Iranian fear in the aftermath of the fighting was that the USSR would exploit the chaos in the area, in order to further bolster its regional influence. Superficially, the Iranian branch of the Policy of the Periphery suffered after the war, as, for the first time, Israel no longer appeared to be invincible. Furthermore, Iran believed that Israel was to blame for the lack of progress in the Arab-Israeli peace talks and it was from this point that the Shah began to connect peace in the region with the implementation of the rights of the Palestinians, demanding that Israel negotiate with the PLO.

Turkish dependence on OPEC oil convinced Ankara to grant the USSR use of its airspace during the war, in order to re-supply the Arab armies, whilst refusing the US request, thereby placing Israel at a strategic disadvantage. After the war, Turkey became an outspoken critic of Israel and it seemed that the Turkish element of the Policy of the Periphery was in danger of collapsing. Due to the rise in the price of oil in the aftermath of the war, Turkey became proactive in its dealings with the Islamic Conference and it sought closer ties with the OPEC Member States. It appeared that the 'positive neutrality' adopted by Prime Minister Bulent Ecevit, was not neutral at all, but rather pro-Arab.

Turkey, like Iran and Ethiopia was vocal at the UN in its opposition to Israeli attempts to alter the status of Jerusalem and re-iterated its commitment to the well-being and safety of the Palestinian refugees, thereby cementing its Muslim credentials. Taking all these factors into account, one can state that Turkey saw the Yom Kippur War as a watershed in its relations with Israel. Israel appeared to be weakened and, for Ankara, acting in the face of Arab opposition in order to develop ties with the Jewish state was becoming an unacceptable risk.

Like Turkey, Ethiopia faced significant regional pressure to sever its ties with Israel as a result of the Yom Kippur War. The OAU, headed by Libya, demanded that Ethiopia ostracise the Jewish state, or the OAU would move its offices from Addis Ababa. Given the Ethiopian fear of the power of Nasserism, one of the issues that the Policy of the Periphery was designed to counter, it duly acquiesced. The severing of the ties between the two countries was accompanied by a statement at the UN by Ethiopian Foreign Minister, Minasse Haile, who expressed the desire of his people to see Israel victorious in its fight against the Arab armies, and was aware that the severing of ties was in Ethiopia's short-term interest only. This statement does indeed withstand scrutiny, as the Ethiopian belief was that, were it to appease the moderate Arab states by severing its ties with Israel, the same moderate Arab states would then placate the radical ones. The following year would see the collapse of the Selassie government, the ascension of the Derg to power and the continuation of the Policy of the Periphery, albeit on a less obvious basis.

After the Iranian Revolution in 1979 and the ascension to power of Ayatollah Khomeini, the Iranian branch of the Policy of the Periphery seemed doomed. Indeed, at the outset of the Lebanon war, a high-ranking Iranian delegation arrived in Damascus, in order to co-ordinate a jihad against the Jewish state, whilst Iraq was prepared to accept an immediate cease-fire in the Iran-Iraq War, in order to concentrate its forces on Israel. The Israeli invasion of Lebanon in 1982 thus had far-reaching regional implications and it appeared that the Policy of the Periphery was failing, in fact uniting two enemies against the Jewish state.

For the new Iranian regime, the Lebanon War presented a superb opportunity to export the Iranian revolution, a concept Khomeini thought vital for its survival and which would eventually furnish Tehran with the framework required to operate proxy allies in its war against Israel. The Israelis knew that, after the Iranian revolution, the US no longer saw Iran as a major regional ally and the invasion of Lebanon revealed that Israel could be counted upon in the US attempt to contain regional Soviet penetration, particularly in the wake of the Soviet invasion of Afghanistan in 1979. Thus, the relationship between Israel and Iran ceased, with Iran embarking on the process that would eventually lead to its spearheading the regional threat to Israel.

For Turkey, the Lebanon War, again, served as a catalyst for its alliance with Israel, whilst the UN proved a suitable sounding board for the Turkish government. In fact, anti-Turkish elements that had trained in Lebanon before the Israeli invasion were exposed, but at the UN, the Turkish delegation openly criticised the Jewish state and held it responsible for the slaughter at Sabra and Shatila.

In addition, well aware that the discovery of PLO fighters captured along with Turkish fighters by Israel could jeopardise its relations with the Arab world, the Turkish government began to distinguish between the Palestinian cause, which it wholeheartedly supported and the various Palestinian terror groups, which it did not necessarily. Indeed, Turkish Foreign Minister Turkmen suggested that it was the duty of the Muslim world to prevent Lebanon from becoming a safe haven for terrorists. The Israeli invasion of Lebanon had shown a link between Armenian, Turkish and PLO terror organisations and, as a result, the intelligence services of Israel and Turkey entered a new era of co-operation.

For Ethiopia, under the Derg regime since 1974, the Lebanon War did little to ameliorate its worsening relationship with Israel. Indeed, as the level of trade between the two countries dropped drastically, the Ethiopian delegation at the UN openly blamed Israel and what it believed to be its imperialist allies, both for the war and the massacres of Sabra and Shatila. For Israel, the Lebanon War sounded the death knell of the Ethiopian branch of the Policy of the Periphery and Israel lost its foothold in Africa. For Ethiopia, the orientation of the new government, and the realisation that the Camp David Accords between Israel and Egypt had drastically reduced its regional strategic importance, were enough to overcome the ebbing Policy of the Periphery, and make Ethiopia retreat to a position of passivity, immersed in the fear that it was weaker than ever in the face of potential regional subversion.

CONCLUSION

By examining the dynamics of Israel's foreign policy with Iran, Turkey and Ethiopia, it emerges that, for much of the period under discussion, the Policy of the Periphery did indeed stand the test of time. The most obvious analysis would reveal that Realpolitik and pragmatism, coupled with political opportunism, cemented the ties. Indeed the alliances between Israel and Iran, Turkey and Ethiopia were some of the most important strategic developments to originate in the Middle East in the twentieth century.

With one pillar of the Policy of the Periphery tenuously intact today, that of Israel and Turkey, it is enlightening to note its formalised, rather ironic, formation at the UN. The Turkish decision to vote against partition was both complex, and fraught with geo-strategic consequences. As a country desperately seeking a formal commitment to its safety from the West, Turkey apparently voted in harmony with the Arab bloc, but Islamic solidarity was a matter of secondary importance, particularly when placed in the context of the Cold War and the resultant Turkish fear that the nascent Jewish state would, through its perceived state of weakness, bring the USSR further into the Middle East.

The military dimension of the eventual relationship would prove to be the future of the Turkish-Israeli alliance, not least because of the trade aspect that it emphasised. The joint projects in particular, which aided Turkey in overcoming internal and external pressure, were the palpable results of its ties with Israel. Indeed, the Turkish-Israeli facet of the Policy of the Periphery would develop, reaching its apogee in 1996–99, when the Ankara-Jerusalem relationship was second only to that between Washington and Jerusalem.

For strategic decision makers and observers in the West, it will be a matter of import to see how Israel challenges regional fundamentalist, destabilising regimes and their proxies, in particular, Iran. Israel will need both to constantly interact with non-fundamentalist regional actors and, concomitantly, to pursue both the strategic and military aspects of the Policy of the Periphery with Turkey, regardless of possible complications arising through administration change in either Ankara, or Jerusalem. In the case of Iran, the temporal nature of politics ensured that regime change in 1979 did not end the relationship with Israel immediately, even with a new administration in Tehran that was ostensibly ill-disposed towards Israel, thus, again, proving the efficacy of the Policy of the Periphery. Moreover, there is an essential need for Jerusalem to nurture other pre-existing, perhaps moribund ties, such as those with Ethiopia, and to attempt to forge fresh alliances with the non-Arab/Muslim, indigenous elements of the region, as prescribed by the Policy of the Periphery.

For proponents of the Israel-Turkey alliance, it must be hoped that the confluence of interests that initiated, and later cemented the relationship, will continue. With the potential for more Islamist Turkish governments in the future, there will, undoubtedly, be additional pressure on Turkey to further reduce its relationship with Israel and it is likely that we shall see additional public diplomatic jousting and gamesmanship between the two countries. However, such behaviour may serve, as the UN did at varying times throughout the period under discussion, and for all parties of the Policy of the Periphery, as a political and diplomatic pressure valve that, when used judiciously, can defray some of the collateral damage absorbed by Israel and Turkey, as a result of their relationship.

NOTES

(Note: It is to be noted that URLs were correct at the time of writing.)

Introduction

1. Excerpt of memo from Ben-Gurion to Eisenhower. Michael Bar-Zohar, 'Ben-Gurion and the Policy of the Periphery', in *Israel in the Middle East: Documents and Readings on Society, Politics, and Foreign Relations, 1948-Present*, Itamar Rabinovich, and Jehuda Reinharz, (eds.) (Oxford University Press: Oxford, 1984), pp.164–171.
2. Eli Podeh, 'Rethinking Israel in the Middle East', *Israel Affairs*, vol.3, nos.3 and 4, (Spring/Summer 1997), pp.280–295.
3. The Arab League was created in 1945, when seven Arab countries: Egypt, Iraq, Lebanon, Saudi Arabia, Syria, Transjordan and Yemen, discussed the idea of an Arab commonwealth. The participants signed a protocol for such an organisation in Alexandria on 7 October, 1944 and the Charter of the Arab league was unveiled on 10 May, 1945. See P.R. Kumaraswamy *Historical Dictionary of the Arab-Israeli Conflict* (Scarecrow Press: Maryland, 2006), p.23.
4. The Arab boycott of Israel was designed to bring about both the economic collapse of the Jewish state, starting before its creation and, ultimately, its physical dissolution. The Arab League began proactively boycotting Zionist goods in 1946 and established a Permanent Boycott Committee, which, in June of the same year, passed resolution 72, declaring it a crime for Member States to sell Arab lands to Zionists. After the Arab defeat in 1948, economic warfare was adopted and not only did the Arab states refuse commercial dealings with Israel, they also ensured that all overland and pipeline routes to and from Israel were ceased. Arab ports and airfields were not to accommodate carriers trading with Israel and pressure was placed on other countries to join the boycott. Secondary and third-party boycotts were also enforced, boycotting those

organisations doing business with Israel and prohibiting them from doing business with members of the League. For a detailed account of the boycott, see Donald L. Losman, 'The Arab Boycott of Israel', *International Journal of Middle East Studies*, vol.3, no.2, (April 1972), pp.99–122 and Kumaraswamy *Historical*, pp.18–19.

5. Podeh, 'Rethinking', p.282.

6. Bar-Zohar, 'Ben-Gurion', pp.165–166, Avi Shlaim, *The Iron Wall: Israel and the Arab World* (Penguin Press: London, 2000), p.192 and Dan Raviv and Yossi Melman, *Every Spy a Prince: The Complete History of Israel's Intelligence Community* (Houghton Mifflin Company: Boston, 1990), p.81.

7. Bar-Zohar, 'Ben-Gurion', p.169.

8. Aharon Klieman, *Statecraft in the Dark: Israel's Practice of Quiet Diplomacy* (Jaffee Centre for Strategic Studies: Israel, 1988), p.77.

9. Bar-Zohar, 'Ben-Gurion', pp.164–171, Raviv and Melman, *Every Spy a Prince*, pp.82–85. For a general survey of this concept, see Gideon Rafael, *Destination Peace: Three Decades of Israeli Foreign Policy: A Personal Memoir* (Weidenfeld and Nicolson: London, 1981), pp.78–86 and Joel Peters, *Israel and Africa: The Problematic Friendship* (I.B.Tauris: London, 1992), p.9.

10. Abba Eban, 'Reality and Vision in the Middle East, an Israeli View', *Foreign Affairs*, vol.3, no.4, (July 1965), pp.634–635.

11. Michael B. Oren, *Six Days of War: June 1967 and the Making of the Modern Middle East* (Oxford University Press: Oxford, 2002), p.8.

12. Shlaim, *The Iron Wall*, p.194.

13. For a detailed analysis of Shiloah, see Haggai Eshed, *Reuven Shiloah: The Man Behind the Mossad. Secret Diplomacy in the Creation of Israel* (Frank Cass: London, 1997). *Mossad: Ha Mossad Le Modi'in Ule Tafkidim Miuchadim* (Heb.), The Institute for Intelligence and Special Tasks.

14. Raviv and Melman, *Every Spy a Prince*, p.21.

15. *Ibid.*

16. Michael Brecher, *The Foreign Policy System of Israel: Setting, Images, Process* (Yale University Press: New Haven, 1972), p.278.

17. Joseph Alpher, 'Israel and the Iran-Iraq War', in *The Iran-Iraq War: Impact and Implications*, Efraim Karsh, (ed.) (The Jaffee Centre for Strategic Studies: Tel Aviv University, Israel, 1987), p.156.

18. Eshed, *Reuven Shiloah*, pp.xxxi and 172.

19. *Ibid,* p.269.

Chapter 1   From the Margins to the Centre: Israel's Policy of the Periphery, Pre-1955

1. See 128th meeting of UNGA, 29 November 1947, *United Nations General Assembly Official Records, 2nd Session, 1947, vol.2*, p.1424. For an account of the financial incentives Israel used to facilitate this recognition, see Uri Bialer, 'The Iranian Connection in Israel's Foreign Policy - 1948–1951', *Middle East Journal*, vol.39, no.2, (Spring 1985), pp.292–315. Iran was a member of UNSCOP, The United Nations Special Committee on Palestine, set up to find a solution to the conflict, along with Representatives from Australia, Canada, Czechoslovakia, Guatemala, India, the Netherlands, Peru, Sweden, Uruguay and Yugoslavia. See 79th meeting of UNGA, 15 May 1947, *United Nations General Assembly Official Records, 1st Special Session, 1947, Plenary Meetings and Committees*, pp.174–177 and Walter Eytan, *The First Ten Years, A Diplomatic History of Israel* (Trinity Press: London, 1958), p.3. Iran was one of three countries, along with India and Yugoslavia, to oppose partition and/or recommend federation. UNSCOP reached a majority decision, recommending the partition of Palestine. See http://www.ipcri.org/files/unscop.html

2. See Adl's reported speech, 11th meeting of Ad Hoc Committee on Palestine, 11 October 1947, *United Nations General Assembly Official Records, 2nd Session, 1947, Various Committees and Resolutions*, pp.68–69.

3. *Ibid*, p.69.

4. See Adl's speech, 124th meeting of UNGA, 26 November 1947, *United Nations General Assembly Official Records, 2nd Session, 1947, vol.2*, pp.1328–1329.

5. *Ibid*.

6. See Adl's speech, 128th meeting of UNGA, 29 November 1947, *United Nations General Assembly Official Records, 2nd Session, 1947, vol.2*, p.1417.

7. *Ibid*.

8. In particular, Iran had been concerned by the refusal of the USSR to remove its troops from Iranian soil after the Second World War. The troops had been stationed there, along with British forces, in order to protect Iranian oilfields. Moreover, the USSR made claims on the northern Iranian province of Azerbaijan. The Soviet troops eventually left in 1946, as a result of US pressure. See Richard Crockatt, *The Fifty Years War: The United States and the Soviet Union in World Politics, 1941–1991* (Routledge: London, 1995), p.59.

9. R.K.Ramazani, *Revolutionary Iran: Challenge and Response in the Middle East* (The John Hopkins University Press: Maryland, 1986), p.148. The Tudeh party was formed by a number of Marxist intellectuals in Tehran in the

aftermath of the Anglo-Soviet invasion of 1941 and within a few years had developed into an influential movement, attracting many from both the intelligentsia and the working class. For this and a detailed account of the Tudeh party, see Ervand Abrahamian, 'Communism and Communalism in Iran: The Tudah and the Firqah-I Dimukrat', *International Journal of Middle East Studies*, vol.1, no.4 (October 1970), pp.291–316.

10. Ramazani, *Revolutionary Iran*, p.148.
11. R.K. Ramazani, 'Iran and the Arab-Israeli Conflict', *The Middle East Journal*, vol.32, no.4, (Autumn 1978), pp.414–415.
12. See 207th meeting of UNGA, 11 May 1949, *United Nations General Assembly Official Records, 3rd Session, 1949, vol.2*, p.330.
13. Bialer, *The Iranian Connection*, p.295.
14. By 1956, some 30,000 Iranian Jews were living in Israel. See M.G. Weinbaum, 'Iran and Israel: The Discreet Entente', *Orbis*, vol.XVIII, no.4, (Winter 1975), pp.1070–1088.
15. His Imperial Majesty Mohammed Reza Shah Pahlavi, *Mission for my Country* (Hutchinson: London, 1961), p.30.
16. Bialer, *The Iranian Connection*, p.295 and Sohrab Sobhani, *The Pragmatic Entente: Israeli-Iranian Relations, 1948–1988*, (Praeger California, 1989), pp.4–5.
17. John P. Miglietta, *American Alliance Policy in the Middle East, 1945–1992: Iran, Israel and Saudi Arabia* (Lexington Books: Maryland, 2002), pp.80–81. The exodus involved not only Iraqi and Persian Jews, but also the Jews of Afghanistan. Many refugees were transported via Turkey and by air, with EL AL, the Israeli national airline, receiving permission to transport immigrants directly from Tehran in 1954. See Weinbaum, 'Iran and Israel', pp.1072–1073.
18. Bialer, *The Iranian Connection*, p.296. Throughout late 1949 and early 1950, Iraqi Jews travelled to Iran at the rate of some 1000 a month. See Sobhani, *The Pragmatic Entente*, p.10.
19. Miglietta, *American Alliance Policy*, p.81.
20. Bar-Zohar, 'Ben-Gurion', p.166.
21. *Ibid.*
22. Sobhani, *The Pragmatic Entente*, p.6.
23. Weinbaum, 'Iran and Israel', p.1076. SAVAK. *Sazmani-Amniyat Va Kisvar*, 'The State Intelligence and Security Organisation'. Raviv and Melman, *Every Spy a Prince*, p.82. This apparatus was conceived as a response to the trying political times for Iran in the 1950s. The Communist Tudeh party was calling for the overthrow of the ruling regime and *Fedayeen Islam* perpetuated a campaign of terrorism. Indeed, it has been stated that one of the main goals of the *SAVAK* from 1954–57 was to destroy the Tudeh party. Sobhani, *The Pragmatic Entente*, pp.21–22.

24. Miglietta, *American Alliance Policy*, p.82 and Weinbaum, 'Iran and Israel', pp.1073–1074.

25. Bialer, *The Iranian Connection*, pp.297–298.

26. Shlaim, *The Iron Wall*, p.195. Iran was keen not to over-involve itself in the Arab-Israeli conflict, and attempted to remain neutral *vis-à-vis* the two sides, whilst pursuing its larger foreign policy goals. This said, however, Iran endorsed the rights of the Palestinian people. See Ramazani, 'Iran and the Arab-Israeli Conflict', pp.413 and 425, Shahram Chubin and Sepher Zabih, *The Foreign Relations of Iran: A Developing State in a Zone of Great-Power Conflict* (University of California Press: California, 1974), p.162 and Weinbaum, 'Iran and Israel', p.1081.

27. See 63rd meeting of Ad Hoc Political Committee, 30 November 1950, *United Nations General Assembly Official Records, 5th Year, 1950*, p.407.

28. Bialer, *The Iranian Connection*, p.308.

29. *Ibid.*

30. Weinbaum, 'Iran and Israel,' p.1073.

31. Bialer, *The Iranian Connection*, p.314.

32. Weinbaum, 'Iran and Israel' p.1073. For a description of this turbulent time in Iranian politics, see Sobhani, *The Pragmatic Entente*, pp.11–13.

33. See Abdoh's reported speech, 35th meeting of Ad Hoc Political Committee, 6 December 1952, *United Nations General Assembly Official Records, 7th Year, 1952*, pp.208–209.

34. See Crockatt, *The Fifty Years War*, p.176. For a detailed account of this period, see Helmut Richards, 'America's Shah, Shahanshan's Iran', *Middle East Research and Information Project*, (1975), pp.3–26. Some ten years after the *coup*, retired CIA director, Allen Dulles, wrote that neither the Truman, nor the Eisenhower doctrine made provisions for a country that, in the face of a Communist take-over, did not call for aid. Cited in *ibid*, p.6.

35. Mossadeq had replaced General Razmara, a pro-Western figure, who had advocated *de jure* recognition of Israel. In the quarter of a century after the removal of Mossadeq, Iran experienced meaningful socio-economic development largely as a result of the increasing oil revenues. In 1953, oil revenues amounted to approximately US$34 million, but by 1973, they had reached US$5 billion and by 1977, had reached US$20 billion. Approximately US$30 billion of these monies were invested in socio-economic projects. See Ervand Abrahamian, 'Structural Causes of the Iranian Revolution', *Middle East Research and Information Project*, (1980), pp.21–22.

36. See, Richards, 'America's Shah', p.7.

37. Sobhani, *The Pragmatic Entente*, p.19. Also, the strengthening of the Iranian defence establishment was achieved by Iran joining the Baghdad pact. *Ibid*, pp.19–20.

38. R.K. Ramazani, 'Emerging Patterns of Regional Relations in Iranian Foreign Policy', *Orbis*, vol.XVIII, no.4, (Winter 1975), pp.1043–1070.

39. See Ardalan's reported speech, 32nd meeting of Ad Hoc Political Committee, 24 November 1954, *United Nations General Assembly Official Records, 9th Year*, p.146.

40. Ramazani, 'Emerging', p.1056. This positive nationalism, *inter alia*, criticised Mossadeq for his negativity and attempted to forge a new Iranian *élan*, based, to an extent, on the character of the Shah. See Richards 'America's Shah', p.7.

41. Ramazani, 'Emerging', p.1056.

42. Shah, *Mission*, p.125.

43. The other elected members of the UNSC in 1955 were: Belgium, Brazil, New Zealand, Peru and Turkey.

44. See www.un.org

45. See 695th meeting of UNSC, 29 March 1955, *United Nations Security Council Official Records, 10th Year, 1955*, p.1. For further details of the incident see despatch from Jerusalem to British Foreign Office, 3 March 1955, *PRO FO 371/115897*.

46. For the full text of the resolution, see www.un.org. What was not included in the resolution was that Israel Radio in English reported that Egyptian units had been active in Israel and that Egyptian soldiers were responsible for the murder of a resident of Qubeiba. Also, the same Egyptian soldiers were responsible for breaking into a government institution near Rishon LeZion where they stole documents and a telephone receiver. The Israelis also revealed that a second Egyptian patrol had been intercepted in Israeli territory in the same period and that one of the Egyptian soldiers had been killed. The Israeli army noted in addition that between 1954–55, 24 Egyptian soldiers had been detained, tried and sentenced to various terms of imprisonment, ten had been killed and five escaped. See BBC memos, 28 February 1955, *PRO FO 371/115897*.

47. See Entezam's speech, 695th meeting of UNSC, 29 March 1955, *United Nations Security Council Official Records, 10th Year, 1955*, p.11.

48. *Ibid*, p.12.

49. For the full text of the resolution, see www.un.org. For voting records, see 696th meeting of UNSC, 30 March 1955, *United Nations Security Council Official Records, 10th Year 1955*, p.32.

50. The United Nations Truce Supervision Organisation (UNTSO) consisted of UN observers who arrived in the region in June 1948. UNTSO had been

created by UNSC Resolution 50 (1948), which called for the cessation of hostilities in Palestine to be supervised by military personnel.

51. For the full text of the resolution, see www.un.org For voting records, see 700th meeting of UNSC, 8 September 1955, *United Nations Security Council Official Records, 10th Year, 1955*, p.22.

52. See Abdoh's speech, *ibid*, p.12.

53. Robert Bruce Reppa, *Israel and Iran: Their Development, Interrelationship and Effect on the Indian Ocean Basin* (PhD thesis, University of Maryland, 1973), p.154.

54. Uri Bialer, *Between East and West: Israel's Foreign Policy Orientation, 1948–1956*, (Cambridge University Press, 1990), p.131.

55. PRO FO 371/114852. See minutes from T.R.D. Belgrave 'Persian Oil For Israel', British Foreign Office, 12 January 1955.

56. *Ibid.* See despatch from British Embassy, Tel Aviv to C.A.E. Shuckburgh, British Foreign Office, 24 January 1955.

57. *Ibid.* See despatch, 'Israel's Purchases of Persian Oil', from British Embassy, Tehran to British Foreign Office, 25 February 1955.

58. *Ibid.* See despatch from British Embassy, Tehran to T.R.D. Belgrave, British Foreign Office, 3 March 1955.

59. *Ibid.* See despatch from D.L. Stewart, 26 February 1955.

60. Bialer, *Between East and West*, pp.131–132. In addition to this, Israel was aware of the development of ties between Soviet-bloc countries and the radical Arab states, thus affording Iranian oil strategic value. Weinbaum, 'Iran and Israel', p.1078.

61. A 1954 oil agreement with a Western consortium had given Iran a quota of oil that could be used either for domestic consumption, or could be sold abroad. The NIOC, however, was forbidden from selling its oil to any market supplied by the consortium. The consortium, in order to placate Arab sentiment, declined from selling oil to Israel, and, thus, presented Iran with a market. Weinbaum, 'Iran and Israel', p.1078.

62. A credit agreement was concluded between Iranian and Israeli banks for the purchase of Iranian oil. However, because of Egypt's control over the Straits of Tiran, the oil could not be delivered. *Ibid.* It should be stated that as long as Israel was receiving oil from Venezuela, Romania and the USSR, the Iranian oil was not vital. *Ibid.*

63. Turkey voted with the Muslim bloc countries: Afghanistan, Egypt, Iran, Iraq, Lebanon, Pakistan, Saudi Arabia, Syria and Yemen. See 128th meeting of UNGA, 29 November 1947, *United Nations General Assembly Official Records, 2nd Session, 1947, vol.2*, pp.1424–1425.

64. See Mim Kemal Oke, 'The Ottoman Empire, Zionism, and the Question of Palestine 1880–1908, *International Journal of Middle East Studies,* vol.14, no.3, (August 1982), pp.329–341.

65. Efraim and Inari Karsh, *Empires of the Sand: The Struggle for Mastery in the Middle East 1789–1923* (Harvard University Press: Harvard, 1999), p.163. Ofra Bengio makes the claim that Abdul Hamid's objection to Herzl's proposal was also based on a combination of Islamic sensitivities and opposition from the Arabs of Palestine. However, he ignored the increasing numbers of Jews immigrating to Palestine. See Ofra Bengio, *The Turkish-Israeli Relationship Changing Ties of Middle Eastern Outsiders* (Palgrave Macmillan: New York, 2004), p.72.

66. Karsh, *Empires,* p.163.

67. *Ibid.*

68. See Oke, 'The Ottoman Empire', p.330.

69. *Ibid.*

70. Karsh, *Empires*, p.164.

71. *Ibid,* pp.164–165.

72. Bengio, *The Turkish-Israeli*, p.73.

73. *Ibid.*

74. *Ibid.*

75. Walter F. Weiker, 'Turkey, the Middle East and Islam', *Middle East Review*, vol.17, no.3, (Spring 1985), pp.27–33.

76. Bengio, *The Turkish-Israeli*, p.73.

77. See Naim Avigdor Guleryuz, 'Turkey', www.jewishvirtuallibrary.org. However, it must also be noted that the Jews, along with other non-Muslim minorities, were subjected to a severe property tax in 1942. See George E. Gruen, *Turkey, Israel and the Palestine Question, 1948–1960, A Study in the Diplomacy of Ambivalence*, (PhD thesis, Columbia University, 1970), p.9.

78. See Guleryuz, 'Turkey'.

79. *Ibid.*

80. Efraim Inbar, *The Israeli-Turkish Entente* (King's College London, Mediterranean Studies, 2002), p.9.

81. *Ibid*, p.2. Moreover, the Turks were not displeased with the defeat of the Arab forces against Israel in 1948. See, Amikam Nachmani, *Israel, Turkey and Greece: Uneasy Relations in the East Mediterranean* (Frank Cass: London, 1987), p.8.

82. See Mahmut Bali Aykan, 'The Palestinian Question in Turkish Foreign Policy from the 1950s to the 1990s', *International Journal of Middle East Studies*, vol.25, no.1, (February 1993), pp.91–110.

83. Arab specialists in the British Foreign Office and the American State Department believed that the creation of a Jewish state against the vehemently expressed wishes of the Arabs would create regional instability. George E. Gruen, 'Dynamic Progress in Turkish-Israeli Relations', *Israel Affairs*, vol.1, no.4, (Summer 1995), pp.40–70.

84. *Ibid*, p.42.

85. Gruen, *Turkey*, p.40.

86. *Ibid*, pp.23–24.

87. Cited in *Ibid*, pp.28–29.

88. See Baydur's speech, 54th meeting of UNGA, 12 May 1947, *United Nations General Assembly Official Records, 1st Special Session, vol.3, 1947, Plenary Meetings and Committees*, p.259.

89. *Ibid*.

90. See 134th meeting of First Committee, 1 May 1948, *United Nations Official Records, 2nd Special Session, vol.2, 1948, Main Committees*, p.197.

91. Gruen, 'Dynamic Progress', p.43.

92. *Ibid*. Indeed, Gruen notes that Turkey, on at least two occasions, declined Arab requests for aid and banned the export of arms to the region by private companies. The Turkish position of neutrality was designed to both prevent extremists from joining the fighting and to show the world that Turkey adopted a truly neutral position over the war. Cited in Gruen, *Turkey*, pp.46–47.

93. See 186th meeting of UNGA, 11 December 1948, *United Nations General Assembly Official Records, 3rd Session, 1948, Plenary Meetings, vol.1*, p.996. Turkey, in supporting the resolution, did not vote with the Muslim states of the Middle East: Iran abstained, while Iraq, Lebanon, Saudi Arabia, Syria, Yemen, Afghanistan and Egypt voted against the resolution. Ethiopia supported the resolution. The committee was conceived in order to resolve the outstanding issues between the warring parties.

94. Gruen, 'Dynamic Progress', p.44. Turkey voted for UN Resolution 212 (III) calling for Assistance to Palestine Refugees. See 163rd meeting of UNGA, 19 November 1948, *United Nations General Assembly Official Records, 1948, vol.1, Plenary Meetings*, p.576. The vote was unanimous.

95. Gruen, 'Turkey', pp.66–67.

96. Meltem Muftuler Bac, *Turkey and Israel: An Evolving Partnership*, (Ariel Centre for Policy Research, Policy Paper 47, 1998). See www.acpr.org.il

97. See 207th meeting of UNGA, 11 May 1949. *United Nations General Assembly Official Records, 3rd Session, 1949, vol.2*, p.330. Turkey did not vote with the Muslim states of the Middle East: Yemen, Afghanistan, Egypt, Iran, Iraq, Lebanon, Saudi Arabia and Syria all voted against Israel's admission to the UN.

98. Cevik Bir and Martin Sherman, 'Formula for Stability: Turkey plus Israel', *Middle East Quarterly*, vol.9, no.4, (Fall 2002), www.meforum.org, and Gruen, 'Dynamic Progress', p.45.

99. Then Turkish Foreign Minister Sadak declared that 42 states had recognised Israel before Turkey did so. *Ibid*, p.44.

100. *Ibid*, p.45.

101. George E. Gruen, 'Turkey's Relations with Israel and its Arab Neighbours: The Impact of Basic Interests and Changing Circumstances', *Middle East Review*, vol.17, no.3, (Spring 1985), pp.33–44.

102. Nachmani, *Israel, Turkey and Greece*, p.5. Israel had Military *Attachés* in only three other capitals: London, Washington and Paris.

103. *Ibid.* Turkey wished to join NATO, *inter alia*, to pursue the Balkan alliance with Greece and Yugoslavia and to finalise a defence pact with Pakistan.

104. Nachmani, *Israel, Turkey and Greece*, p.7. This led Moshe Sharett, then Israeli Foreign Minister to lament, 'to our regret, this assumption of ours was not borne out.' *Ibid.*

105. Ankara believed that a powerful Israel would have the same effect in the event of hostility towards Turkey from a unified Arab bloc. Orhan Soysal, *An Analysis of the Influences of Turkey's Alignment with the West and of the Arab-Israeli Conflict upon Turkish-Israeli and Turkish-Arab Relations, 1947–1977,* (PhD thesis, Princeton University, 1983), p.32.

106. Cited in Suha Bolukbasi, 'Behind the Turkish-Israeli Alliance: A Turkish View', *Journal of Palestine Studies*, vol.29, no.1, (Autumn 1999), pp.21–35.

107. Ankara was particularly concerned about Israel's left-wing Mapam party. Mapai, Israel's ruling labour party was tolerated, but Israeli politicians and diplomats visiting Turkey were instructed to define Mapai as a labour rather than socialist party. See Nachmani, *Israel, Turkey and Greece*, pp.48–49.

108. For an enlightening account of this factor in Israeli foreign policy see Alan Dowty, 'Israeli Foreign Policy and the Jewish Question' *MERIA*, vol.3, no.1, (March 1999). www.meria.idc.ac.il

109. Nachmani, *Israel, Turkey and Greece*, p.48.

110. See Michael B. Bishku, 'How Has Turkey Viewed Israel?', *Israel Affairs*, vol.12, no.1, (January 2006), pp.177–194.

111. Nachmani, *Israel, Turkey and Greece*, p.48.

112. *Ibid.*

113. For examples of these restrictions see, Weiker, 'Turkey', p.28.

114. Weiker, 'Turkey, the Middle East and Islam', p.29.

115. Nachmani, *Israel, Turkey and Greece*, p.45.

116. See Ronnie Margulies and Ergin Yildizoglu, 'The Political Uses of Islam in Turkey, *Middle East Report, (July-August 1988)*, pp.12–17.

117. Nachmani, *Israel, Turkey and Greece*, p.45.

118. Turkey's relationship with the West was complicated by issues such as its record on human rights, the Cyprus question, and the treatment of the Kurds. These points had caused the US Congress to attempt to scale down

Western contacts with Turkey. See Amikam Nachmani, 'A Triangular Relationship: Turkish-Israeli Co-operation and its Implications for Greece,' *Cahiers d'études sur la Méditerranée Orientale et le Monde Turco-Iranien, no. 28, (Juin-Decembre 1999)*, www.ceri-sciencespo.com. See also M.C. Geokas and A.T. Papathanasis, 'The Turkish-Israeli Axis, Greece and the Middle East', *Washington Report on Middle East Affairs*, (1999). http://www.econ.ccsu. edu/Papathanasis/Research/herald.htm. Then Turkish Prime Minister, Menderes stated on 5 June 1954, that 'one should recognise the existence of Israel and the Arabs', a statement perhaps tailored to the Jewish community. Soysal, *An Analysis*, p.33.

119. Nachmani, *Israel, Turkey and Greece*, p.50. Ankara was unsure whether a violation of its border with the USSR would be a *casus belli* for the West, or whether Anatolia would be sacrificed before Western intervention was forthcoming. However, a telegram sent from Ankara to the British Foreign Office noted that an 'Israeli minister made yesterday a statement to the Istanbul press that Israel would fully support any UN decision if Turkey were attacked' See Inward Saving Telegram from British Embassy Ankara, to British Foreign Office, 6 December 1950, *PRO FO 371/82522*.

120. Except 1947, when it was in fourth place. Gruen, 'Dynamic Progress', p.45.

121. Nachmani, *Israel, Turkey and Greece*, p.61.

122. For a full account of the flow of goods between the countries in this period see Gruen, 'Dynamic Progress', p.45. *Solel Boneh* also built the road from Yesilkoy airport to Istanbul and a housing complex for members of the Turkish parliament. Symbolically, both Israeli and Turkish firms were awarded contracts to build NATO military bases on Turkish soil, such as Incirlik. Gruen, 'Dynamic Progress', p.46.

123. Gruen, 'Dynamic Progress', p.45.

124. See Bishku, 'How Has Turkey Viewed Israel?', p.181.

125. Nachmani, *Israel, Turkey and Greece*, p.51.

126. *Ibid.*

127. Nicole and Hugh Pope, *Turkey Unveiled: A History of Modern Turkey* (The Overlook Press: New York, 2004), p.89.

128. *Ibid.*

129. The Israeli Foreign Ministry issued a paper outlining the advantages and disadvantages of the possible stances Israel might adopt on the issue, which was constructed in terms favourable to Turkey from the outset. Nachmani, *Israel, Turkey and Greece*, pp.68–69.

130. Cited in *Ibid*, p.68.

131. *Ibid.*

132. See Savut's reported speech, 33rd meeting of Ad Hoc Political Committee, 7 January 1952, *United Nations General Assembly Official Records, 6th Year, 1952*, p.175.

133. See Savut's reported speech, 46th meeting of Ad Hoc Political Committee, 21 January 1952, *United Nations General Assembly Official Records, 6th Year, 1952*, p.253.

134. William Hale, *Turkish Foreign Policy 1774–2000* (Frank Cass: London 2000), p.124.

135. Cited in Nachmani, *Israel, Turkey and Greece*, p.71.

136. See Amikam Nachmani, *Turkey: Facing A New Millennium Coping With Intertwined Conflicts* (Manchester University Press: Manchester, 2003), p.203.

137. Nachmani, *Israel, Turkey and Greece*, p.71. Dulles allegedly told the Israelis 'stand aside till we have the Arabs in the net'. Gruen, 'Dynamic Progress', p.46.

138. In the 1950s, there were plans to upgrade the relations between Israel and Turkey to those of embassy status. These were scrapped however, by the efforts of the Eisenhower administration to establish a Middle East defence pact against the USSR. Gruen, 'Dynamic Progress', p.46.

139. The Baghdad Pact was originally a Turkish-Pakistani bilateral security treaty signed in 1954 under the auspices of the US. Britain pushed for, and succeeded, in obtaining the inclusion of Iraq, Iran and itself to the treaty, which evolved into the Baghdad Pact. The US did not join, but had observer status. See Crockatt, *The Fifty Years War*, p.179.

140. Although the Arabs had been disinterested in the plan, the 'northern tier' states, Turkey, Iran, Iraq and Pakistan were sympathetic, and were suitably positioned geographically. The aim was to encircle the USSR with air bases from which US bombers could be launched as a second-strike capability. US Foreign Secretary, John Foster Dulles had made a trip to the area in 1953 and, in a meeting with Turkish leaders, was informed that Turkey would do its utmost to ensure the US initiative was carried out. The Turks believed they could persuade the Arab states to join, an idea the British liked. To this end, Turkey floated the idea of making concessions to Iraq over the question of Palestine, which concerned the Israelis, but Prime Minister Menderes made it clear to the leadership of the Jewish state that it was simply a tactical move on the part of his government. See Nadav Safran, *From War To War: The Arab-Israeli Confrontation, 1948–1967*, (Pegasus: New York, 1969), p.104, Hale, *Turkish*, p.125, and Aysegul Sever, 'The Compliant Ally? Turkey and the West in the Middle East 1954–58', Middle Eastern Studies, vol. 34, no.2, (April 1998), p.75.

141. Nachmani, *Israel, Turkey and Greece*, pp.72–73.

142. *Ibid*, p.73.

143. *PRO FO 371/115821*. During this time, Turkey found itself publicly denying its ties with Israel. For example, BBC monitoring stated that 'Ankara radio has broadcast a definitive denial regarding publications in the Egyptian press' concerning 'Egyptian press reports of a political and military agreement between Turkey and Israel'. See B37, 'Ankara Radio on Egyptian Lies About Pact With Israel', 4 February 1955.

144. Cited in Nachmani, *Israel, Turkey and Greece*, p.74.

145. *PRO FO 371/115821*. See despatch from British Embassy, Tel Aviv to E.M. Rose, British Foreign Office, 9 August 1955.

146. *PRO FO 371/115488*. See despatch from British Embassy, Tel Aviv to Sir Anthony Eden, British Foreign Office, 1 February 1955.

147. *Ibid*. The British Embassy in Tel Aviv also reported that, when asked about the Turkish-Iraqi relationship, the Israeli prime minister had not 'made up his mind whether Israel stood to gain or to lose in the long run'. See Inward Saving Telegram, from British Embassy, Tel Aviv to British Foreign Office, 18 January 1955, *PRO FO 371/115485*.

148. The other elected members of the UNSC at the time were: Belgium, Brazil, Iran, New Zealand and Peru.

149. See www.un.org

150. *Ibid*.

151. *Ibid*.

152. See Sarper's speech, 695th meeting of UNSC, 29 March 1955, *United Nations Security Council Official Records*, 10th Year, 1955, p.19.

153. *Ibid*, p.20.

154. *Ibid*.

155. See 20th meeting of Ad Hoc Political Committee, 23 November 1955, *United Nations General Assembly Official Records, 10th Year, 1955*, p.83.

156. Bar-Zohar, 'Ben-Gurion', p.165.

157. Adam Garfinkle, *Politics and Society in Modern Israel: Myths and Realities* (M.E. Sharpe: New York, 1997), p.239.

158. Peters, *Israel and Africa*, p.13.

159. Interview with Israeli Ambassador Yaakov Shimoni, 'Israel, the Arabs and Africa', *Africa Report*, vol.21, no.4, (July-August 1976), pp.51–55.

160. Peters, *Israel and Africa*, p.15 and Nadav Safran, *The United States and Israel* (Harvard University Press: Harvard, 1963), p.266.

161. For examples of such aid, see Aaron Segal, 'Israel in Africa', *Africa Report*, vol.8, no.4, (April 1963), pp.19–21.

162. Interview with Shimoni, p.52. Shimoni also states that Burma, when looking to set up a car plant, turned to Israel rather than Detroit, as the Burmese felt Israel to be more helpful in this context. *Ibid*.

163. Israel was keen to make its citizens aware of both African history and the parallels between Blacks and Jews. See Segal, 'Israel in Africa', p.20. For an African view on the shared suffering of Africans and Jews see 'Africans, Arabs and Israelis: A Triad of Suffering Peoples.' Interview with President Senghor of Senegal, *Africa Report*, vol.17, no.7, (July–August 1972), pp.11–13.

164. Moshe Pearlman, *Ben Gurion Looks Back in Talks with Moshe Pearlman* (Weidenfeld and Nicolson: London, 1965), p.171.

165. Samuel Decalo, *Israel and Africa: Forty Years, 1956–1996* (Florida Academic Press: Florida, 1998), pp.36–37.

166. Peters, *Israel and Africa*, p.14.

167. Cited in *Ibid.*

168. Segal, 'Israel in Africa', p.19.

169. Interview with Shimoni, 'Israel, the Arabs and Africa', p.51.

170. Segal, 'Israel in Africa', p.19.

171. Mitchell G. Bard 'The Evolution of Israel's Africa Policy, http://www.jewishvirtuallibrary.org/jsource/Politics/africa.html

172. Golda Meir, *My Life* (Weidenfeld and Nicolson: London, 1975), p.264.

173. *Ibid*, p.265.

174. Theodore Herzl, *Old-Newland* (Bloch Publishing Company: New York, 1960), p.170.

175. Haggai Erlich, *Ethiopia and the Challenge of Independence* (Lynne Rienner Publishers: Colorado, 1986), p.254.

176. Howard Sachar, *A History of Israel: From the Rise of Zionism To Our Time* (Basil Blackwell: Oxford, 1977), p.474.

177. *Ibid.*

178. Raviv and Melman, *Every Spy a Prince*, pp.84–85.

179. Meir, *My Life*, p.283.

180. See Derek Tulloch, *Wingate* (Macdonald and Company: London, 1972), p.49.

181. *Ibid*, p.50.

182. See Tesemma's speech, 127th meeting of UNGA, 28 November 1947, *United Nations General Assembly Official Records, 2nd Year, 1947*, pp.1405–1406.

183. *Ibid.*

184. Peters, *Israel and Africa*, p.8.

185. See Medhen's reported speech, 68th meeting of Ad Hoc Political Committee, 4 December 1950, *United Nations General Assembly Official Records, 5th Year, 1950*, p.441.

186. See Dawit's reported speech, 5th meeting of Ad Hoc Political Committee, 28 October 1952, *United Nations General Assembly Official Records, 7th Year, 1952*, p.20.

187. See 35th meeting of Ad Hoc Political Committee, 26 November 1954, *United Nations General Assembly Official Records, 9th Year, 1954*, p.165.
188. Sachar, *A History Of Israel*, p.939.
189. Peter Schwab, *Haile Selassie I: Ethiopia's Lion of Judah* (Nelson Hall: Chicago, 1979), p.93.
190. Shlaim, *The Iron Wall*, p.196.
191. Bard 'The Evolution'.
192. See Aklilou's speech, 531st meeting of UNGA, 3 October 1955, *United Nations General Assembly Official Records, 10th Year, 1955*, p.204.
193. *Ibid.*

Chapter 2   Iran and Israel, 1956–72: Calculated Ambivalence?

1. For authoritative accounts of the Suez War, see Mordechai Bar-On, *The Gates of Gaza: Israel's Road to Suez and Back, 1955–1957* (Palgrave Macmillan: New York, 1994), Sydney D. Bailey, *Four Arab-Israeli Wars and the Peace Process* (Macmillan: London, 1990), Keith Kyle, *Suez* (Weidenfeld and Nicolson: London, 1991), and Selwyn Ilan Troen and Moshe Shemesh, *The Suez-Sinai Crisis 1956: Retrospective and Reappraisal* (Frank Cass: London, 1990).
2. Cited in Leopold Laufer, *Israel and the Developing Countries: New Approaches to Co-Operation* (Twentieth Century Fund: New York, 1967), pp.21–22.
3. See Entezam's speech, 748th meeting of UNSC, 30 October 1956, *United Nations Security Council Official Records, 11th Year, 1956*, p.5.
4. *Ibid.*
5. See Entezam's speech, 750th meeting of UNSC, 30 October 1956, *United Nations Security Council Official Records, 11th Year, 1956*, p.13.
6. *Ibid.*
7. See www.un.org
8. See 749th meeting of UNSC, 30 October 1956, *United Nations Security Council Official Records, 11th Year, 1956*, p.31.
9. For voting pattern see 751st meeting of UNSC, 31 October 1956, *United Nations Security Council Official Records, 11th Year, 1956*, p.22.
10. See Entezam's speech, 567th meeting of UNGA, 7 November 1956, *United Nations General Assembly Official Records, First Emergency Special Session*, p.120.
11. *Ibid.*
12. See Entezam's speech, 652nd meeting of UNGA, 2 February 1957, *United Nations General Assembly Official Records, 11th Year, 1956–57, vols. 2–3*, p.1082.

13. Weinbaum, 'Iran and Israel', pp.1078–79.

14. *Ibid*, p.1079.

15. *PRO FO 371/127126*. See letter from British Embassy, Tehran, to British Foreign Office, 17 April 1957.

16. *Ibid*. See letter from British Foreign Office to British Embassy, Tehran, 29 April 1957. It is interesting to note that some four months later, the BBC received a report that Iran had informed Syria and the other Arab states that it had refused permission to the Israeli Finance Minister to visit the country, in accordance with its relations with the Arab states. In response, an official from the British Levant Department stated that 'Iran is adept at hunting with the Arabs while running with the Israelis. Apart from oil deals. I believe there is an unofficial Israeli agent permanently resident in Tehran'. See statement from BBC, 6 August 1957, *PRO FO 371/128097*.

17. *PRO FO 371/120719*. Letter from British Embassy, Tehran to Eastern Department, British Foreign Office, 10 October 1956.

18. *Ibid*.

19. *Ibid*.

20. Ramazani, 'Iran and the Arab-Israeli Conflict', p.416.

21. *Ibid*.

22. Sobhani, *The Pragmatic Entente*, p.46.

23. *Ibid*, p.47. Also, in 1958, Israel's international development co-operation programme began. It was known as the Centre for International Co-operation (MASHAV) and was a department within the Ministry of Foreign Affairs. See Haim Divon, 'MASHAV in Africa: the Israeli Government's Development Co-operation Program', *Israel and Africa: Assessing the Past, Envisioning the Future*, (The Africa Institute, American Jewish Committee, The Harold Hartog School: Tel Aviv University, Israel, 2006), p.16, www.ajc.org

24. *Statistical Analysis of Iran's Foreign Trade Years: 1956/57–1958/59*, CENTO unclassified document, 14 September 1960.

25. *PRO FO 371/142289*. Letter from British Embassy, Tel Aviv, to the Levant Department, British Foreign Office, 5 June 1959.

26. *Ibid*.

27. *Ibid*.

28. *Ibid*. Letter from F. J. Leishman, British Embassy, Tehran, to A.K. Rothnie, British Foreign Office, 12 November 1959.

29. Weinbaum, 'Iran and Israel', p.1074.

30. Avner Yaniv, *Deterrence without the Bomb: The Politics of Israeli Strategy* (Lexington Books: Maryland, 1987), p.94. In 1966, Nasser explained his decision thus: 'The Shah declared ... that his country recognised Israel. And

so, a country said to be an Islamic member of the Baghdad Pact opened all opportunities of activity to Israel and helped it to work against the Arab homeland'. Cited in Chubin and Zabih, *The Foreign Relations of Iran*, p.158.

31. Cited in Sobhani, *The Pragmatic Entente*, pp.40–41.

32. *Ibid*. The Shah used this opportunity to clarify the status of ties between Iran and Israel in a response to a Muslim cleric. See *Ibid*, p.41.

33. *Middle East Record*, vol.1, 1960, Israel Oriental Society, Reuven Shiloah Research Centre (Weidenfeld and Nicolson: London, 1960) p.216.

34. For details of this period see 'Iran, The Arab Countries and Israel, Iran's *de facto* Recognition of Israel and Arabs' reactions', *Ibid*, pp.216–219.

35. Weinbaum, 'Iran and Israel', p.1074.

36. B. Souresrafil, *Khomeini and Israel* (I. Research Inc: England, 1988), p.22.

37. *PRO FO 371/142289*. See letter from British Embassy, Tehran, to G.F. Hiller, Eastern Department, British Foreign Office, 14 July 1959.

38. Sobhani, *The Pragmatic Entente*, p.38.

39. Cited in *Middle East Record*, 1960, p.307.

40. *Ibid*.

41. *Ibid*.

42. Weinbaum, 'Iran and Israel', p.1075.

43. *Middle East Record*, 1961, p.328.

44. *Ibid*.

45. *PRO FO 371/157753*. See letter from British Embassy, Tehran to British Foreign Office, 11 April 1961.

46. Yaniv, *Deterrence*, p.94. The Shah visited the area worst affected by the earthquake in (January 1974), and was moved by the progress that had been made by the Iranian-Israeli project. See Sobhani, *The Pragmatic Entente*, p.115.

47. Sobhani, *The Pragmatic Entente*, pp.55–56. For the advantages and disadvantages of the two well types, see Reppa, *Israel and Iran*, pp.228–229.

48. E.A. Bayne, *Persian Kingship in Transition: Conversations with a Monarch whose Office is Traditional and whose Goal is Modernisation* (American Universities Field Staff Inc, 1968), pp.100–101.

49. Cited in Reppa, *Israel and Iran*, p.228.

50. Weinbaum, 'Iran and Israel', p.1075.

51. *Ibid*, p.1076 and cited in *Middle East Record*, 1961, p.328.

52. *PRO FO 317/164300*. See letter from British Embassy, Tehran to A.E. Saunders, British Foreign Office, 22 October 1962.

53. Ramazani, 'Emerging', p.1048.

54. *Ibid*.

55. *PRO FO 371/164300*. See letter from British Embassy, Tehran to British Foreign Office, 17 January 1962, This suspicion was strengthened by the

Military *Attaché* at the British Embassy, Tehran, who had seen General Mirjahangiri amongst the passengers on his son's plane. See letter from Military *Attaché's* Office, British Embassy, Tehran to British Foreign Office, 17 January 1962. *Ibid.*

56. *Ibid.* See letter from British Embassy, Tel Aviv to British Foreign Office, 23 January 1962.

57. *Ibid.* See letter from British Embassy, Tehran to C.L.S. Cope, British Foreign Office, 14 March 1962.

58. Yaniv, *Deterrence*, p.95. These guns were later on display by Iranian soldiers during King Faisal's visit to Tehran in 1965. See Sobhani, *The Pragmatic Entente*, p.50.

59. Sobhani, *The Pragmatic Entente*, pp.47–48.

60. *Ibid*, p.49.

61. The essential characteristics of the White Revolution were agrarian reform, nationalisation of forests and pasture land, transformation of state enterprises into anonymous companies, with the ensuing shares' revenue guaranteeing agrarian reform, workers sharing in company profits, electoral law reform, including universal suffrage and the creation of an education corps, consisting of bachelors who would teach in urban areas to fulfil their national service duties. A health corps, reconstruction and development corps, rural courts of justice, nationalisation of waterways, national reconstruction and educational and administrative revolution. For further detail see Mohammad Reza Pahlavi, *The Shah's Story* (Michael Joseph London, 1980), pp.71–161, William Shawcross, *The Shah's Last Ride: The Story of the Exile, Misadventures and Death of the Emperor* (Chatto and Windus: London, 1989), pp.87–88 and Richards, 'America's Shah', p.20.

62. Ramazani, 'Emerging' , p.1043.

63. *Ibid*, p.1046.

64. It must be noted, however, that the Shah did not envisage any reform of the monarchy within the framework of his socio-political revolution. For a detailed analysis of this subject, see R.K. Ramazani, 'Iran's 'White Revolution': A Study in Political Development', *International Journal of Middle East Studies*, vol.5, no.2, (April 1974), pp.124–139.

65. Shahram Chubin, 'Iran's Foreign Policy 1960–1976: an Overview', in Hossein Amirsadeghi (ed.), *Twentieth Century Iran* (Heinemann: London, 1977), pp.197–223.

66. Ramazani, 'Emerging', pp.1048–1050.

67. Indeed, in August 1970, the British Embassy in Tel Aviv revealed that the Shah thought the British withdrawal from the Persian Gulf 'irreversible'.

See despatch from E.J.W. Barnes, British Embassy, Tel Aviv, to J.P. Tripp, British Foreign Office, 5 August 1970, *PRO FO 248/1666*. After the British announcement, the Shah volunteered his armed forces as the defenders of the Persian Gulf, an initiative that was welcomed by the West. Initially, the main task was to ensure there were no interruptions to the oil routes in the Gulf, which, in the early 1970s, saw some 20 million barrels of oil pass through it every day. See Khosrow Fatemi, 'The Iranian Revolution: Its Impact on Economic Relations with the United States', *International Journal of Middle East Studies*, vol.12, no.3, (November 1980), pp.303–317.

68. Ramazani, 'Emerging', p.1052.

69. For a detailed account of the Six Day War, see Oren, *Six Days of War*, Chaim Herzog, *The Arab-Israeli Wars: War and Peace in the Middle East* (Random House: New York, 1984), and Randolph S. Churchill, *The Six Day War* (Heinemann: London, 1967).

70. See Zahedi's speech, 1530th meeting of UNGA, 21 June 1967, *United Nations General Assembly Official Records, Fifth Emergency Special Session*, p.11.

71. *Ibid.*

72. See 1548th meeting of UNGA, 4 July 1967, *United Nations General Assembly Official Records, 1967, Fifth Emergency Special Session,* pp.14–15.

73. *Ibid*, pp.15–16.The withdrawal of Israeli forces was apparently a subject of some importance to the Shah. He is quoted as saying 'The days of occupation and retention of one country's territory by another are over ... that part of Arab territory occupied by Israel ... should be returned to them as soon as possible'. See Zahedi's speech, 1530th meeting of UNGA, 21 June 1967, *United Nations General Assembly Official Records, Fifth Emergency Special Session*, p.11.

74. From 2–5 May, Turkish Prime Minister Demirel visited Tehran for talks with Iranian Prime Minister Hoveyda. They discussed closer co-operation between Turkey, Iran and Pakistan in the framework of Regional Co-operation for Development. In addition, from 16–21 June of the same year, The Shah and Empress of Iran visited Turkey, where they conveyed their intention to develop the friendly ties between the two countries. See *Middle East Record, 1967*, p.152.

75. See 1548th meeting of UNGA, 4 July 1967, *United Nations General Assembly Official Records, 1967, Fifth Emergency Special Session*, p.16.

76. See Zahedi's speech, 1530th meeting of UNGA, 21 June 1967, *United Nations General Assembly Official Records, Fifth Emergency Special Session*, p.10.

77. *Ibid.*

78. See 1548th meeting of UNGA, 4 July 1967, *United Nations General Assembly Official Records, 1967, Fifth Emergency Special Session*, p.17.

79. *Ibid.*

80. See Zahedi's speech, 1530th meeting of UNGA, 21 June 1967, *United Nations General Assembly Official Records, Fifth Emergency Special Session*, p.10.

81. *Ibid*, p.11.

82. Cited in Reppa, *Israel and Iran*, p.189.

83. Sobhani, *The Pragmatic Entente*, pp.81–82.

84. See 1748th meeting of UNGA, 19 December 1968, *United Nations General Assembly Official Records, 23rd Session 1968*, p.7. This resolution forms the political basis for the Palestinian right of return.

85. See 633rd meeting of Special Political Committee, 11 December 1968, *United Nations General Assembly Official Records, 23rd Session 1968*, p.3.

86. See 743rd meeting of the Special Political Committee, 4 December 1970, *United Nations General Assembly Official Records, 25th Session 1970*, p.301 and 792nd meeting of the Special Political Committee, 1 December 1971, *United Nations General Assembly Official Records, 25th Session 1971*, p.251.

87. See 1548th meeting of UNGA, 4 July 1967, *United Nations General Assembly Official Records, 1967, Fifth Emergency Special Session*, p.18.

88. See 1554th meeting of UNGA, 14 July 1967, *United Nations Official Records, 1967, Fifth Emergency Special Session*, pp.8–9.

89. Iranian opposition to any change in the status of Jerusalem is also conveyed in subsequent years. See Khalatbari's speech, 1940th meeting of UNGA, 27 September 1971, *United Nations General Assembly Official Records, 26th Session, 1971*, p.13 and Hoveyda's speech, 2006th meeting of UNGA, 8 December 1971, *United Nations General Assembly Official Records, 26th Session, 1971*, p.26.

90. See Zahedi's speech, 1776th meeting of UNGA, 23 October 1969, *United Nations General Assembly Official Records, 24th Session 1969*, p.14. Zahedi also believed that it was this act of arson which led to the first Islamic Summit Conference, held in Rabat from 22–25 September 1969. *Ibid*.

91. See 1558th meeting of UNGA, 21 July 1967, *United Nations Official Records, 1967, Fifth Emergency Special Session*, p.16 and 1559th meeting of UNGA, 18 September 1967, *Ibid*, p.1. Iraq, Jordan, Kuwait, Lebanon, Libya, Morocco, Saudi Arabia, Syria, Tunisia, the UAR and Yemen voted against draft resolution A/L 529/Rev.1 See 1558th meeting of UNGA, 21 July 1967, *Ibid*, p.16.

92. See Ghafari's reported speech, 592nd meeting of the Special Political Committee, 15 December 1967, *United Nations General Assembly Official Records, 22nd Session 1967*, pp.295–296. Princess Pahlavi noted that the Iranian government went on to double its contribution to UNWRA in 1970. See Princess Pahlavi's reported speech, 781st meeting of the Special Political Committee, 17 November 1971, *United Nations General Assembly Official Records, 26th Session, 1971*, p.175.

93. See Ansari's reported comments, 619th meeting of the Special Political Committee, 21 November 1968, *United Nations General Assembly Official Records, 23rd Session 1968*, p.3.

94. See 834th meeting of the Special Political Committee, 10 November 1972, *United Nations General Assembly Official Records, 27th Session, 1972*, p.188.

95. See Princess Pahlavi's speech, 1887th meeting of UNGA, 28 October 1970, *United Nations General Assembly Official Records, 25th Session 1970*, p.1.

96. *PRO 17/1276*. Despatch from J.S. Champion, British Embassy, Tehran to D.J. Makinson, Near Eastern Department, British Foreign Office, 13 August 1970.

97. *Ibid.* Despatch from E.J.W. Barnes, British Embassy, Tel Aviv, to J.P. Tripp, Near Eastern Department, British Foreign Office, 13 July 1970.

98. *Ibid.*

99. *Ibid.* Despatch from D.J. Makinson, Near Eastern Department, British Foreign Office, 17 June 1970.

100. *Ibid.* Despatch from D.A.H. Wright, British Embassy, Tehran, to The Rt. Hon. Michael Stewart, British Foreign Office, on Irano-Israeli Relations, 10 June 1970.

101. *Ibid.*

102. *Ibid.*

103. *Ibid.*

104. *Ibid.* The British Embassy in Tehran also revealed that 'there have of course been a number of Israeli pilots working for Iranair here since about 1965'. Despatch from Donald F. Murray, British Embassy, Tehran, to S.L. Egerton, Near Eastern Department, British Foreign Office, 15 April 1970. *Ibid.*

105. *PRO FO 248/1666*. See despatch from C.D.S. Drace-Francis, British Embassy, Tehran to British Foreign Office, 5 June 1970.

106. *Ibid.* See despatch from C.D.S. Drace-France, British Embassy, Tehran to British Foreign Office, 8 June 1970.

107. *PRO 17/1276*. Despatch from D.A.H. Wright, British Embassy, Tehran to The Rt. Hon. Michael Stewart, British Foreign Office, 'Irano-Israeli Relations', 10 June 1970.

108 *Ibid.*

109. *Ibid* and despatch from Donald F. Murray, British Embassy, Tehran, to S.L. Egerton, Near Eastern Department, British Foreign Office, 15 April 1970.

110. *PRO FO 248/1666*. See despatch from D.F. Murray, British Embassy, Tehran, to C.T. Brant, British Foreign Office, 22 October 1970.

111. *Ibid.* Despatch from D.A.H. Wright, British Embassy, Tehran to The Rt. Hon. Michael Stewart, British Foreign Office, 'Irano-Israeli Relations', 10 June 1970.

112. See 1896th meeting of UNGA, 4 November 1970, *United Nations General Assembly Official Records (Vol III) Resolutions, Special Political Committee, 25th Session*, 1970, p.12.

113. *PRO 17/1276.* Despatch from D.A.H. Wright, British Embassy, Tehran, to The Rt. Hon. Michael Stewart, British Foreign Office, 'Irano-Israeli Relations', 10 June 1970 and despatch from Donald F. Murray, British Embassy, Tehran, to S.L. Egerton, Near Eastern Department, British Foreign Office, 15 April 1970, *ibid.*

114. See *Index to Proceedings of United Nations General Assembly, 26th Session*, 1971, p.59 and 2016th meeting of UNGA, 13 December 1971, *United Nations General Assembly Official Records, 26th Session 1971*, p.34.

115. On 8 September, Iranian Foreign Minister Zahedi arrived in Ankara for a one day visit. After a meeting with his Turkish counterpart, Caglayangil, Zahedi revealed that their views on the Middle East were very close. See *Middle East Record*, 1969–1970, parts 1–4, vol.5, p.663.

116. *PRO 17/1276.* Despatch from D.A.H. Wright, British Embassy, Tehran, to The Rt. Hon. Michael Stewart, British Foreign Office, 'Irano-Israeli Relations', 10 June 1970.

117. *Ibid.*

118. *Ibid.*

119. See Khalatbari's speech, 1940th meeting of UNGA, 27 September 1971, *United Nations General Assembly Official Records, 26th Session, 1971*, p.13.

120. See Hoveyda's speech, 2006th meeting of UNGA, 8 December 1971, *United Nations General Assembly Official Records, 26th Session 1971*, p.26.

121. Bakhtiar was dismissed from the Shah's regime in 1962, as rumours began to surface that he was, *inter alia*, intending to overthrow the Shah. From exile in Europe, Bakhtiar supported himself with monies he had invested whilst director of SAVAK. He left behind a fourteen storey tower block in Tehran that was under construction and thought to be financed by drug money. See Richards, 'America's Shah', p.17.

122. Sobhani, *The Pragmatic Entente*, p.73.

123. Ibid, p.73.

124. *Ibid*, p.77.

125. See Khalatbari's speech, 2046th meeting of UNGA, 29 September 1972, *United Nations General Assembly Official Records, 27th Session, 1972*, p.5.

126. Cited in Chubin and Sabih, *The Foreign Relations of Iran*, pp.160–161.

127. Sobhani, *The Pragmatic Entente*, p.78.

128. The Nixon Doctrine stated that the US expected its allies to manage the expense of their own defence; it provided a shield to those of its allies threatened by a nuclear power and provided military aid to Iran and Saudi Arabia, in order to stabilise the region.

129. Henry Paolucci, *Iran, Israel and the United States* (Griffon House Publications: New York, 1991), p.12.

130. See Hoveyda's speech, 1723rd meeting of UNSC, 12 June 1973, *United Nations Security Council Official Records, 28th Year, 1973*, p.8. The questionnaire was sent to the governments of the UAR on 5 March, Jordan on 8 March, Israel on 9 March and Lebanon on 14 March 1969. The questions were based on each country's readiness to refrain from war and allow the other countries in the region to live peacefully. For a list of the questions, see www.jewishvirtuallibrary.org and www.mfa.gov.il

131. See Hoveyda's speech, 1723rd meeting of UNSC, 12 June 1973, *United Nations Security Council Official Records, 28th Year, 1973*, p.8.

132. *Ibid*, p.9.

Chapter 3   Iran and Israel, 1973–82: From Consolidation to Revolution

1. For a more detailed account of the war, see Uri Bar-Joseph, *The Watchman Fell Asleep: The Surprise of Yom Kippur and its Sources* (State University of New York Press: New York, 2005), Abraham Rabinovich, *The Yom Kippur War: The Epic Encounter that Transformed the Middle East* (Schocken Books: New York, 2004) and P.R. Kumaraswamy (ed.) *Revisiting the Yom Kippur War* (Frank Cass: Oregon, 2000).

2. Sobhani, *The Pragmatic Entente* pp.88–89.

3. Weinbaum, 'Iran and Israel', p.1081. However, Israel did receive Iranian crude oil during the war, along with a number of 160mm heavy mortars from the Iranian army. Sobhani, *The Pragmatic Entente*, p.89 and letter from H.J. Arbuthnott, British Embassy, Tehran to R. Hunt, British Foreign Office, 1 November 1973, *PRO FCO 8/2053*.

4. *Ibid*. See interview with the Shah, *Kayhan*, vol.16, no.4901, 25 November 1973.

5. *Ibid*.

6. Ramazani, 'Iran and the Arab-Israeli Conflict', p.419.

7. *PRO FCO 8/2053*. See letter from H.J. Arbuthnott, British Embassy, Tehran to R. Hunt, British Foreign Office, 1 November 1973.

8. OPEC is the Organisation of the Petroleum Exporting Countries, consisting of Algeria, Angola, Indonesia, Iran, Iraq, Kuwait, Libya, Nigeria, Qatar,

Saudi Arabia, the UAE and Venezuela. It is a permanent, inter-governmental organization, created at the Baghdad Conference, 10–14 September 1960, by Iran, Iraq, Kuwait, Saudi Arabia and Venezuela. See, www.opec.org

9. *PRO FCO 8/2053*. The Shah had admitted to the British that he would continue to supply NIOC oil to Israel via Eilat. See letter from H.J. Arbuthnott, British Embassy, Tehran to R. Hunt, British Foreign Office, 1 November 1973. It has been noted that the OPEC oil price rise in 1973 was one of the causes of the Shah's downfall. He used the oil revenue, thought to be in the region of US$17 billion, to finance increases in investments and armaments that the country could ill afford. Iran faced increasing inflation and a shortage of housing that was exacerbated by a migration from rural to urban areas. See Nikki R. Keddie, 'Iranian Revolutions in Comparative Perspective', *American Historical Review*, vol.88, no.3, (June 1983), pp.579–598, p.588 and Fatemi, 'The Iranian Revolution', p.314.

10. Chubin 'Iran's Foreign Policy', pp.201–204.

11. *PRO FCO 8/2053*. See interview with the Shah, *Kayhan*, vol.16, no.4901, 25 November 1973.

12. Ramazani, 'Iran and the Arab-Israeli Conflict', pp.423–424.

13. See Khalatbari's speech, 2127th meeting of UNGA, 25 September 1973, *United Nations General Assembly Official Records, 28th Session, 1973, vol.1*, p.19.

14. Hoveyda cited in 885th meeting of Special Political Committee, 13 November 1973, *United Nations General Assembly Official Records, 28th Session, 1973*, p.148.

15. See Khalatbari's speech, 2264th meeting of UNGA, 10 October 1974, *United Nations General Assembly Official Records, 29th Session, 1974*, p.628.

16. Resolution 3210 (**XXIX**), sponsored by Syria, was adopted by 105 votes to 4, with 20 abstentions. The US and Israel were amongst those states opposing the resolution, while Britain abstained. Both Turkey and Ethiopia supported the resolution. See 2268th meeting of UNGA, 14 October 1974, *United Nations General Assembly Official Records, 29th Session*, pp.677–678.

17. See 2289th meeting of UNGA, 18 November 1974, *United Nations General Assembly Official Records, 29th Session, 1974*, p.949, http://unispal.un.org/unispal.nsf/udc.htm. and cited in Ramazani, 'Iran and the Arab-Israeli Conflict', p.426.

18. Resolution 3237 (**XXIX**) was adopted by 95 votes to 17, with 19 abstentions. Britain, the US and Israel were amongst those states opposing the resolution, while Ethiopia and Turkey supported it. See 2296th meeting of UNGA, 22 November 1974, *United Nations General Assembly Official Records,*

29th Session, 1974, p.1066 and Rory Miller, *Ireland and the Palestine Question: 1948–2004* (Irish Academic Press: Dublin, 2005), p.81.

19. Cited in Alpher, 'Israel and the Iran-Iraq War', p.157.

20. See 2400th meeting of UNGA, 10 November 1975, www.un.org and www.mfa.gov.il

21. Cited in Ramazani, 'Iran and the Arab-Israeli Conflict', p.427. Also, an upsurge in urban violence in Iran at the beginning of 1971 was blamed on individuals who had received training in Palestinian camps. See Weinbaum, 'Iran and Israel', p.1081. In fact, the origins of the guerrilla movement can be traced back to 1963, when SAVAK put down demonstrations organised by the political opposition. This led Amnesty International, in its report of 1974–75, to state that the Shah 'retains his benevolent image despite the highest rate of death penalties in the world, no valid system of civilian courts and a history of torture which is beyond belief'. Cited in Ervand Abrahamian, 'The Guerrilla Movement in Iran, 1963–1977', *Middle East Research and Information Project*, no.86, (March-April 1980), pp.3–15.

22. Ramazani, 'Iran and the Arab-Israeli Conflict', p.427.

23. UNDOF was established in 1974, following the agreed disengagement of the Israeli and Syrian forces on the Golan Heights.

24. See Khalatbari's speech, 14th meeting of UNGA, 1 October 1976, *United Nations General Assembly Official Records, 31st Session, 1976, vol.I*, p.239.

25. See Fard's speech, 73rd meeting of UNGA, 19 November 1976, *United Nations General Assembly Official Records, 31st Session, 1976, vol.II*, p.1133.

26. See Mokri's speech, 91st meeting of UNGA, 7 December 1976, *United Nations General Assembly Official Records, 31st Session, vol.III*, p.1385.

27. See Khalatbari's speech, 9th meeting of UNGA, 27 September 1977, *United Nations General Assembly Official Records, 32nd Session, vol.1*, p.128.

28. See 52nd meeting of UNGA, 28 October 1977, *United Nations General Assembly Official Records, 32nd Session*, p.940.

29. Gawdat Bahgat, 'The Islamic Republic and the Jewish State', *Israel Affairs*, vol.II, no.3, (July 2005), pp.517–534.

30. Ehsassi cited in 17th meeting of Special Political Committee, 4 November 1977, *United Nations General Assembly Official Records, 32nd Session, 1977*, p.12.

31. Sobhani, *The Pragmatic Entente*, p.100.

32. *Ibid*, p.107. The year 1975 also saw parliamentary elections in Iran. On 2 March, the Shah dissolved all existing political parties at a news conference, an order which was summarily obeyed by the members of the suddenly disbanded parties, all of whom declared their support for a one-party system. The Iranian People's Resurgence Party was the result of this process. See Hassan

Mohammadi-Nejad, 'The Iranian Parliamentary Elections of 1975', *International Journal of Middle East Studies*, vol.8, no.1, (January 1977), pp.103–116.

33. *Ibid*, p.108.

34. James A. Bill, *The Eagle and the Lion; The Tragedy of American-Iranian Relations* (Yale University Press: Yale, 1988), p.365.

35. Sobhani, *The Pragmatic Entente*, p.116.

36. *Ibid*, p.131.

37. Bill, *The Eagle and the Lion*, p.430. The same year also saw the zenith of US economic involvement in Iran. That year, US investments were in excess of US$682 million; there were approximately 50,000 US citizens living and working in Iran; military commitments from US firms totalled approximately US$12 billion and the US was the second largest supplier of Iran's non-military imports, to the tune of US$12.7 billion. It is thought that the Iranian revolution directly resulted in the loss of approximately US$12.5 billion in military hardware sales and US$1–2 billion in the prevented sale of spare parts for the US. See Fatemi, 'The Iranian Revolution', pp.303 and 306.

38. Sobhani, *The Pragmatic Entente*, pp.117–118.

39. They were aided by the findings of Amnesty International and the statements of US President Jimmy Carter. See Keddie, 'Iranian Revolutions', p.588.

40. *Ibid*, p.589.

41. Cited in Ali M. Ansari, *Confronting Iran: The Failure of American Foreign Policy and the Roots of Mistrust* (Hurst and Company: London, 2006), pp.80–81.

42. The revolution was to serve as a serious challenge to the durability of Turco-Iranian relations. After the Shah was deposed, Iran's ties with the US were massively impacted and, as a result, Iran a central building block of the relationship, was gone. Moreover, Iran sought to undermine the Arab Gulf rulers who were at odds with the Islamic nature of the new regime, while Turkey desired to remain on cordial terms with them. The Turks viewed the ensuing Iran-Iraq war with trepidation, not least because Iraq had become one of Turkey's foremost energy suppliers. There was also a Turkish fear that the Islamic rhetoric emanating from Tehran may serve to exacerbate the political unrest that Turkey was experiencing, particularly in 1980, when the army instigated martial law. In particular, the regime in Ankara believed that Iranians living in Turkey were potential 'fifth columnists' and Tehran believed that Turks living in Iran were 'counter-revolutionaries'. See John Calabrese, 'Turkey and Iran: Limits of a Stable Relationship', *British Journal of Middle Eastern Studies*, vol.25, no.1, (May 1998), pp.75–94, pp.77–78.

43. Ramazani, *Revolutionary Iran*, p.154.

44. *Ibid*, p.152.
45. See Shemirani's speech, 2124th meeting of UNSC, 12 March 1979, *United Nations Security Council Official Records, 34th Year, 1979*, p.10.
46. *Ibid*.
47. *Ibid*, pp.10–11.
48. In fact, Israeli military sales to Iran continued until the Iran-Contra affair of 1985–86. See Baghat, 'The Islamic Republic', p.524.
49. Alpher, 'Israel and the Iran-Iraq War', p.158.
50. Ramazani, *Revolutionary Iran*, pp.152–153.
51. See Shemirani's speech, 2148th meeting of UNSC, 14 June 1979, *Provisional Verbatim Record of United Nations Security Council, 34th Year, 1979*, p.32.
52. *Ibid*, pp.33–35.
53. The Israel-Iran Connection', the Washington Report on Middle East Affairs, *Journal of Palestine Studies*, vol.16, no.3, (Spring 1987), pp.210–212.
54. Ibid.
55. Sobhani, *The Pragmatic Entente*, p.143.
56. Ramazani, *Revolutionary Iran*, pp.149–150.
57. Paolucci, *Iran, Israel and the United States*, p.240.
58. See David Menashri, 'Iran, Israel and the Middle East Conflict', *Israel Affairs*, vol.12, no.1, (January 2006), pp.107–122.
59. David Menashri, *Post-Revolutionary Politics in Iran: Religion, Society and Power* (Frank Cass: London, 2001), p.263.
60. Bahgat, 'The Islamic Republic' p.521.
61. *Ibid*.
62. Sobhani, *The Pragmatic Entente*, p.144 However, it must also be noted that many more Muslims were killed. See Bahgat, 'The Islamic Republic', p.521.
63. Ali Rahnema and Farhad Nomani, *The Secular Miracle: Religion, Politics and Economic Policy in Iran* (Zed Books: London, 1990), p.181.
64. See Yazdi's speech, 21st meeting of UNGA, 4 October 1979, *United Nations General Assembly Official Records, 34th Session, 1979*, p.444.
65. Ramazani, *Revolutionary Iran*, pp.158–159.
66. 'The Israel-Iran Connection', p.211.
67. See 104th meeting of UNGA, 14 December 1979, *Provisional Verbatim Record of United Nations General Assembly, 34th Session, 1979*, p.49.
68. Cited in Rahnema and Nomani, *The Secular Miracle*, p.343. It was on 7 June 1981, that Israel destroyed the Iraqi 'Osirak' nuclear reactor.
69. Rahnema and Nomani, *The Secular Miracle*, p.343. It should be noted that the Iranian clerical leadership saw these deals with Israel as permissible for the maintenance and expansion of the Islamic order. *Ibid*.

70. See Moussavi's speech, 26th meeting of UNGA, 5 October 1981, *United Nations General Assembly Official Records, 36th Session, 1981*, p.551.

71. See Velayati's speech, 8th meeting of UNGA, 3 February 1982, *United Nations Official Records, Ninth Emergency Special Session*, p.77.

72. *Ibid.*

73. *Ibid*, pp.77–78.

74. *Ibid*, pp.78–79.

75. See Rajaie-Khorassani's speech, 8th meeting of UNGA, 3 February 1982, *United Nations Official Records, Ninth Emergency Special Session*, p.88.

76. See Rajaie-Khorassani's speech, 2340th meeting of UNSC, 30 March 1982, *United Nations Security Council Official Records, 37th Year, 1982*, p.1.

77. *Ibid*, p.2.

78. *Ibid.*

79. *Ibid*, p.3.

80. See Rajaie-Khorassani's speech, 2354th meeting of UNSC, 15 April 1982, *United Nations Security Council Official Records, 37th Year*, p.7.

81. *Ibid*, p.8.

82. *Ibid*, p.9.

83. For detailed accounts of the Lebanon War, see Ze'ev Schiff and Ehud Ya'ari, *Israel's Lebanon War* (Unwin Paperbacks: London, 1986) and Itamar Rabinovich, *The War for Lebanon: 1970–1985* (Cornell University Press: Ithaca, 1985).

84. Dilip Hiro, *Iran Under The Ayatollahs* (Routledge: London, 1987), p.211.

85. Yosef Olmert, 'Iranian-Syrian Relations: Between Islam and Realpolitik' in David Menashri (ed.) *The Iranian Revolution and the Muslim World* (Westview Press: Colorado, 1990), p.180.

86. Hiro, *Iran*, p.211. Khomeini rejected the offer, claiming that Iraq was utilising the same methods in war as Israel: namely occupying cities and then seeking a cease-fire. *Ibid.*

87. Ansari, *Confronting Iran*, p.101.

88. See Velayati's speech, 27th meeting of UNGA, 12 October 1982, *United Nations General Assembly Official Records, 37th Session, 1982*, pp.516–517.

89. *Ibid.*

90. *Ibid.*

91. Ramazani, *Revolutionary Iran*, pp.180–181. Indeed, Ramazani suggests that the timing of the Israeli invasion coincided with Iranian military successes in the war with Iraq in March and May of 1982. *Ibid.*.

92. See Velayati's speech, 27th meeting of UNGA, 12 October 1982, *United Nations General Assembly Official Records, 37th Session, 1982*, p.516–517.

Chapter 4   Turkey and Israel, 1956–72:
Alignment and Ambivalence

1. See Sarper's speech, 562nd meeting of UNGA, 1 November 1956, *United Nations General Assembly Official Records, First Emergency Special Session, 1956,* p.19.

2. *Ibid.*

3. See 565th meeting of UNGA, 5 November 1956, *United Nations General Assembly Official Records, First Emergency Special Session,* p.89.

4. However, at a meeting of the Special Political Committee, under the chairmanship of Selim Sarper, Turkish Representative Bayramoglu revealed that the refugee problem was one of the main causes of instability in the Middle East and that Turkey wanted the issue resolved quickly. He also revealed that Turkey had supported the work of UNRWA and had made modest contributions to its finances. See 27th meeting of Special Political Committee, 19 February 1957, *United Nations General Assembly Official Records, 11th Session, 1956–57,* p.123.

5. See Sarper's speech, 567th meeting, 7 November 1956, *United Nations General Assembly Official Records, First Emergency Special Session,* p.120.

6. *Ibid,* p.120.

7. See Sarper's speech, 564th meeting of UNGA, 4 November 1956, *United Nations General Assembly Official Records, Second Emergency Special Session,* p.18.

8. Cited in Gruen, *Dynamic Progress,* p.46.

9. *Ibid.*

10. *PRO FO 371/121700.* See telegram 1034 from British Embassy, Ankara, to British Foreign Office, 27 November 1956. Also cited in Gruen, *Dynamic Progress,* p.47.

11. *PRO, FO 371/121700.* The Israeli Ambassador was recalled on 19 December 1956. See telegram 1145 from British Embassy, Ankara to British Foreign Office, 20 December 1956.

12. *Middle East Record,* 1960, p.308. In 1956, the Israeli Commercial Secretary informed Thomas Brimelow of the British Embassy in Ankara that Turkey owed Israel approximately US$5.7 million and had exceeded the limit set for 'swing'. In addition, he stated that Israel had no use for Turkish cotton, that the price of Turkish oil cake was too high and that Turkey did not seem to have any exportable commodities attractive to Israel. See despatch from Thomas Brimelow, British Embassy, Ankara to D. M. O'Brien, British Foreign Office, 11 May 1956, *PRO FO 371/124026.*

13. *PRO FO 371/121700.* See letter from Sir J. Bowker, British Embassy, Ankara to the Rt. Hon. Selwyn Lloyd, British Foreign Office, 28 December 1956.

14. *PRO FO 371/128099.* See letter from British Embassy, Ankara, to British Embassy, Tel Aviv, 31 October 1957.

15. See Esin's speech, 692nd meeting of UNGA, 27 September 1957, *United Nations General Assembly Official Records, 12th Session, 1957*, pp.199–200.

16. Gruen, *Turkey's Relations*, p.36.

17. *PRO FO 371/121700.* See telegram 1019 from British Embassy, Ankara to British Foreign Office, 24 November 1956, and Bolukbasi, *Behind*, p.23.

18. Cited in Bar-Zohar, *Ben-Gurion*, p.169.

19. *Ibid,* pp.169–170.

20. *Ibid,* p.170.

21. Bengio, *The Turkish-Israeli*, p.43.

22. *PRO FO 371/134331.* See Letter from C.B.B Heathcote-Smith, British Embassy, Ankara to J.S. Sadler, British Board of Trade, 17 September 1958.

23. *PRO FO 371/142349.* See BBC memo, KO B71, 4 February 1959. The same year also saw a visit to Turkey by the Israeli Chief of Staff, which was understood by the British Foreign Office to signify potential Turkish aid to Israel. See British Embassy, Ankara, to British Foreign Office, 14 April 1959, *PRO FO 371/142292* and Bengio, *The Turkish-Israeli*, p.53.

24. See Zorlu's speech, 809th meeting of UNGA, 25 September 1959, *United Nations General Assembly Official Records, 14th Session, 1959*, p.201.

25. 158th meeting of Special Political Committee, 25 November 1959, *United Nations General Assembly Official Records, 14th Session, 1959*, p.139.

26. *Middle East Record*, 1961, pp.82–84.

27. *Middle East Record*, 1960, p.308.

28. *Middle East Record*, 1961, pp.84–85 and 329.

29. *Middle East Record*, 1960, p.308.

30. The other elected members of the UNSC in 1961 were: Ceylon, Chile, Ecuador, Liberia and the UAR. See 921st meeting of UNSC, 4 January 1961, *United Nations Security Council Official Records, 16th Year, Jan-June, 1961*, p.1.

31. Draft proposal S/4777 took the form of a letter from the government of the Hashemite Kingdom of Jordan, complaining that Israel was intending to hold a military parade in Jerusalem on 20 April, 1961. Moreover, the letter continued, on 17 March, Israel had held a dress rehearsal for the parade with 'heavy military armament'. See *United Nations Security Council Official Records, 16th Year, 1961, Supplements for April, May and June 1961*, pp.1–2.

32. See Menemencioglu's speech, 948th meeting of UNSC, 10 April 1961, *United Nations Security Council Official Records, 16th Year, 1961*, p.8.

33. Four Mixed Armistice Commissions were created to protect and develop agreements between Israel, Egypt, Jordan, Lebanon and Syria. See P.R. Kumaraswamy *Historical*, p.167.

34. See Menemencioglu's speech, 948th meeting of UNSC, 10 April 1961, *United Nations Security Council Official Records, 16th Year, 1961*, p.9.

35. See 322nd meeting of Special Political Committee, 18 December 1961, *United Nations General Assembly Official Records, 16th Session, 1961*, p.331.

36. See Sarper's speech 1021st meeting of UNGA, 2 October 1961, *United Nations General Assembly Official Records, 16th Session, 1961*, p.195.

37. *Ibid.*

38. *Ibid.*

39. Cited in Bengio, *The Turkish-Israeli*, p.54.

40. On 2 June 1964, the Turkish government had planned to invade Cyprus. See Hale, *Turkish*, p.149.

41. For a more detailed account of this episode, see *ibid*, pp.149–150.

42. Alon Liel, *Turkey in the Middle East: Oil, Islam and Politics* (Lynne Rienner: Colorado, 2001), p.191. At the World Islamic Congress held in Somalia in December 1964–January 1965, a resolution was endorsed which called for a federation on Cyprus which would be based on equal rights for both the Turkish and Greek populations of the island. However, at the UN, Turkey did not have support on the same issue, even from many Muslim countries. Cited in Bishku, 'How Has Turkey Viewed Israel?', p.184.

43. Philip Robins, *Turkey and the Middle East* (Chatham House, 1991), pp.77–78 and Philip Robins, *Turkish-Israeli Relations: From the Periphery to the Centre* (The Emirates Centre for Strategic Studies and Research, 2001), p.3.

44. See Hale, *Turkish*, p.150.

45. Cited in Bolukbasi, 'Behind the Turkish', p.26.

46. As early as 1 February 1965, then Turkish Foreign Minister, Feridun Cemal Erkin, had revealed that disagreements between the Arab world and Turkey would be overcome by their mutual concern for the Palestinians and ties between the two parties would subsequently strengthen. Cited in *Ibid,* p.26.

47. Bengio, *The Turkish-Israeli*, pp.56–57.

48. On 9–10 May 1964, the Israeli College for National Defence visited Ankara and Inonu and Eshkol met in Paris in July of the same year to discuss, *inter alia*, the Cyprus issue. *Ibid,* p.58.

49. *Ibid*, pp.58–59.

50. *Ibid*, p.55.

51. Robins, *Turkey and the Middle East*, p.78.

52. Cited in Bengio, *The Turkish-Israeli*, p.59.

53. See Erkin's speech, 1321st meeting of UNGA, 25 January 1965, *United Nations General Assembly Official Records, 19th Session, 1965*, p.5.

54. See 447th meeting of Special Political Committee, 4 November 1965, *United Nations General Assembly Official Records, 20th Session, 1965*, p.1.

55. Cited in Bengio, *The Turkish-Israeli*, p.60.
56. For more details of this episode see *ibid*, p.64.
57. Cited in *ibid*, pp.59–67.
58. *Ibid*.
59. See Caglayangil's speech, 1532nd meeting of UNGA, 22 June 1967, *United Nations General Assembly Official Records, Fifth Emergency Special Session*, p.1.
60. *Ibid*.
61. *Ibid*.
62. *Ibid*, pp.1–2.
63. See Caglayangil's speech, 1577th meeting of UNGA, 3 October 1967, *United Nations General Assembly Official Records, 1967, 22nd Session, 1967*, p.9.
64. It is worth nothing that Turkey did not participate in efforts made to reopen the Gulf Of Aqaba to Israeli shipping and denied the US access to the Incerklik airbase during the Six Day War. See Bengio, *The Turkish-Israeli*, p.74. In addition, it has been reported that the Turkish government relayed information to the Arab world *vis-à-vis* Israel's plans of attack, purportedly including an attack on Egypt's air bases. Cited in Jacob Abadi, 'Israel and Turkey: From Covert to Overt Relations' http://www.lib.unb.ca. Turkey also informed the Syrian government that it would not position troops along its border with Syria and furnished Syria with humanitarian aid, such as foodstuffs, clothing and medical equipment. This action was publicly lauded on 21 August 1967, when then Syrian Foreign Minister Ibrahim Mahous, expressed the gratitude Syria felt towards Turkey for its actions during the war. See Liel, *Turkey in the Middle East*, p.194.
65. See 1548th meeting of UNGA, 4 July 1967, *United Nations General Assembly Official Records, 1967, Fifth Emergency Special Session*, pp.14–15.
66. *Ibid*, pp.15–16.
67. *Ibid*, p.16.
68. *Ibid*, p.17.
69. See 1558th meeting of UNGA, 21 July 1967, *United Nations General Assembly Official Records, 1967, Fifth Emergency Special Session*, p.16 and 1559th meeting of UNGA, 18 September 1967, *Ibid*, p.1.
70. See Caglayangil's speech, 1532nd meeting of UNGA, 22 June 1967, *United Nations General Assembly Official Records, 1967, Fifth Emergency Special Session*, pp.1–2.
71. See Caglayangil's speech, 1577th meeting of UNGA, 3 October 1967, *United Nations General Assembly Official Records, 22nd Session, 1967*, p.10.
72. *Ibid*, p.9.
73. See 591st meeting of Special Political Committee, 15 December 1967, *United Nations General Assembly Official Records, 22nd Session, 1967*, p.291.

74. See 1748th meeting of UNGA, 19 December 1968, *United Nations General Assembly Official Records, 23rd Session 1968*, p.7.

75. See 633rd meeting of the Special Political Committee, 11 December 1968, *United Nations General Assembly Official Records, 23rd Session*, p.3.

76. See 743rd meeting of the Special Political Committee, 4 December 1970, *United Nations General Assembly Official Records, 25th Session 1970*, p.301.

77. See 792nd meeting of the Special Political Committee, 1 December 1971, *United Nations General Assembly Official Records, 26th Session 1971*, p.251.

78. See 1896th meeting of UNGA, 4 November 1970, *United Nations General Assembly Official Records (Vol III) Resolutions, Special Political Committee, 25th Session, 1970*, p.12.

79. See 2016th meeting of UNGA, 13 December 1971, *United Nations General Assembly Official Records, 26th Session 1971*, p.34.

80. See 1548th meeting of UNGA, 4 July 1967, *United Nations General Assembly Official Records, 1967, Fifth Emergency Special Session*, p.18 and 1554th meeting of UNGA, 14 July 1967, *United Nations Official Records, 1967, Fifth Emergency Special Session*, pp.8–9.

81. See Caglayangil's speech, 1532nd meeting of UNGA, 22 June 1967, *United Nations General Assembly Official Records, 1967, Fifth Emergency Special Session*, p.2.

82. On 10 March 1968, an extension of the Turkish-Israeli trade agreement for another year was signed in Jerusalem. Israeli Foreign Minister, Abba Eban, called upon Turkey to balance its relations with countries in the Middle East, rather than attempt to improve its relations with Arab countries only. He suggested that Turkish-Israeli ties should be raised to embassy level from that of legation. *See Middle East Record*, 1968, p.197. The following year saw the abrogation of the trade agreement as a result of 'increasing difficulties' in implementing it. A protocol was signed between Turkey and Israel concerning the settlement of trade balances and a Turkish official noted that, because of the protocol, future trade with Israel would be conducted on the basis of free foreign exchange. See *Middle East Record*, 1969–1970, parts 1–4, p.650.

83. See Caglayangil's speech, 1772nd meeting of UNGA, 30 September 1969, *United Nations General Assembly Official Records, 24th Session, 1969*, p.18.

84. It is worth noting that, despite the admission of guilt from and the deportation of Rohan, certain sectors of the Arab world refused to believe that Israel had not been behind the arson. For example, a statement from the Organisation of the Islamic Conference (OIC) from 19 August 2004, refers to the fire as an 'atrocious arson attempt carried out against the Blessed Mosque by Israeli extremists'. See http://domino.un.org/. Moreover, in a

letter dated 14 March 1983 from the Permanent Representative of Jordan, Abdullah Salah, to the United Nations Secretary-General, Salah stated that the act of arson was one of 'the Israeli assaults on the blessed Al Aqsa Mosque in Jerusalem from June 1967 to 11 March 1983.' Salah also claimed that the fire was 'the first of the conspicuous attempts to destroy and demolish this Islamic Holy Place ... when a Zionist, of Australian nationality, Michael Rohan, started a fire in the Mosque ...' See http://domino.un.org

85. See Mahmut Bali Aykan, 'The Palestinian Question', p.95.

86. Cited in *Ibid*, p.96. Indeed, in 1970, Representative Eren drew the attention of the Special Committee to the existence of unused empty shelters, schools, health centres and food distribution centres in Jericho. 728th meeting of Special Political Committee, 19 November 1970, *United Nations General Assembly Official Records, 25th Session, 1970*, p.200.

87. On 9 April 1970, the Lebanese paper, *al-Hayat*, reported that the Turkish Students' Federation refused to allow the Israeli consul in Istanbul, Efraim Elrom, to visit its centre and accused him of being a spy. Also, on 11 April 1970, fifteen Turkish students demonstrated in front of the Israeli Consulate in Istanbul. Finally, on 15 May, students from the Middle East Technical University held a protest on the 22nd anniversary of the birth of Israel. See *Middle East Record*, 1969–1970, parts 1–4, p.650.

88. See 786th meeting of Special Political Committee, 24 November 1971, *United Nations General Assembly Official Records, 26th Session, 1971,* pp.199–200.

89. See Bayulken's speech, 1886th meeting of UNGA, 27 October 1970, *United Nations General Assembly Official Records, 25th Session, 1970*, p.2.

90. *Ibid.*

91. *Ibid.*

92. *Ibid.*

93. However, from 1970–82, Turkish exports to the Middle East increased from US$54 million to US$1.9 billion and its imports for the same period. increased from US$64 million to US$2.6 billion. See Bishku, 'How Has Turkey Viewed Israel?', p.185. For additional details of the turmoil see, Roger P. Nye, 'Civil-Military Confrontation in Turkey: The 1973 Presidential Election', *International Journal of Middle East Studies*, vol.8, no.2, (April 1977), pp.209–228.

94. Nicole and Hugh Pope, *Turkey*, p.105. For a detailed account of this turmoil, see *ibid*, pp.100–107.

95. *Ibid*, p.106.

96. *Ibid.*

97. www.jewishvirtuallibrary.org

98. See 834th meeting of Special Political Committee, 10 November 1972, *United Nations General Assembly Official Records, 27th Session, 1972*, p.186.
99. *Ibid.*
100. See Olcay's speech, 2095th meeting of UNGA, 1 December 1972, *United Nations General Assembly Official Records, 27th Session, 1972*, p.1.
101. *Ibid.*
102. Inbar, *The Israeli-Turkish Entente*, p.9.
103. See Olcay's speech, 2095th meeting of UNGA, 1 December 1972, *United Nations General Assembly Official Records, 27th Session, 1972*, p.1.

Chapter 5   Turkey and Israel, 1973–82: Rejection and Realignment

1. See Bayulken's speech, 2132nd meeting of UNGA, 28 September 1973, *United Nations General Assembly Official Records, 28th Session, 1973, vol.1*, p.5.
2. Abadi, 'Israel and Turkey'. In addition, ties between Turkey and Syria had been improving for some time. In 1972–73, the foreign ministers of the two countries, Haluk Bayulken and Abd-al-Halim Khaddam, visited each other and discussed commerce, air links, tourism, cultural affairs, Cyprus and border problems and the two countries finalised a compromise over nationalised property belonging to Syrian citizens in the Hatay province (Alexandretta) and to Turkish citizens in Syria. See Liel, *Turkey in the Middle East*, p.194.
3. Bolukbasi, 'Behind the Turkish', p.2t66.
4. Cited in Jacob Abadi, *Israel's Quest for Recognition and Acceptance in Asia: Garrison State Diplomacy* (Frank Cass: London, 2004), p.18.
5. See Gunes's speech, 2241st meeting of UNGA, 24 September 1974, *United Nations General Assembly Official Records, 29th Session, 1974, vol.I*, p.133.
6. See Olcay's speech, 2292nd meeting of UNGA, 20 November 1974, *United Nations General Assembly Official Records, 29th Session, 1974, vol.II*, p.988.
7. *Ibid*, p.989.
8. *Ibid.* The apparent Turkish empathy for the Palestinian cause was readily observable in Turkey's support of UNGA Resolutions 3210 (**XXIX**) and 3237 (**XXIX**). See 2268th and 2296th meetings of UNGA, 14 October and 22 November 1974, *United Nations General Assembly Official Records, 29th Session, 1974*, pp. 677–678 and 1066.
9. See 944th meeting of the Special Political Committee, 4 December 1974, *United Nations General Assembly Official Records, 29th Session, 1974*, p.229.

10. *Ibid.*
11. See www.un.org
12. Abadi, 'Israel and Turkey' and www.mfa.gov.il
13. Abadi, 'Israel and Turkey'.
14. See Caglayangil's speech, 8th meeting of UNGA, 28 September 1976, *United Nations General Assembly Official Records, 31st Session, 1976*, p.114.
15. See 13th meeting of Special Political Committee, 4 November 1976, *United Nations General Assembly Official Records, 31st Session, 1976*, pp.12–13.
16. See Turkmen's speech, 73rd meeting of UNGA, *United Nations General Assembly Official Records, 31st Session, 1976*, p.1134.
17. *Ibid.*
18. See, Liel, *Turkey in the Middle East*, pp.199–200.
19. See Turkmen's speech, 82nd meeting of UNGA, 25 November 1977, *United Nations General Assembly Official Records, 32nd Session, 1977*, p.1388.
20. See Akiman's speech, 67th meeting of UNGA, 1 December 1978, *Provisional Verbatim Records of United Nations General Assembly, 33rd Session, 1978*, p.31.
21. See Eralp's speech, 2124th meeting of UNSC, 12 March 1979, *United Nations Security Council Official Records, 34th Year, 1979*, p.4.
22. *Ibid.*
23. In addition, the law stated that: 'the Holy Places shall be protected from desecration and any other violation and from anything likely to violate the freedom of access of the members of the different religions to the places sacred to them or their feelings towards those places. The Government shall provide for the development and prosperity of Jerusalem and the well-being of its inhabitants by allocating special funds, including a special annual grant to the Municipality of Jerusalem (Capital City Grant) with the approval of the Finance Committee of the Knesset. Jerusalem shall be given special priority in the activities of the authorities of the State so as to further its development in economic and other matters'. It was signed by then Israeli Prime Minister, Menachem Begin and then Israeli President, Yitzhak Navon. See www.knesset.gov.il
24. Gruen, 'Dynamic Progess', p.48.
25. See Eralp's speech, 2236th meeting of UNSC, 26 June 1980, *Provisional Verbatim Records of United Nations Security Council, 35th Year, 1980*, p.27.
26. *Ibid,* p.28.
27. *Ibid,* p.31.
28. See Turkmen's speech, 19th meeting of UNGA, 1 October 1980, *United Nations Security Council Official Records, 35th Session, 1980*, p.352.
29. *Ibid,* p.352.
30. See Kirca's speech, 80th meeting of UNGA, 3 December 1980 *United Nations Security Council Official Records, 35th Session, 1980*, pp.1378–1379.

31. Gruen, 'Dynamic Progress', p.48.

32. Erbakan, whose National Salvation Party (NSP) was a coalition partner in the two National Front governments that were in power from April 1975 until January 1978, for many years spoke of the goals of Zionism being the dissection of the Arab world, a process which would start with Turkey. The creation of the state of Israel was a tool for such purposes, he believed. He also claimed that Herzl dreamed of incorporating areas of Turkey into the Zionist enterprise and that the European Common Market was the result of Zionist conspiracies and, as a result, Turkey should never join. See Bengio, *The Turkish-Israeli*, p.76, Mahmut Bali Aykan, 'The Palestinian Question', p.98 and Bishku, 'How Has Israel?', p.178.

33. See Liel, *Turkey in the Middle East*, p.208.

34. Gruen, 'Turkey's Relations', pp.36–37.

35. *Ibid*, p.37 However, there was not complete consensus within the Turkish elites regarding the government's stance on Israel. Former Defence Minister, Hasan Isik, stated that the closure of the Turkish consulate was a mistake, because the consulate general, which could be traced back to the days of the Ottoman Empire, was not a diplomatic mission attributed to the Israeli government. Ibid.

36. See Bengio, *The Turkish-Israeli*, p.75.

37. See Gruen, 'Turkey's Relations', p.37.

38. *Ibid*.

39. Bolukbasi, 'Behind the Turkish', p.28.

40. *Ibid*.

41. *Ibid*.

42. Abadi, 'Israel and Turkey'.

43. See Bishku, 'How Has Turkey Viewed Israel?', p.185.

44. See Bengio, *The Turkish-Israeli*, p.75.

45. See Gruen, 'Turkey's Relations', p.38. In the same year, Turkey's trade union president, Ibrahim Denizcier, was explicitly criticised for his trip to Israel in September 1981, as a guest of the *Histadrut*. This visit led the Turkish government to state that the trip had been carried out without its knowledge. See Liel, *Turkey in the Middle East*, p.210.

46. See Turkmen's speech, 16th meeting of UNGA, 28 September 1981, *United Nations General Assembly Official Records, 36th Session, 1981*, p.314.

47. *Ibid*, p.315.

48. The subsequent Golan Heights Law stated that: 'The Law, jurisdiction and administration of the state shall apply to the Golan Heights, as described in the Appendix. This Law shall become valid on the day of its passage in the Knesset. The Minister of the Interior shall be charged with the

implementation of this Law, and he is entitled, in consultation with the Minister of Justice, to enact regulations for its implementation and to formulate in regulations transitional provisions concerning the continued application of regulations, orders, administrative orders, rights and duties which were in force on the Golan Heights prior to the application of this Law'. See www.jewishvirtuallibrary.org

49. See Kirca's speech, 99th meeting of UNGA, 15 December 1981, *United Nations General Assembly Official Records, 36th Session, 1981*, pp.1775–1776.

50. *Ibid*, p.1776.

51. Cited in Gruen, 'Turkey's Relations', p.34. Indeed, Turkish UN Representative Turkmen stated that: 'Armenian terrorists have in recent years brutally assassinated more than 20 Turkish diplomats and officials. In the first week of August, Armenian terrorists launched an attack at Ankara airport in which nine people lost their lives and some 70 were wounded'. See Turkmen's speech, 15th meeting of UNGA, 4 October 1982, *United Nations General Assembly Official Records, 37th Session, 1982*, p.256.

52. See Kirca's speech, 12th meeting of UNGA, 5 February 1982, *United Nations General Assembly Official Records, Ninth Emergency Special Session*, p.143.

53. For the full text of the resolution, see www.mfa.gov.il. For the voting records see, 12th meeting of UNGA, 5 February 1982, *United Nations General Assembly Official Records, Ninth Emergency Special Session, Annexes*, pp.139–140.

54. See Kirca's speech, 12th meeting of UNGA, 5 February 1982, *United Nations General Assembly Official Records, Ninth Emergency Special Session*, p.143.

55. See Kirca's speech, 2338th meeting of UNSC, 26 March 1982, *United Nations Security Council Official Records, 37th Year, 1982*, p.5.

56. *Ibid*, p.6.

57. See Kirca's speech, 2354th meeting of UNSC, 15 April 1982, *United Nations Security Council Official Records, 37th Year, 1982*, p.6.

58. See Gruen, 'Turkey's Relations', p.34. The criticism of Israel may have been made in the context of Turkey's exports to Arab countries which, in the same year, comprised approximately 47 per cent of its total exports. See M. Hakan Yavuz, 'Turkish-Israeli Relations Through the Lens of the Turkish Identity Debate', *Journal of Palestine Studies*, vol.27, no.1, (Autumn 1997), pp.22–37, p.27.

59. See Turkmen's speech, 15th meeting of UNGA, 4 October 1982, *United Nations Security Council Official Records, 37th Session, 1982*, p.255.

60. *Ibid*.

61. See 37th meeting of Special Political Committee, 26 November 1982 *United Nations Security Council Official Records, 37th Session, 1982*, p.13.

62. See Gokce's speech, 94th meeting of UNGA, 7 December 1982, *United Nations General Assembly Official Records, 35th Session, 1982*, p.1565.
63. *Ibid*, p.1566.
64. See Kirca's speech, 108th meeting of UNGA, 16 December 1982, *United Nations General Assembly Official Records, 35th Session, 1982*, p.1839.
65. See Jacob Abadi, 'Constraints and Adjustments in Greece's Policy Toward Israel', *Mediterranean Quarterly*, vol.11, no.4, (2000), pp.40–70, http://muse.jhu.edu/
66. Cited in Gruen, 'Turkey's Relations', p.35.

Chapter 6   Ethiopia and Israel, 1956–72: From Partner to Pariah

1. See Deressa's speech, 562nd meeting of UNGA, 1 November 1956, *United Nations General Assembly Official Records, First Emergency Special Session, 1956*, p.41.
2. *Ibid*.
3. *Ibid*, p.42.
4. See Deressa's speech, 567th meeting of UNGA, 7 November 1956, *United Nations General Assembly Official Records, First Emergency Special Session, 1956*, p.113.
5. *Ibid*.
6. See Deressa's speech, 601st meeting of UNGA, 29 November 1956, *United Nations General Assembly Official Records, 11th Session, 1956–1957, vol.1*, p.412.
7. *Ibid*.
8. *Ibid*, p.413.
9. *Ibid*.
10. *Shifta* is a term used in Ethiopia to describe armed bandits. Richard Greenfield, *Ethiopia: A New Political History* (Pall Mall Press: London, 1965), p.19.
11. Haggai Erlich, *Ethiopia and the Middle East* (Lynne Rienner: Colorado, 1994), p.134.
12. See Peter Schwab, 'Cold War on the Horn of Africa', *African Affairs*, vol.77 (January, 1978), no.306, p.10.
13. Cited in Erlich, *Ethiopia*, p.134.
14. Yaniv, *Deterrence*, p.96.
15. Statement to a British journalist, cited in Erlich, *Ethiopia*, p.134.
16. Yaniv, *Deterrence*, p.96.
17. *PRO FO 371/142277*. Letter from G.W. Furlonge, British Ambassador to Ethiopia, British Embassy, Addis Ababa, to The Rt. Hon. Selwyn Lloyd, British Foreign Secretary, 30 May 1959. However, the figures for exports

from Ethiopia to Israel in 1958 alone have also been published as $1.7 million, with $0.2 million in exports from Israel to Ethiopia. *Middle East Record*, 1960, pp.57–58.

18. *PRO FO 371/142277*. See Letter from G.W. Furlonge, British Ambassador to Ethiopia, British Embassy, Addis Ababa, to The Rt. Hon. Selwyn Lloyd, British Foreign Secretary, 30 May 1959. 1958 also saw a visit a visit by Ben Gurion's political advisor to Addis Ababa. *Ibid.*

19. *Ibid.*

20. Haggai Erlich, *The Struggle over Eritrea: 1962–1978, War and Revolution in the Horn of Africa* (Hoover International Press: California, 1983), p.57.

21. Yaniv, *Deterrence*, p.96.

22. *Ibid.*

23. For example, the Afro-Asian Institute for Labour Studies and Co-operation commenced its first course in Tel Aviv on 10 October. See *Middle East Record*, 1960, p.302.

24. *Ibid*, p.184.

25. *Ibid*, p.306.

26. Cited in *Ibid*, p.184.

27. Cited in *Ibid*, pp.306–307. In June 1961, the Ethiopian National Transport Company agreed that 75 buses be built in Israel on English chassis. Egged agreed to co-operate on this project for five years. See *Middle East Record*, 1961, p.327.

28. *Ibid.*

29. Cited in *Middle East Record*, 1960 p.307.

30. *Ibid.*

31. Cited in *Middle East Record*, 1961, p.82.

32. Cited in Erlich, *The Struggle*, p.57. On 24 October, it was announced that Ethiopia had extended *de jure* recognition to Israel. The hope was that the recognition would encourage Iran to do the same. See *Middle East Record*, 1961, p.327.

33. Erlich, *The Struggle,* p.57.

34. Cited in *Middle East Record*, 1961, p.190. Selassie, was happy to have an Israeli doctor attend the Empress and to receive an Israeli shipment of medicine for relief of flood victims in Ogaden. Notable Ethiopian visitors to Israel in that year included: Haddis Alemayehoo, Minister of State and Acting Minister of Education and Araya Wassieh, Deputy Minister of Health. See *Middle East Record*, 1961, p.328.

35. Cited in *Middle East Record*, 1960, p.190.

36. Laufer, *Israel*, p.133.

37. Cited in *ibid*, p.133.

38. *Ibid.*

39. *Ibid*, p.135.
40. *Ibid*.
41. Bard, 'The Evolution'.
42. Cited in Abel Jacob, 'Israel's Military Aid to Africa, 1960–1966', *Journal of Modern African Studies*, vol.9, no.2, (August 1971), pp.165–187. This point serves to highlight the Israeli belief that a significant presence in Ethiopia would act as both a deterrent to Egypt and help contain Eastern Africa.
43. Erlich, *The Struggle*, p.38.
44. *Ibid*, p.38. By 1966, the size of the Israeli military delegation in Ethiopia was second only in size to the US military presence in the country. Peters, *Israel and Africa*, p.8.
45. Erlich, *The Struggle*, p.58.
46. Bard, 'The Evolution' and Erlich, *The Struggle*, p.58.
47. Erlich, *The Struggle*, p.39.
48. *Ibid,* p.58.
49. Bard, 'The Evolution'.
50. See Makonnen's speech, 1345th meeting of UNSC, 31 May 1967, *United Nations Security Council Official Records, 22nd Year, 1967*, p.12.
51. See Makonnen's speech, 1346th meeting of UNSC, 3 June 1967, *United Nations Security Council Official Records, 22nd Year, 1967*, p.22.
52. See Makonnen's speech, 1369th meeting of UNSC, 24/25 October 1967, *United Nations Security Council Official Records, 22nd Year, 1967*, p.14.
53. See 348th meeting of UNSC, 6 June 1967, *United Nations Security Council Official Records, 22nd Year, 1967*, pp.1–2.
54. See *Ibid*, p.2 and www.un.org
55. At the time of the Six Day War, Ethiopia was an elected member of the UNSC for the years 1967–68, with Representative Makonnen fulfilling the role of president in December 1968. The other elected members for the period 1967–68 were for 1967: Argentina. Brazil, Bulgaria, Canada, Denmark, India, Japan, Mali, and Nigeria, and for 1968: Algeria, Brazil, Canada, Denmark, Hungary, India, Pakistan, Paraguay and Senegal. See 1341st meeting of UNSC, 24 May 1967, *United Nations Security Council Official Records, 22nd Year, 1967*, p.1 and www.un.org
56. See Makonnen's speech, 1348th meeting of UNSC, 6 June 1967, *United Nations Security Council Official Records, 22nd Year, 1967*, p.3.
57. *Ibid*, p.3.
58. *Ibid*.
59. *Ibid*.
60. See 1350th meeting of UNSC, 7 June 1967, *United Nations Security Council Official Records, 22nd Year, 1967*, p.2 and www.un.org

61. See 1352nd meeting of UNSC, 9 June 1967, *United Nations Security Council Official Records, 22nd Year, 1967*, p.4.

62. See *ibid*, p.4 and www.un.org

63. See El-Kony's speech, 1355th meeting of UNSC, 10 June 1967, *United Nations Security Council Official Records, 22nd Year, 1967*, p.11.

64. See El-Farra's speech, *ibid*, p.11.

65. See Makonnen's speech, *ibid*, pp.11–12.

66. *Ibid*, p.12.

67. *Ibid*.

68. *Ibid*.

69. See Oren, *Six Days of War*, p.296, Odd Bull, *War and Peace In The Middle East: The Experiences and Views of a UN Observer* (Leo Cooper: London, 1976), p.120 and *Sydney D. Bailey: The Making of Resolution 242* (Martinus Nijhoff, Dordrect: The Netherlands, 1985), pp.87–89.

70. See *United Nations Security Council Index to Proceedings 1964–1974 22nd Year, 1967*, p.21.

71. www.un.org

72. See Makonnen's speech, 1360th meeting of UNSC, 14 June 1967, *United Nations Security Council Official Records, 22nd Year, 1967*, p.8.

73. See *United Nations Security Council Index to Proceedings 1964–1974, 22nd Year, 1967*, p.21.

74. See, 1361st meeting of UNSC, 14 June 1967, *United Nations Security Council Official Records, 22nd Year, 1967*, p.9 and www.un.org

75. See *United Nations Security Council Index to Proceedings 1964–1974, 22nd Year*, p.21.

76. See 1371st meeting of UNSC, 25 October 1967, *United Nations Security Council Official Records, 22nd Year, 1967*, p.1 and www.un.org

77. See *Index to Proceedings of the Security Council 1964–1974, 22nd Year, 1967*, p.22.

78. See 1382nd meeting of UNSC. 22 November 1967, *United Nations Security Council Official Records, 22nd Year, 1967*, p.8 and www.un.org

79. See Lord Caradon on Security Council Resolution 242, Lord Caradon, Arthur J. Goldberg, Mohammad H. El-Zayyat, and Abba Eban, *UN Security Council Resolution 242: A Case Study In Diplomatic Ambiguity, Institute for the Study of Diplomacy, Edmund A. Walsh School of Foreign Service* (Georgetown University: Washington D.C., 1981), p.vii, and http://domino.un.org

80. See Caradon *et al*, p.4.

81. *FCO 17/523*. See telegram no.1836, UK mission, New York, to British Foreign Office, 21 July 1967.

82. See Makonnen's speech, 1382nd meeting of UNSC, 22 November 1967, *United Nations Security Council Official Records, 22nd Year, 1967*, p.4.

83. Cited in, Bailey, *The Making*, p.153.
84. Bull quoted in *Ibid*, p.155.
85. See Caradon *et al*, *UN*, p.13.
86. *Ibid*, p.13.It should also be noted that then US Ambassador to the UN, Arthur J. Goldberg, argued that 'the Resolution speaks of withdrawal from occupied territories, without defining the extent of withdrawal, except that it is clear from the debates that less than total withdrawal is contemplated on all fronts. And the notable presence of the words 'secure and recognised boundaries' by implication contemplates that the parties could make territorial adjustments in their peace settlements encompassing less than a complete withdrawal of Israeli forces from occupied territories'. *Ibid*, p.22.
87. See Jillian Becker, *The PLO: The Rise and Fall of the Palestine Liberation Organisation* (Weidenfeld and Nicolson: London, 1984), p.62.
88. *Ibid*, and www.jewishvirtuallibrary.org
89. See Herzog, *The Arab-Israeli Wars*, p.205.
90. *Ibid*.
91. For a more detailed account of the operation in Safi, see *Ibid*.
92. See Makonnen's speech, 1402nd meeting of UNSC, 21 March 1968, *United Nations Security Council Official Records, 22nd Year, 1968*, p.10.
93. See 1407th meeting of UNSC, 24 March 1968, *United Nations Security Council Official Records, 23rd Year, 1968*, p.2.
94. *Ibid*.
95. See *Index to Proceedings of the Security Council, 1964–1974, 23rd Year, 1968*, p.23.
96. See Makonnen's speech, 1411th meeting of UNSC, 2 April 1968, *United Nations Security Council Official Records, 23rd Year, 1968*, p.7.
97. See 1417th meeting of UNSC, 27 April 1968, *United Nations Security Council Official Records, 23rd Year, 1968*, p.17 and www.un.org
98. See www.un.org
99. See *Index to Proceedings of the Security Council, 1964–1974, 23rd Year*, 1968, p.23.
100. See Makonnen's speech, 1417th meeting 27 April 1968, *United Nations Security Council Official Records, 23rd Year, 1968*, pp.4–5.
101. See www.un.org
102. See *Index to Proceedings of the Security Council, 1964–1974, 23rd Year, 1968*, p.23.
103. See 1426th meeting of UNSC, 21 May 1968, *United Nations Security Council Official Records, 23rd Year, 1968*, p.7 and www.un.org
104. See www.un.org
105. See Erlich, *Ethiopia*, p.169.
106. *Ibid*.

107. Habte-Wold and Ras Asrate Kassa competed for the position of Emperor as Selassie grew frailer and Selassie was happy to perpetuate the situation. *Ibid*, pp.171–172.

108. See *Index to Proceedings of the Security Council, 1964–1974, 23rd Year, 1968*, p.23.

109. See 1440th meeting of UNSC, 16 August 1968, *United Nations Security Council Official Records, 23rd Year, 1968*, p.2 and www.un.org

110. See Makonnen's speech, 1449th meeting of UNSC, 10 September 1968, *United Nations Security Council Official Records, 23rd Year, 1968*, pp.4–5.

111. *Ibid*, p.5.

112. See *Index to Proceedings of the Security Council, 1964–1974, 23rd Year, 1968*, p.24.

113. See 1452nd meeting of UNSC, 18 September 1968, *United Nations Security Council Official Records, 23rd Year, 1968*, p.2 and www.un.org

114. See ibid.

115. *Ibid*. The request for a Special Representative was included in the text of resolution 242 (1967).

116. See *Index to the Proceedings of the Security Council, 1964–1974, 23rd Year, 1968*, p.24.

117. See 1454th meeting of UNSC, 27 September 1968, *United Nations Security Council Official Records, 23rd Year, 1968*, p.24.

118. See, www.un.org

119. *Ibid*.

120. See Makonnen's speech, 1454th meeting of UNSC, 27 September 1968, *United Nations Security Council Official Records, 23rd Year, 1968*, p.17.

121. See Makonnen's speech, 1457th meeting of UNSC, 4 November 1968, *United Nations Security Council Official Records, 23rd Year, 1968*, p.8.

122. *Ibid*.

123. See *Index to the Proceedings of the Security Council, 1964–1974, 23rd Year, 1968*, p.24.

124. *Ibid* and 1462nd meeting of UNSC, 31 December 1968, *United Nations Security Council Official Records, 23rd Year, 1968*, p.2.

125. See www.un.org

126. *Ibid* and 1462nd meeting of UNSC, 31 December 1968, *United Nations Security Council Official Records, 23rd Year, 1968*, pp.1–2.

127. *Ibid*.

128. See statement to the Knesset by Israeli Prime Minister Levi Eshkol, 31 December 1968, www.mfa.gov.il. and Samuel M. Katz, *Guards without Frontiers: Israel's War against Terrorism* (Arms and Armour: London, 1990), p.38 and Becker, *The PLO*, p.94.

129. See Makonnen's speech, 1547th meeting of UNGA, 4 July 1967, *United Nations General Assembly Official Records, 1967, Fifth Emergency Special Session,* p.5.

130. Co-sponsored by Afghanistan, Burundi, Cambodia, Ceylon, Congo, Cyprus, Guinea, India, Indonesia, Malaysia, Mali, Pakistan, Senegal, Somalia, United Republic of Tanzania, Yugoslavia and Zambia. See *Index to Proceedings of United Nations General Assembly, Fifth Emergency Special Session, 22nd Session, 1967,* p.7.

131. See 1548th meeting of UNGA, 4 July 1967, *United Nations General Assembly Official Records, 1967, Fifth Emergency Special Session,* pp.14–15.

132. See Makonnen's' speech, 1547th meeting of UNGA, 4 July 1967, *United Nations General Assembly Official Records, 1967, Fifth Emergency Special Session,* p.5.

133. *Ibid.*

134. See 1548th meeting of UNGA, 4 July 1967, *United Nations General Assembly Official Records, 1967, Fifth Emergency Special Session,* p.16.

135. The draft proposal was co-sponsored by Argentina, Barbados, Bolivia, Brazil, Chile, Colombia, Costa Rica, Dominican Republic, Ecuador, El Salvador, Guatemala, Guyana, Honduras, Jamaica, Mexico, Nicaragua, Panama, Paraguay, Trinidad and Tobago and Venezuela. *Index to Proceedings of United Nations General Assembly, Fifth Emergency Special Session, 22nd Session, 1967,* p.7.

136. See 1548th meeting of UNGA, 4 July 1967, *United Nations General Assembly Official Records, 1967, Fifth Emergency Special Session,* p.17.

137. The draft resolution was co-sponsored by Afghanistan, Argentina, Austria, Belgium, Brazil, Canada, Chile, Denmark, Ethiopia, Finland, Iceland, India, Iran, Ireland, Italy, Japan, Liberia, Niger, Nigeria, Norway, Pakistan, Rwanda, Singapore, Sweden, Turkey and Yugoslavia. See *Index to Proceedings . of United Nations General Assembly, Fifth Emergency Special Session, 22nd Session, 1967,* p.7.

138. See 1548th meeting of UNGA, 4 July 1967, *United Nations General Assembly Official Records, 1967, Fifth Emergency Special Session,* p.17.

139. See www.un.org

140. The draft proposal was co-sponsored by Guinea, Iran, Mali, Niger, Pakistan and Turkey. See *Index to Proceedings of United Nations General Assembly, Fifth Emergency Special Session, 22nd Session, 1967,* p.7.

141. *Ibid,* p.8.

142. See 'Law and Administration Ordinance (Amendment No.11) Law, 27 June 1967. Municipal Corporation Ordinance (Amendment) Law, 1967', in Meron Medzini (ed.) *Israel's Foreign Relations, Selected Documents 1947–1974, vol.1* (Ministry for Foreign Affairs, Jerusalem, 1976), p.245 and Miller, *Ireland,* p.38. It should be noted that then Israeli Prime Minister Levi Eshkol, stated that 'no harm whatsoever shall come to the places

sacred to all religions' and that the religious leaders of the Old City 'may continue their spiritual activities unhindered' whilst 'arrangements in connection with the Moslem Holy Places shall be made by a council of Moslem clerics.' See 'Prime Minister Levi Eshkol's Address to the Spiritual Leaders of all communities in Jerusalem, 7 June 1967', Medzini, *Israel's Foreign*, p.244. This approach was also taken by then Israeli Defence Minister, Moshe Dayan, when he declared on the day that the IDF liberated the Old City of Jerusalem and ended nineteen years of Jordanian rule, 'to our Arab neighbours we extend, also at this hour-and with added emphasis at this hour-our hand in peace. And to our Christian and Muslim fellow citizens, we solemnly promise full religious freedom and rights'. See 'Statement at the Western Wall by Defence Minister Dayan, 7 June 1967', *Ibid*, p.243.

143. See 1548th meeting of UNGA, 4 July 1967, *United Nations General Assembly Official Records, 1967, Fifth Emergency Special Session*, p.18.

144. The draft proposal was co-sponsored by Afghanistan, Guinea, Iran, Malaysia, Mali, Pakistan, Somalia and Turkey. See *Index to Proceedings of United Nations General Assembly, Fifth Emergency Special Session, 22nd Session, 1967*, p.7.

145. *Ibid*, p.8.

146. See 1554th meeting of UNGA, 14 July 1967, *United Nations General Assembly Official Records, 1967, Fifth Emergency Special Session*, pp.8–9.

147. See www.un.org

148. Co-sponsored by Austria, Finland and Sweden. See *Index to Proceedings of United Nations General Assembly, Fifth Emergency Special Session, 22nd Session, 1967*, p.7.

149. *Ibid*, p.8.

150. Co-sponsored by Austria, Finland, and Sweden. See *Index to Proceedings of United Nations General Assembly, Fifth Emergency Special Session, 22nd Session, 1967*, p.7.

151. *Ibid*, p.8.

152. See 1558th meeting of UNGA, 21 July 1967, *United Nations General Assembly Official Records, 1967, Fifth Emergency Special Session*, p.16. Iraq, Jordan, Kuwait, Lebanon, Libya, Morocco, Saudi Arabia, Syria, Tunisia, UAR, Yemen, and Algeria voted against the draft resolution. *Ibid*.

153. See 1559th meeting of UNGA, 18 September 1967, *United Nations General Assembly Official Records, 1967, Fifth Emergency Special Session*, p.1.

154. See Yifru's speech, 1683rd meeting of UNGA, 7 October 1968, *United Nations General Assembly Official Records, Plenary Meetings, Resolutions, 23rd Session, 1968*, pp.2–3.

155. *Ibid*, p.3.
156. See Yifru's speech, 1776th meeting of UNGA, 2 October 1969, *United Nations General Assembly Official Records, Plenary Meetings, 24th Session, 1969*, p.5.
157. See UNGA resolution 2443 (XXIII), Respect for and Implementation of Human Rights in Occupied Territories, 19 December 1968, see www.un.org. The committee consisted of three Member States: Malaysia, Senegal and Sri Lanka. For an account of the structure and role of the Committee, see www.un.org
158. See www.un.org
159. See 1748th meeting of UNGA, 19 December 1968, *United Nations General Assembly Official Records, 23rd Session, 1968*, p.7.
160. Co-sponsored by Argentina, Iran, Pakistan, Senegal, Turkey and Yugoslavia. See *Index to Proceedings of United Nations General Assembly, 23rd Session, 1968*, p.69 and 633rd meeting of the Special Political Committee, 11 December 1968, *United Nations General Assembly Official Records, 23rd Session*, p.3.
161. See 633rd meeting of the Special Political Committee, 11 December 1968, *United Nations General Assembly Official Records, 23rd Session*, p.3.
162. See Selassie's speech, 1882nd meeting of UNGA, 23 October 1970, *United Nations General Assembly Official Records, Plenary Meetings, vols.I and II, 25th Session, 1970*, p.3.
163. See 1896th meeting of UNGA, 4 November 1970, *United Nations General Assembly Official Records (vol. III) Resolutions, Special Political Committee, 25th Session, 1970*, p.12.
164. See UNGA Resolution 2628, www.un.org
165. Co-sponsored by Afghanistan, Guinea, Indonesia, Malaysia, Mali, Mauritania, Pakistan and Somalia. See *Index to Proceedings of United Nations General Assembly, 25th Session 1970*, p.75 and 743rd meeting of the Special Political Committee, 4 December 1970 *United Nations General Assembly Official Records, 25th Session 1970*, p.301.
166. *Ibid*.
167. The Organisation of African Unity (OAU) was established on 25 May 1963, in Addis Ababa, Ethiopia. In that year, it comprised 32 independent Member States. The OAU was disbanded in 2002 and became the African Union.
168. See Tseghe's speech, 1963rd meeting of UNGA, 12 October 1971, *United Nations General Assembly Official Records Plenary Meetings, volume 2, 26th Session, 1971*, p.2.
169. See 792nd meeting of the Special Political Committee, 1 December 1971, *United Nations General Assembly Official Records, 26th Session 1971*, p.251.

170. Co-sponsored by Afghanistan, Indonesia, Malaysia, Mali, Pakistan, Senegal, Somalia and Yugoslavia, See *Index to Proceedings of United Nations General Assembly, 26th Session, 1971*, p.65.

171. See Haile's speech, 2063rd meeting of UNGA, 11 October 1972, *United Nations General Assembly Official Records, Plenary Meetings, Volume II, 27th Session, 1972*, p.15.

172. Ethiopia voted in favour of the draft resolution, co-sponsored by Afghanistan, Cameroon, Congo (People's Republic), Cyprus, Equatorial Guinea, Ethiopia, Guinea, India, Indonesia, Iran, Malaysia, Mali, Mauritania, Mauritius, Nigeria, Pakistan, Somalia, Spain, United Republic of Tanzania, Yugoslavia and Zambia. See *Index to Proceedings of United Nations General Assembly, 26th Session, 1971*, pp.58–59 and 2016th meeting of UNGA, 13 December 1971, *United Nations General Assembly Official Records, 26th Session 1971*, p.34.

173. See 2016th meeting of UNGA, 13 December 1971, *United Nations General Assembly Official Records, 26th Session 1971*, p.34.

174. See www.unispal.un.org/. The *aide-memoire* called on Israel, *inter alia*, 'to withdraw forces from occupied United Arab Republic territory to the former international boundary between Egypt and the British mandate of Palestine, on the understanding that satisfactory arrangements are made for establishing de-militarised zones; practical security arrangements in the Sharm-el-Sheikh area for guaranteeing freedom of navigation through the Straits of Tiran and freedom of navigation through the Suez Canal'. See *United Nations Security Council Official Records, 26th Year, Supplements for October, November and December 1971*, p.58. It is worth noting that Ambassador Gunnar Jarring, then Special Representative to the Secretary-General for the Middle East, imagined guaranteeing freedom of navigation through the Straits of Tiran to mean '... a United Nations force in the area for this purpose'. See *Ibid.*

175. See www.unispal.un.org/

176. Bard, 'The Evolution'.

177. Erlich, *Ethiopia*, p.172.

Chapter 7   Ethiopia and Israel, 1973–82: Pressure and Resistance

1. Haile Selassie had reached the age of 80 in 1972 and the issue of succession became a divisive factor in Ethiopian politics. In October 1973, the political element that had pushed for appeasement with the Arab world trumped its

rivals and the emperor was persuaded. See, Erlich, *Ethiopia and the Middle East*, p.165.

2. Bard, 'The Evolution'. It was not only Ethiopia that felt Arab pressure. Indeed, members of the OAU succeeded in garnering support for their policy on the Middle East in black Africa. This was largely due to African countries being adversely affected by the oil crisis and the financial inducements that the OAU offered for compliant countries. See Lawrence P. Frank, 'Israel and Africa; the Era of Tachlis', *Journal of Modern African Studies*, vol.26, no.1, (March 1988), pp.151–155, p.152.

3. Cited in Peters, *Israel and Africa*, pp.45–46.

4. For more details see, *Ibid*, p.43.

5. *Ibid*, p.150.

6. *Ibid*, pp.151 and 154. The relationship would become its most problematic when allegations arose that Israel and South Africa were co-operating in the production of a nuclear bomb.

7. Indeed, between 1972–73, 28 African countries severed their relations with Israel. Only three, Lesotho, Swaziland and Malawi, resisted. See Decalo, *Israel and Africa*, p.135.

8. Cited in Erlich, *Ethiopia and the Middle East*, p.173. Joel Peters maintains there is scant evidence to suggest that Islamic solidarity was a meaningful factor behind the severance of ties. Rather, Islam had been a divisive issue between Arab and African countries in the past. See Peters, *Israel and Africa*, p.48.

9. Erlich, *Ethiopia*, p.174.

10. Bard, 'The Evolution'. In 1973, the fruits of co-operation between the two countries included a blood bank, a geological survey, a hotel training programme, instruction on port development and fisheries and a joint microbiology teaching and research project. These were in addition to the military interactions. See 'Israel and Ethiopia', *Journal of Palestine Studies*, vol.14, no.4, (Summer 1985), pp.194–196, p.195.

11. See Kassim Shehim, 'Israel-Ethiopian Relations: Change and Continuity', *Northeast African Studies*, vol.10, no.1, (1988), pp.25–39.

12. Bard, 'The Evolution'. The Provisional Military Administrative Committee, which was behind the overthrow of Selassie, vowed to eradicate the feudal social system. For a description of the taxation system, see Schwab, 'Cold War', p.11. Chanan Aynor, a former Israeli Ambassador to Ethiopia, blamed the US for Selassie's decision and his subsequent removal. According to Aynor, in the spring of 1973, Selassie had asked the Nixon administration for urgent aid in combating the Eritrean threat. However, Nixon was in the midst of

the Watergate scandal and was not forthcoming. See Bard, 'The Evolution'. In 1973, there were 19 Israeli experts working in Africa on a short-term basis and 19 on a long-term basis. The severing of diplomatic relations generally did not affect trade between Israel and Africa. In fact, Israeli exports to Africa amounted to approximately 4–5 per cent of the total volume of Israeli exports and Israeli imports were a small fraction of Africa's total imports. Ethiopia, though, claimed the highest proportion of Israeli imports, approximately 2.5 per cent of its imports and exports to Israel accounted for approximately 1.5 per cent of its exports. In 1973, Israeli exports to Ethiopia totalled approximately US$4 million, while Israel's imports from Ethiopia totalled US$4.4 million. See Peters, *Israel and Africa*, pp.65–70.

13. See Haile's speech, 2127th meeting of UNGA, 25 September 1973, *United Nations General Assembly Official Records, 28th Session, 1973*, p.14.

14. *Ibid.*

15. See Gabre-Sellassie's speech, 2257th meeting of UNGA, 4 October 1974, *United Nations General Assembly Official Records, 29th Session, 1974*, p.479.

16. *Ibid.*

17. Erlich, *Ethiopia*, p.174.

18. 'Israel and Ethiopia', p.196. In 1974, Israeli exports to Ethiopia totalled some US$5.5 million, while Israel's imports from Ethiopia totalled US$4.6 million. See Peters, *Israel and Africa*, pp.69–70.

19. Asher Naim, Israel's first ambassador to Ethiopia after diplomatic ties between Israel and Ethiopia resumed in 1989, is reported to have said that, had Israel still had a presence in Ethiopia in 1974, it is possible that the revolution may never have occurred. Interview with Asher Naim in Jennifer A. Joyce, *Ethiopia's Foreign Relations with Israel, 1955–1998*, (MA thesis, Howard University: Washington D.C., 2000), p.52.

20. The US may also have benefited from data acquired by the advisors as its presence in the country lessened. Bard, 'The Evolution' and 'Israel and Ethiopia', p.196. In particular, the Israelis are reported to have been involved with the training of Addis Abba police and an elite guard unit. *Ibid.* The US, by 1974, had virtually closed their base, Kagnew, near Asmara, and opened a new one on Diego Garcia. See Schwab, 'Cold War', p.12. The US was losing its influence in Ethiopia, while the USSR was strengthening its presence in Somalia. *Ibid,* p.9. Among the fruits of the military co-operation between Israel and Ethiopia were bases that the Israelis had constructed on Ethiopian islands in the *Bab el-Mandeb* straits. See Ethan A. Nadelmann, 'Israel and Black Africa: A Rapprochement?' *Journal of Modern African Studies,* vol.19, no.2 (June 1981), pp.183–219. Also, on 28 February 1977, the presidents of Egypt, Syria and Sudan met in Khartoum and issued a joint

statement, suggesting that the issue of stability in the Red Sea area had become a matter of urgency for the Arabs, and that Ethiopia and Israel were colluding to make possible moves against peace in the area. Moreover, Assad of Syria revealed to the press that the three Arab leaders viewed the Red Sea as an Arab sea, as Ethiopia had lost its foothold there in the wake of the success of the Eritrean struggle. See Erlich, *The Struggle*, p.82. At the OAU summit of July 1975, the Arab states, led by Libya, demanded that Israel be expelled from the UN, a demand which was rejected. As a result, the meeting adopted an alternative proposal from Egypt, calling on the members of the OAU to work with other states, with the aim of removing Israel from the UN, as long as it refused to withdraw from 'occupied Arab territories'. In addition, it was decided that the OAU should not boycott Israel, as the Arab states had done. See Peters, *Israel and Africa*, p.74.

21. Cited in Erlich, *The Struggle*, p.103. The worsening relations between Ethiopia and her Arab neighbours were exacerbated by the death of General Andom, an Eritrean with ties to Sudan. Mengistu Haile Mariam was allegedly involved in this incident. As a result, many Arab states strengthened their support for the Eritrean cause.

22. Shehim, 'Israel', p.33.

23. In 1975, Ethiopia had seven trainees in Israel. Israel's exports to Ethiopia totalled US$ 4.4 million and Israel's imports from Ethiopia totalled US$5.6 million. See Peters, *Israel and Africa*, pp.68–69.

24. In 1975, the Ethiopian regime had requested approximately US$25 million from the US in order to combat the Eritrean secessionist forces. After much deliberating, the US sent aid to the value of approximately US$7 million. This was the beginning of the end of the US-Ethiopian relationship. See Schwab, 'Cold War', p.16.

25. Cited in Erlich, *The Struggle*, p.104. The IAF, sent pilots to Ethiopia to aid in the airlift of goods to Ethiopian forces in the fight against Eritrea. Israeli aid did not cease there and eventually saw the Jewish state supply Ethiopia with T-54 and T-55 tanks captured from Arab forces during the Yom Kippur war and vital spare parts for F5 fighter aircraft. See Peters, *Israel and Africa*, p.71.

26. See Wodajo's speech, 2374th meeting of UNGA, 3 October 1975, *United Nations General Assembly Official Records, 30th Session, 1975*, p.430.

27. See 2400th meeting of UNGA, 10 November 1975, www.mfa.gov.il

28. See Wodajo's speech, 28th meeting of UNGA, 12 October 1976, *United Nations General Assembly Official Records, 31st Session, 1976*, p.541.

29. *Ibid.*

30. See Bekele's speech, 77th meeting of UNGA, 24 November 1976, *United Nations General Assembly Official Records, 31st Session, 1976*, p.1195.
31. It is noteworthy that in 1976, Israeli exports to Ethiopia totalled US$ 7.6 million, an increase of US$ 3.2 million from the previous year, whilst Israel's imports from Ethiopia totalled US$ 4.5 million. See Peters, *Israel and Africa*, pp.69–70.
32. See Olusola Ojo, *Africa and Israel: Relations in Perspective* (Westview Press: Colorado, 1988), p.73.
33. Bard, 'The Evolution'. Indeed, in September 1977, the Soviets delivered 48 MIG fighters, 200 T-54 and T-55 tanks and SAM-3 and SAM-7, anti-aircraft missiles. In addition to the military hardware, a number of Cuban military advisors arrived in Ethiopia in the summer of 1977, in order to mould a civilian force that would aid in countering the Eritrean forces. This, the USSR did in the hope that it would not jeopardise its relationship with Somalia. To this end, Fidel Castro's trip to both Somalia and Ethiopia in 1977 was an attempt to bring the two countries together. For the USSR, even though it was expelled from Somalia in 1977, control of the port of Massawa allowed it access to Israel and would allow it the potential of turning the Red Sea into a Soviet asset. It could then disrupt international communication and trade lines. See, Schwab, 'Cold War', p.17.
34. After being elected in 1977, Menachem Begin attempted to convince Carter to restore US aid to Ethiopia, to no avail. Bard, 'The Evolution'.
35. See Schwab, 'Cold War', p.10.
36. Dayan's *faux pas* may not have been inadvertent, as it came at a time of increased Soviet activity in Ethiopia. Ojo, *Africa*, p.75.
37. See Moshe Dayan, *Breakthrough: A Personal Account of the Egypt-Israel Peace Negotiations* (Alfred A. Knopf: New York, 1981), p.52.
38. See Gedle Giorgis's speech, 31st meeting of UNGA, 11 October 1978, *Provisional Verbatim Records of United Nations General Assembly, 33rd Session, 1978*, pp.67–68.
39. *Ibid,* p.68.
40. See Ibrahim's speech, 66th meeting of UNGA, 30 November 1978, *Provisional Verbatim Records of United Nations General Assembly, 33rd Session, 1978*, p.28.
41. *Ibid.*
42. *Ibid,* pp.28–30.
43. Peters, *Israel and Africa*, p.94.
44. Bard, 'The Evolution'. Begin's desire to introduce a Jewish element in Israel's relationship with Ethiopia was not accepted unanimously by his cabinet. See Israel and Ethiopia', p.196. Begin had asked Mengistu in 1977 to allow

200 Jews to leave Ethiopia and fly to Israel on an Israeli military jet that had been emptied of its cargo. Mengistu obliged and, what was in effect the precursor to Operation Moses, was a success. However, the fledgling exodus was terminated by Dayan's *faux pas*. It was not until 11 March 1975, that an inter-ministerial committee decreed that Israel grant automatic citizenship and benefits to Ethiopian Jews, under the Jewish state's Law of Return. Shehim, 'Israel', p.25.

45. Edward Alexander, 'Operation Moses, *Commentary*, (July 1985), pp.45–50. It is worth noting that Ethiopian Jews were being smuggled in and out of Sudan, on both large and small scales, from the 1970s. For more on this matter, see, Ahmed Kardawi, 'The Smuggling of the Ethiopian Falasha to Israel through Sudan, *African Affairs*, vol.90, no.358, (January 1991), pp.23–49. In addition, Sudan's President, Jaafar Nimeiry, allowed Israel to open a Mossad office in Khartoum as a result of the growing co-operation between the two countries. For more on this matter, see Jacob Abadi, 'Israel and Sudan: the Saga of an Enigmatic Relationship', *Middle Eastern Studies*, vol.35, no.3, (July 1999) pp.19–41.

46. See Gedle-Giorgis's speech, 21st meeting of UNGA, 4 October 1979, *United Nations General Assembly Official Records, 34th Session, 1979*, p.434.

47. *Ibid*.

48. *Ibid*.

49. Peters, *Israel and Africa*, p.94.

50. See Deressa's speech, 83rd meeting of UNGA, 29 November 1979, *Provisional Verbatim Records of United Nations General Assembly, 34th Session*, p.33.

51. *Ibid*.

52. *Ibid*, pp.33–35.

53. *Ibid,* pp.34–35.

54. Alexander, 'Operation Moses', p.46.

55. 'The Flight of the Ethiopian Jews', *Africa Now,* no.45 (January 1985), p.11.

56. *Ibid*.

57. Peters, *Israel and Africa*, p.94.

58. See Gedle-Giorgis's speech, 22nd meeting of UNGA, 1 October 1981, *United Nations General Assembly Official Records, 36th Session, 1981*, p.445.

59. *Ibid*.

60. See Gedle-Giorgis's speech, 22nd meeting of UNGA, 7 October 1982, *United Nations General Assembly Official Records, 37th Session, 1982*, p.403.

BIBLIOGRAPHY

Primary Sources

1. **Archival Material**
   The Public Records Office of the United Kingdom
   Foreign Office (FO)
   Foreign and Commonwealth Office (FCO)

2. **Official Documents**

CENTO unclassified document

Israel's Foreign Relations: Selected Documents, vol. 1, 1947–1974, Ministry of Foreign Affairs: Jerusalem
Official Records of the United Nations General Assembly, Sessions 1–37, 1946–1982, United Nations: New York
Official Records of the United Nations Security Council, Sessions 1–37, 1946–1982, United Nations: New York

3. **Memoirs**

Ben-Gurion, David. *'Al ha-hityashvut: kovets devarim, 1915–1956*, (ha-Kibbutz ha-me'uhad: Tel Aviv, 1986)
———— *Ba-ma'arakhah*, (Mifleget Poaley Erets Yisrael: Tel Aviv, 1947)
———— *Medinat Yisra'el ha mehudeshet*, (Am Oved: Tel Aviv, 1969)
Dayan, Moshe. *Breakthrough: A Personal Account of the Egypt-Israel Peace Negotiations*, (Alfred A. Knopf: New York, 1981)
Eytan, Walter. *The First Ten Years: A Diplomatic History of Israel*, (Simon and Schuster: New York, 1958)
Meir, Golda. *My Life*, (Weidenfeld and Nicolson: London, 1975)
Pahlavi, Mohammed Reza. *Mission for my Country*, (Hutchinson: UK, 1961)
Pahlavi, Mohammed Reza. *The Shah's Story*, (Michael Joseph: London, 1980)
Rafael, Gideon. *Destination Peace: Three Decades of Israeli Foreign Policy, A Personal Memoir*, (Weidenfeld and Nicolson: London, 1981)
Sharett, M., *Yoman Ishi*, (Sifriat Ma'ariv: Tel Aviv, 1978)

4. Newspapers

Daily Express
Financial Times
The Guardian
Haaretz
The Independent
The Jerusalem Post
London Evening Standard
Maariv
The New Republic
New Statesman
The New York Times
The Observer
The Spectator
Sunday Express
The Sunday Independent
The Times (London)
The Weekly Standard
The Washington Post
Yediot Ahoronot

Journals

'Africans, Arabs and Israelis, a Triad of Suffering Peoples.' Interview with President Senghor of Senegal in *Africa Report*, vol.17, no.7 (July-August 1972), pp.11–13

'Israel, the Arabs and Africa', interview with Israeli Ambassador Yaakov Shimoni *Africa Report*, vol.21, no.4, (July-August 1976), pp.51–55

Secondary Material

1. Books

Abadi, J., *Israel's Quest for Recognition and Acceptance in Asia: Garrison State Diplomacy*, (Frank Cass: London, 2004)

Aksin, S., *Turkey: from empire to revolutionary republic: the emergence of the Turkish nation from 1789 to the present*, (Hurst and Company: London, 2007)

Amirsadeghi, H., (ed.) *Twentieth Century Iran*, (Heinemann: London, 1977)

Ansari, A.M., *Confronting Iran: The Failure of American Foreign Policy and the Roots of Mistrust*, (Hurst and Company: London, 2006)

Bailey, S.D., *The Making of Resolution 242*, (Martinus Nijhoff: Dordrect, The Netherlands, 1985)

————— *Four Arab-Israeli Wars and the Peace Process*, (Macmillan: London, 1990)

Bard, M.G., *From Tragedy to Triumph: the Politics Behind the Rescue of Ethiopian Jewry*, (Praeger: Westport, Conn., 2002)

Bar-Joseph, U., *The Watchman Fell Asleep: The Surprise of Yom Kippur and its Sources*, (State University of New York Press: New York, 2005)

Bar-On, M., *The Gates of Gaza: Israel's Road to Suez and Back, 1955–1957*, (Palgrave Macmillan: New York, 1994)

Bayne, E.A., *Persian Kingship in Transition: Conversations with a Monarch Whose Office Is Traditional and Whose Goal is Modernisation*, (American Universities Field Staff Inc, 1968)

Becker, J., *The PLO; The Rise and Fall of the Palestine Liberation Organisation* (Weidenfeld and Nicolson: London, 1984)

Bengio. O., *The Turkish-Israeli Relationship Changing Ties of Middle Eastern Outsiders*, (Palgrave Macmillan: New York, 2004)

Bill, J.A., *The Eagle and the Lion: The Tragedy of American-Iranian Relations*, (Yale University Press: Yale, 1988)

Brecher, M., *The Foreign Policy System of Israel: Setting, Images, Process*, (Yale University Press: Yale, 1972)

Brenchley, F., *Britain, The Six Day War and its Aftermath*, (I.B.Tauris: London, 2005)

Bull, O., *War and Peace In The Middle East: The Experiences and Views of a UN Observer*, (Leo Cooper: London, 1976)

Caradon, Lord, Goldberg A.J., El-Zayyat M.H., and Eban, A., *UN Security Council Resolution 242: A Case Study In Diplomatic Ambiguity*, (Institute for the Study of Diplomacy, Edmund A. Walsh School of Foreign Service, Georgetown University: Washington D.C., 1981)

Çarkoglu, A. and Rubin, B., *Religion and Politics in Turkey*, (Routledge: London, 2006)

Chubin, S., and Sabih, S., *The Foreign Relations of Iran: A Developing State in a Zone of Great-Power Conflict*, (University of California Press: California, 1974)

Churchill, R.S., *The Six Day War*, (Heinemann: London, 1967)

Crockatt, R., *The Fifty Years War: The United States and the Soviet Union in World Politics, 1941–1991*, (Routledge: London, 1995)

Decalo, S., *Israel and Africa: Forty Years, 1956–1996*, (Florida Academic Press: Florida, 1998)

Eliav, A.L., *Te'ome Tseviyah*, ('Am 'oved: Tel Aviv, 2005)

Elm, M., *Oil, Power, and Principle: Iran's Oil Nationalization and its Aftermath*, (Syracuse University Press: New York, 1992)

Erlich, H., *Ethiopia and the Challenge of Independence*, (Lynne Rienner Publishers: Colorado, 1986)

———— *Ethiopia and the Middle East*, (Lynne Rienner Publishers: Colorado, 1994)

———— *The Struggle over Eritrea, 1962–1978: War and Revolution in the Horn of Africa*, (Hoover International Press, Stanford University: California, 1983)

Eshed, H., *Reuven Shiloah The Man Behind the Mossad Secret Diplomacy in the Creation of Israel*, (Frank Cass: London, 1997)

Garfinkle, A., *Politics and Society in Modern Israel Myths and Realities*, (M.E. Sharpe: New York, 1997)

Golan, S., *Gevul ha milhamah ha karah: hitgabshut mediniyut ha-bitahon shel Yisra'el, 1949–1953*, (Tsahal, Hotsa'at 'Ma'arakhot', Mi'srad ha-bitahon: Tel Aviv, 2000)

Gonzalez, N., *Engaging Iran: the Rise of a Middle East Powerhouse and America's Strategic Choice*, (Praeger Security International: Westport, Conn., 2007)

Greenfield, R., *Ethiopia: A New Political History*, (Pall Mall Press: London, 1965)

Hakan, M.Y., and Esposito, J., (eds.), *Turkish Islam and the Secular State: the Gülen Movement*, (Syracuse University Press: New York, 2003)

Hale, W., *Turkish Foreign Policy 1774–2000*, (Frank Cass: London, 2000)

Halliday, F., and Molyneux, M., *The Ethiopian Revolution*, (Verso: London, 1981)

Harbeson, J.H., *The Ethiopian Transformation: the Quest for the Post-Imperial State*, (Westview Press: Colorado, 1988)

Herman, T., and Twite, R., (eds.) *ha-Ma'sa u-matan ha-Yi'sre'eli-'Arvi : 'amadot mediniyot u-misgarot mu'sagiyot*, (Papirus, Merkaz Tami Shtainmets le-me-hkere shalom: Tel Aviv, 1993)

Herzl, T., *Old-Newland*, (Bloch Publishing Company: New York, 1960)

Herzog, H., *The Arab-Israeli Wars: War and Peace in the Middle East*, (Random House: New York, 1984)

Hiro, D., *Iran Under The Ayatollahs*, (Routledge: London, 1987)

Hoveyda, F., *The Shah and the Ayatollah: Iranian Mythology and Islamic Revolution*, (Praeger: Colorado, 2003)

Inbar. E., *The Israeli-Turkish Entente*, (Mediterranean Studies: King's College London, 2002)

Kalaycioglu, E., *Turkish Dynamics: Bridge Across Troubled Lands*, (Palgrave Macmillan: Basingstoke, 2005)

Karniel, M., *Menahem Begin: deyokan shel manhig*, (R. Mass: Jerusalem, 1998)

Karsh, E., (ed.), *The Iran-Iraq War: Impact and Implications*, (The Jaffee Centre for Strategic Studies: Tel Aviv University, Israel, 1987)

Karsh E., and Karsh, I., *Empires of the Sand: The Struggle for Mastery in the Middle East 1789–1923*, (Harvard University Press: Harvard, 1999)

Katz, S.M., *Guards without Frontiers: Israel's War against Terrorism*, (Arms and Armour: London, 1990)

Klieman, A., *Statecraft in the Dark: Israel's Practice of Quiet Diplomacy*, (Jaffee Centre for Strategic Studies: Israel, 1988)

Kumaraswamy, P.R., *Historical Dictionary of the Arab-Israeli Conflict*, (Scarecrow Press: Maryland, 2006)

———— (ed.), *Revisiting the Yom Kippur War*, (Frank Cass, Oregon, 2000)

Kyle, K., *Suez*, (Weidenfeld and Nicolson: London, 1991)

Laufer, L., *Israel and the Developing Countries: New Approaches to Co-Operation*, (Twentieth Century Fund: New York, 1967)

Liel, A., *Turkey in the Middle East: Oil, Islam and Politics*, (Lynne Rienner Publishers: Colorado, 2001)

Medzini, M., (ed.), *Israel's Foreign Relations: Selected Documents 1947–1974, vol.1*, (Ministry for Foreign Affairs: Jerusalem, 1976)

Meeker, M.E., *A Nation of Empire: the Ottoman Legacy of Turkish Modernity*, (University of California Press: California, 2002)

Menashri, D., *Post-Revolutionary Politics in Iran, Religion, Society and Power*, (Frank Cass: London, 2001)

———— (ed.), *The Iranian Revolution and the Muslim World*, (Westview Press, Colorado, 1990)

Miglietta. J.P., *American Alliance Policy in the Middle East, 1945–1992: Iran, Israel and Saudi Arabia*, (Lexington Books: Maryland, 2002)

Miller, R., *Ireland and the Palestine Question 1948–2004*, (Irish Academic Press: Dublin, 2005)

Nachmani. A., *Israel, Turkey and Greece: Uneasy Relations in the East Mediterranean*, (Frank Cass: London, 1987)

———— *Turkey: Facing A New Millennium Coping With Intertwined Conflicts*, (Manchester University Press: Manchester, 2003)

Ojo, O., *Africa and Israel: Relations in Perspective*, (Westview Press: Colorado, 1988)

Oren, M., *Six Days of War: June 1967 and the Making of the Modern Middle East*, (Oxford University Press: Oxford, 2002)

Panah, M., *The Islamic Republic and the World: Global Dimensions of the Iranian Revolution*, (Pluto Press: London, 2007)

Paolucci, H., *Iran, Israel and the United States*, (Griffon House Publications: New York, 1991)

Pearlman, M., *Ben Gurion Looks Back in Talks with Moshe Pearlman*, (Weidenfeld and Nicolson: London, 1965)

Peters, J., *Israel and Africa: The Problematic Friendship*, (I.B.Tauris: London, 1992)

Pope, N., and Pope, H., *Turkey Unveiled: A History of Modern Turkey*, (The Overlook Press: New York, 2004)

Rabinovich, A., *The Yom Kippur War: The Epic Encounter that Transformed the Middle East*, (Schocken Books: New York, 2004)

Rabinovich, I., *The War for Lebanon, 1970–1985*, (Cornell University Press: Ithaca, 1985)

Rabinovich, I., and Reinharz, J., (eds.), *Israel in the Middle East: Documents and Readings on Society, Politics and Foreign Relations, 1948-present*, (Oxford University Press: Oxford, 1984)

Rahnema, A., and Nomani, F., *The Secular Miracle: Religion, Politics and Economic Policy in Iran*, (Zed Books: London, 1990)

Ramazani, R.K., *Revolutionary Iran: Challenge and Response in the Middle East*, (The John Hopkins University Press: Maryland, 1986)

Raviv, D., and Melman,Y., *Every Spy a Prince The Complete History of Israel's Intelligence Community*, (Houghton Mifflin Company: Boston, 1990)

Ridgeon, L., (ed.), *Religion and Politics in Modern Iran: A Reader*, (I.B.Tauris: London, 2005)

Robins, P., *Turkey and the Middle East*, (Chatham House: London, 1991)

────── *Turkish-Israeli Relations: From the Periphery to the Centre*, (The Emirates Centre for Strategic Studies and Research, 2001)

Rubinstein, A., *Me-Hertsel ad Rabin: ve-hal'ah, me'ah shenot Tsiyonut*, (Schocken: Tel Aviv, 1997)

Sachar, H.M., *A History of Israel: From the Rise of Zionism To Our Time*, (Basil Blackwell: Oxford, 1977)

Safran, N., *From War To War: The Arab-Israeli Confrontation, 1948–1967*, (Pegasus: New York, 1969)

────── *The United States and Israel*, (Harvard University Press: Harvard, 1963)

Schiff, Z., and Ya'ari, E., *Israel's Lebanon War*, (Unwin Paperbacks: London, 1986)

Schwab, P., *Haile Selassie I: Ethiopia's Lion of Judah*, (Nelson Hall: Chicago, 1979)

Selwyn. I.T., and Shemesh, M., *The Suez-Sinai Crisis 1956: Retrospective and Reappraisal*, (Frank Cass: London, 1990)

Shalom, Z., *Ke-esh be-'atsmotav : David Ben Gurion u-ma'ava ka v'al demut ha-medinah, 1963–1967*, (Kiryat 'Sedeh-Boker, Mekhon Ben-Guryon le-heker Yi'sra'el, ha-Tsiyonut u-moreshet Ben-Gurion, Hotsa'at ha-sefarim shel Universitat Ben-Gurion ba-Negev, 765: Be'er Sheva, Israel, 2004)

Shawcross, W., *The Shah's Last Ride: The Story of the Exile, Misadventures and Death of the Emperor*, (Chatto and Windus: London, 1988)

Shimshi, E., *Bahem yoter mi-kol: 'al sod ha-hatsla hah shel Tsahal*, (Mi'srad ha-bitahon: Tel Aviv, 2005)

Shlaim, A., *The Iron Wall: Israel and the Arab World*, (Penguin Press: London, 2000)

Sobhani. S., *The Pragmatic Entente: Israeli-Iranian Relations, 1948–1988*, (Praeger California, 1989)

Souresrafil, B., *Khomeini and Israel*, (I. Research Inc: England, 1988)

Teferra, H., *The Ethiopian Revolution, 1974–1991: from a Monarchical Autocracy to a Military Oligarchy*, (Kegan Paul International: London, 1997)

Tulloch, D., *Wingate*, (Macdonald and Company: London, 1972)

Yaniv, A., *Deterrence without the Bomb: The Politics of Israeli Strategy*, (Lexington Books: Maryland, 1987)

2. Articles

Abadi, J., 'Constraints and Adjustments in Greece's Policy Toward Israel', *Mediterranean Quarterly*, vol.11, no.4, (2000), pp.40–70

———— 'Israel and Sudan: the Saga of an Enigmatic Relationship', *Middle Eastern Studies*, vol.35, no.3, (July 1999), pp.19–41

———— 'Israel and Turkey: From Covert to Overt Relations' http://www.lib.unb.ca

Abrahamian, E., 'Communism and Communalism in Iran: The Tudeh and the Firqah-I Dimukrat', *International Journal of Middle East Studies*, vol.1, (1970), pp.291–316

———— 'Structural Causes of the Iranian Revolution', *MERIP Reports*, no.87, Iran's Revolution: The Rural Dimension, (May 1980), pp.21–26

———— 'The Guerrilla Movement in Iran, 1963–1977', *MERIP Reports*, no.86, The Left Forces in Iran, (March-April 1980), pp.3–15

Alexander, E., 'Operation Moses, *Commentary*, vol.80, no.1, (July 1985), pp.45–50

Alpher, J., 'Israel and the Iran-Iraq War', in *The Iran-Iraq War Impact and Implications*, Efraim K., (ed.), (The Jaffee Centre for Strategic Studies: Tel Aviv University, Israel, 1987), pp.154–170

Bahgat, G., 'The Islamic Republic and the Jewish State', *Israel Affairs*, vol.11, no.3, (July 2005), pp.517–534

Bali Aykan, M., 'The Palestinian Question in Turkish Foreign Policy from the 1950s to the 1990s', *International Journal of Middle East Studies*, vol.25, no.1, (February 1993), pp. 91–110

Bard, M.G., The Evolution of Israel's Africa Policy, http://www.jewishvirtual-library.org/jsource/Politics/africa.html

Bar-Zohar, M., 'Ben-Gurion and the Policy of the Periphery', in *Israel in the Middle East: Documents and Readings on Society, Politics, and Foreign Relations, 1948-present*, Itamar Rabinovich, and Jehuda Reinharz, (eds.) (Oxford University Press: Oxford, 1984)

Ber, C., and Sherman, M., 'Formula for Stability: Turkey plus Israel', *Middle East Quarterly*, vol.9, no.4, (Fall 2002), http://www.meforum.org

Bialer, U., 'The Iranian Connection in Israel's Foreign Policy - 1948–1951', *Middle East Journal*, vol.39, no.2, (Spring 1985), pp.292–315

Bishku, M. B., 'How Has Turkey Viewed Israel?' *Israel Affairs*, vol.12, no.1, (January 2006), pp.177–194

Bolukbasi, S., 'Behind the Turkish-Israeli Alliance: A Turkish View', *Journal of Palestine Studies*, vol.29, no.1, (Autumn, 1999), pp.21–35

Calabrese, J., 'Turkey and Iran: Limits of a Stable Relationship', *British Journal of Middle Eastern Studies*, vol.25, no.1, (May 1998), pp.75–94

Divon, H., 'MASHAV in Africa: the Israeli Government's Development Co-operation Program', *Israel and Africa, Assessing the Past, Envisioning the Future*, The Africa Institute, American Jewish Committee, The Harold Hartog School: Tel Aviv University, (2006), http://www.ajc.org

Eban, A., 'Reality and Vision in the Middle East an Israeli View', *Foreign Affairs*, vol.3, no.4, (July 1965), pp. 634–635

Editorial, 'Africans, Arabs and Israelis: a Triad of Suffering Peoples', Interview with President Senghor of Senegal in *Africa Report*, vol.17, no.7, (July-August 1972), pp.11–13

Editorial, 'Israel and Ethiopia', *Journal of Palestine Studies*, vol.14, no.4, (Summer 1985), pp.194–196

Editorial, 'Israel, the Arabs and Africa', *Africa Report*, vol.21 no.4, (July-August 1976), pp.51–55

Editorial, 'The Flight of the Ethiopian Jews, *Africa Now*, no.45, (January 1985), p.11

Editorial, 'The Israel-Iran Connection', Washington Report on Middle East Affairs *Journal of Palestine Studies*, vol.16, no.3, (Spring 1987), pp.210–212

Fatemi, K., 'The Iranian Revolution: Its Impact on Economic Relations with the United States', *International Journal of Middle East Studies*, vol.12, no.3, (November 1980), pp.303–317

Frank, L.P., 'Israel and Africa; the Era of Tachlis', *Journal of Modern African Studies*, vol.26, no.1, (March 1988), pp.151–155

Geokas, M.C., and Papathanasis, A. T., 'The Turkish-Israeli Axis, Greece and the Middle East', *Washington Report on Middle East Affairs*, (1999), http://www.demokritos.org/Axis_eng.htm

Gruen, G.E., 'Dynamic Progress in Turkish-Israeli Relation', *Israel Affairs*, vol.1, no.4, (Summer 1995), pp.40–70

——— 'Turkey's Relations with Israel and its Arab Neighbours: The Impact of Basic Interests and Changing Circumstances', *Middle East Review*, vol.17, no.3, (Spring 1985), pp.33–44

Jacob, A., 'Israel's Military Aid to Africa, 1960–1966', *Journal of Modern African Studies*, vol.9, no.2, (August 1971), pp.165–187

Kardawi, A., 'The Smuggling of the Ethiopian Falasha to Israel through Sudan', *African Affairs*, vol.90, no.358, (January 1991), pp.23–49

Keddie, N.R., 'Iranian Revolutions in Comparative Perspective', *American Historical Review*, vol.88, no.3, (June 1983), pp.579–598

Losman, D.L., 'The Arab Boycott of Israel', *International Journal of Middle East Studies*, vol.3, no.2, (April 1972), pp.99–122.

Margulies, R., and Yildizoglu, E., 'The Political Uses of Islam in Turkey', *Middle East Report*, (July-August 1988), p.12–17

Menashri, D., 'Iran, Israel and the Middle East Conflict', *Israel Affairs*, vol.12, no.1, (January 2006), pp.107–122

Mohammadi-Nejad, H., 'The Iranian Parliamentary Elections of 1975', *International Journal of Middle East Studies*, vol.8, no.1, (January 1977), pp.103–116

Nachmani, A., 'A Triangular Relationship: Turkish-Israeli Co-operation and its Implications for Greece,' *Cahiers d'études sur la Méditerranée Orientale et le Monde Turco-Iranien, no. 28, (Juin-Decembre 1999)*, www.ceri-sciencespo.com

Nadelmann, E.A., 'Israel and Black Africa: A Rapprochement?', *Journal of Modern African Studies*, vol.19, no.2, (June 1981), pp. 183–219

Nye, R.P., 'Civil-Military Confrontation in Turkey: The 1973 Presidential Election', *International Journal of Middle East Studies*, vol.8, (1977), pp.209–228

Oke, K., 'The Ottoman Empire, Zionism, and the Question of Palestine 1880–1908_International Journal of Middle East Studies,_ vol.14, no.3, (August 1982), pp.329–341

Podeh, E., 'Rethinking Israel in the Middle East', _Israel Affairs,_ vol.3, issue 3 and 4, (Spring 1997), pp.280–295

Ramazani, R.K., 'Emerging Patterns of Regional Relations in Iranian Foreign Policy' _Orbis,_ vol.18, no.4, (Winter 1975), pp.1043–1070

——— 'Iran and the Arab-Israeli Conflict', _Middle East Journal,_ vol.32, no.4, (Autumn 1978), pp. 414–415

——— 'Iran's 'White Revolution': A Study in Political Development', _International Journal of Middle East Studies,_ vol.5, no.2, (April 1974), pp.124–139

Richards, H., 'America's Shah, Shahanshah's Iran', _MERIP Reports,_ no.40, (September 1975), pp. 3–26

Schwab, P., 'Cold War on the Horn of Africa, _African Affairs,_ vol.77, no.306, (January 1978), pp.6–20

Segal, A., 'Israel in Africa', _Africa Report,_ vol.8, no.4, (April 1963), pp.19–21

Sever, A., 'The Compliant Ally? Turkey and the West in the Middle East 1954–58', _Middle Eastern Studies,_ vol.34, no.2, (April 1998), pp.73–90

Shehim, K., 'Israel-Ethiopian Relations: Change and Continuity', _Northeast African Studies,_ vol.10, no.1, (1988), pp.25–39

Weiker, W.F., 'Turkey, the Middle East and Islam', _Middle East Review,_ vol.17, no.3, (Spring 1985), pp.27–33

Weinbaum, M.G., 'Iran and Israel: The Discreet Entente', _Orbis,_ vol.18, no.4, (Winter 1975), pp.1070–1088

Yavuz, M.H., 'Turkish-Israeli Relations: Through the Lens of the Turkish Identity Debate', _Journal of Palestine Studies,_ vol.27, no.1, (Autumn 1997), pp.22–37

3. Policy Papers

Gronau, R., _Globalization's Implications for the Economy,_ Policy Paper no.36, (2002), The Israel Democracy Institute, http://www.idi.org.il

Kramer, M., and Kepel, G., _Islam, Islamists and US Foreign Policy,_ PolicyWatch 907, (11 October 2004), The Washington Institute for Near East Policy, http://www.washingtoninstitute.org

Makovsky, A., _Israeli-Turkish Co-operation: Full Steam Ahead,_ PolicyWatch 292, (6 January 1998), The Washington Institute for Near East Policy, http://www.washingtoninstitute.org

Muftuler Bac, M., _Turkey and Israel: An Evolving Partnership,_ Ariel Centre for Policy Research, Policy Paper 47, (1998), http://www.acpr.org.il

4. Journals

Middle East Record (Israel Universities Press: London, 1960–1970)

5. Theses

Gruen, G., *Turkey, Israel and the Palestine Question, 1948–1960: A Study in the Diplomacy of Ambivalence*, (PhD thesis, Columbia University, 1970)

Joyce, J., *Ethiopia's Foreign Relations with Israel, 1955–1998*, (MA thesis, Howard University, Washington D.C., 2000)

Reppa. R.B., *Israel and Iran: Their Development, Interrelationship and Effect on the Indian Ocean Basin* (PhD thesis, University of Maryland, 1973)

Soysal, O., *An Analysis of the Influences of Turkey's Alignment with the West and of the Arab-Israeli Conflict upon Turkish-Israeli and Turkish-Arab Relations, 1947–1977* (PhD thesis, Princeton University, 1983)

INDEX

Addis Ababa, 139, 140, 141, 145, 162
Abdoh, Djalal, 8–9, 11
Abyssinia, 31–2
Ad Hoc Committee on Palestine, 4
Adl, Mostafa, 4–5
Africa, Israeli's policy toward, 28–35,
    141–2, 163
Aklilou, Representative, 34
Al Aqsa Mosque, 50, 69, 94, 97, 105,
    199n83
Aliyah Bet, 6–7, 156
Almogi, Yosef, 90
Al-Quds, 77–8, 105–6
Anglo Iranian Oil Company (AIOC),
    6, 8, 9
anti-Jewish violence, 15
apartheid, 142
Arab boycott, 1, 12, 22, 166n4
Arab-Israeli peace process, 61, 64, 103,
    108, 161
Arab-Israeli war, 19, 46–58, 91–7, 123,
    124–40
Arab League, 1, 26, 166n3
Arab nationalism, 2, 16, 31, 39, 118
Arafat, Yasser, 68, 70
Ardalan, Ali Gholi, 10
Argov, Shlomo, 78–9
arms sales, 57, 66, 67, 73

Asia, 28
Atatürk, Kemal, 15, 16
atheism, 22
Aynor, Chanan, 143, 214n12

Baghdad Pact, 25, 39, 41, 177n139
Bakhtiar, Teymour, 56, 187n120
Balkan Defence Pact, 24–5
Bank of Israel, 12
Bayar, Prime Minister, 17
Baydur, Hüseyin Ragip, 18–19
Bayne, E.A., 43
Begin, Menachem, 64, 65, 78, 217n44
Ben-Gurion, David, 1–3, 28, 42, 44,
    45, 84, 119–20, 121
Britain, 36–9, 44, 119, 161
British Mandate, 89
British Petroleum (BP), 12, 39

Caglayangil, Ihsan Sabri, 91–4, 101–2,
    160
Camp David accords, 74, 75, 108, 151,
    152
Caradon, Lord, 127, 128, 129
Carter, Jimmy, 147
Castro, Fidel, 217n33
Christianity, 22
Coffee Project, 132, 140

Cohen, David Ha, 36
Cold War, 20, 164
colonisation, 142
communism, 2, 16, 17, 21, 22, 23,
    25, 30
Consul of Rhodes, 16
Cuban missile crisis, 88
Cyprus, 23–4, 87–91, 97, 107–8, 200n2

Dayan, Moshe, 44, 64, 121
Deressa, Yilma, 116–17, 151–2
Derg, 144–5, 148, 162, 163
development projects, 42–4, 52,
    118–19, 121
Druze, 2
Dulles, John Foster, 25, 84, 177n140

economic alliances, 1, 12, 22–3, 42–3
Egged, 121–2
Egypt, 2, 26, 31, 37, 38, 41, 49, 56–7,
    59, 60, 81, 97, 103, 117, 151, 157
Egyptian Revolution, 10
Eisenhower, Dwight, 84
Elrom, Efraim, 96
Entezam, Nasrollah, 11, 37, 38
Eralp, Orhan, 104–5
Erbakan, Necmettin, 107, 202n32
Eritrea, 32–3, 118, 122–3, 139, 145, 147
Eshkol, Levi, 51, 90
Ethiopia, 2, 156–7
    1956–1972, 116–40
    1973–1982, 141–54
    Arab relations, 124–5
    Jews in, 31, 150–4
    Lebanon War and, 163
    pre-1955 relations with, 28–35
    Six Day War and, 124–40, 160
    Somalia and, 118, 139, 147–8
    Suez War and, 116–17, 118, 158–9
    trade with, 120, 150, 153
    at the UNGA, 135–40
    at the UNSC, 124–35
    Yom Kippur War and, 141–2,
        145, 162

Europe, 3
Evren, Kenan, 107

First World War, see World War I
Fischer, Maurice, 83
foreign policy, 2
    see also Policy of the Periphery
    non-alignment policy, 5, 6
    pre-1955, 4–35
    of Turkey, 16
France, 16, 20, 36, 37
Freemasonry, 22

Gaza, 26–7, 64
Gedle-Giorgis, Feleke, 148–9, 151,
    153–4
Germany, 16, 22
Gideon Force, 31
Gocke, Onur, 113–14
Golan Heights, 109–10, 202n48
Goldberg, Arthur J., 208n86
Goodman, Allan, 77
Great Britain, 6, 8, 12, 13
Greece, 23–4, 88–91, 107–8, 120
Gunes, Turan, 98–9

Habt-Wold, Akilu, 132
Haile, Minasse, 142, 144, 162
Hamid, Abdul, 14, 15
Hatay, 16
Herzl, Theodore, 14, 30
Heywot, Ato Zaude, 33
Hezbollah, 80
Horn of Africa, 33, 34
Hoveyda, Fereydoun, 55, 57–8, 184n74
Hussein, King of Jordan, 46–7, 66
Hussein, Saddam, 56, 65, 69

Imperial Charter for the Colonisation of
    Palestine, 14–15
imperialism, 29, 31, 36, 72, 141–2,
    149–50
Inbar, Efraim, 97
India, 131

Indian Ocean, 34
Inonu, Ismet, 17
Iran, 2, 156
  1956–1972, 36–58
  1973–1982, 59–80
  Arab relations, 12, 13, 40–2, 55–6
  arms embargo on, 72–3
  Ayatollah Khomeini, 67–73
  domestic sphere in, 7
  Islamic Republic of, 68–73
  Jews in, 6, 71–2
  Lebanon War and, 73–80, 162–3
  oil sales by, 12–13, 38–9, 53–4, 57, 66
  pre-1955 relations with, 4–13
  revolution in, 67, 162–3, 191n42
  Shah of, 9–11, 38, 41–3, 45, 52, 55,
    56, 60–5, 67, 70, 72, 184n73,
    189n9
  Six Day War and, 46–58, 159
  Soviet Union and, 5, 9–10, 44, 168n8
  Suez War and, 37, 38, 158
  trade with, 40
  U.S. and, 5, 9, 72–3, 74, 191n37
  White Revolution, 45–6, 183n61
  Yom Kippur War and, 59–67, 161
Iranian National Jamboree, 42
Iran-Iraq war, 69, 75, 162
Iraq
  Baghdad Pact, 25, 39
  Jews in, 6–7
  Kurds, 65
  revolution in, 40, 46, 84
  Soviet Union and, 56
  Turkey and, 25–6
Islam, 21–2
Israel
  1956–1972, 36–58, 81–97, 116–40
  1973–1982, 59–80, 98–115, 141–54
  Africa and, 28–35
  Arab boycott of, 1, 12, 22, 166n4
  Asia and, 28
  emigration to, 19
  establishment of, 4–5
  Ethiopia and, 28–35, 116–54, 156–7

exclusion of, 1
foreign policy, 2. see also Policy of the
    Periphery
  Iran and, 4–13, 36–58, 59–80
  Lebanon and, 79–80, 110–15, 153–4
  Turkey and, 13–28, 81–97, 98–115,
    156, 165
  U.S. and, 19–20, 65–6, 79–80, 84
Israeli Defence Forces (IDF), 11, 78,
    130, 135
Izmir International Fair, 18

Javits, Jacob, 65–6
Jerusalem, 9, 49–50, 68, 93–4, 104–10,
    136–7, 201n23
Jerusalem Law, 104, 105, 107
Jewish Agency, 2, 17–18
Jewish community
  in Ethiopia, 31, 150–4
  in Iran, 6, 71–2
  in Iraq, 6–7
  in Palestine, 13–14, 15
  in Soviet Union, 21
  in Turkey, 18
Jews, immigration of, to Israel, 6–7, 19,
    150, 152
Johnson, Lyndon, 88
Jordan, 31, 46–7, 50, 97, 125
Judaism, 22

Kassa, Asrate, 119, 122–3, 139
Kemalism, 22
Khalatbari, Ali, 55, 60, 62, 63, 64
Khomeini, Ruhollah, 56, 67–73, 162
Khuzestan, 42
kibbutz movement, 17
Kirca, Representative, 106, 109, 110–11
Kissinger, Henry, 57, 75
Koprulu, Fuat, 21
Korean War, 23
Kurds, 2, 25, 40, 65

Lebanon, 2, 63
  civil war in, 118

Lebanon War, 73–80, 110–15, 153–4, 162–3
Levant Fair, 15–16
Libya, 141
Litani Operation, 73

Maccabi games, 15
Makonnen, Lij Endalkachew, 123–8, 130, 131, 133, 134–6, 160
Marmarah, Abravaya, 15
Maronite Christian community, 2
MEDO, 167n6
Meir, Golda, 3, 30, 56
Menderes, Adnan, 21, 82, 84
Middle East
    end of imperialism in, 31
    regional stability in, 5
    ties with, 1–3
    U.S. interests in, 3
military, 52, 57, 66
Mirza, Iskandar, 82
Mossad, 2, 6
Mossadeq, Mohammad, 8, 9, 170n35

Naim, Asher, 215n19
Nasser, Gamal Abdel, 2, 31, 36, 39, 41, 57, 82, 118, 157
Nasserist expansionism, 2, 16, 155
National Iranian Oil Company (NIOC), 39, 53–4, 172n61
nationalism, 10–11, 16, 31
NATO, 23, 45, 88
Nile, River, 34
Nixon, Richard, 57, 214n12
non-alignment policy, 5, 6
non-Arab minorities, 2–3

Ogaden, 118
oil, 8, 9, 12–13, 38–9, 46, 49, 53–4, 57, 80, 144–5
oil embargo, 98–9, 144
oils-for-arms agreement, 66
Olcay, Osman, 99–100

Oman, 46
OPEC (Organisation of Petroleum Exporting Countries), 61, 98–9, 161
Operation Flower, 66
Operation Moses, 150, 152
Organisation of African Unity, 141, 142, 143, 212n167, 214n2
Ottoman Empire, 14, 15, 16

Pahlavi, Ashraf, 50–1
Pakistan, 25, 82, 131
Palestine
    partition of, 4–5, 32
    pre-state Jewish community in, 13–14, 15
Palestine Conciliation Commission (PCC), 19–20
Palestine Manufacturers' Association, 18
Palestinian Liberation Organisation (PLO), 62, 100, 107, 112, 114, 152, 163
Palestinian refugees, 10, 24, 27, 33, 34, 49, 50, 61–2, 85, 92–3, 161–2
Pan-Arabism, 31
partition, 4–5, 13, 16, 17, 19, 32, 155
Persian-Arab relations, 12, 13
Policy of the Periphery, 2–3, 155–63, 164–5
    1956–1972, 36–58, 81–97, 116–40
    1973–1982, 59–80, 81–97, 98–115, 141–54
    pre-1955, 4–35
political alliances, 1
positive nationalism, 10–11
pragmatism, 164

Rajaie-Khorassani, Said, 75–8
Ramazani, R.K., 6
Realpolitik, 164
Red Sea, 33, 34, 140, 145, 157, 159
Rehovot Science Conference, 42

Resolution 3379, 216n20
Rohan, Dennis Michael, 94

Sadat, Anwar, 66, 75, 103
Sarper, Selim, 18, 24, 26–7, 81, 87,
    194n4
Saudi Arabia, 31, 66, 108
SAVAK, 7, 56, 72
Second World War, see World War II
Selassie, Haile, 31, 32, 34, 119–20, 121,
    138, 143, 145, 205n34, 213n1,
    214n12
Senegal, 131
Pahlavi, Mohammad Reza, Shah of
    Iran, 9–11, 38, 41–5, 52, 55, 56,
    60–5, 67, 70, 72, 184n73, 189n9
Shell Oil, 12
Shi'a fundamentalists, 6
Shiloah, Reuven, 2, 3
Shimoni, Yaakov, 28, 29
shipping lanes, 34, 140, 144
Shuckburgh, C.A.E., 12
Sinai Campaign, 12, 28
Six Day War, 46–58, 91–7, 123–40,
    159–60
slave trade, 29
Snunnit, 85–6
Solel Boneh, 23, 25, 42, 119
Somalia, 118, 139, 147–8
South Africa, 142
Soviet Union, 2, 5, 9–10, 16, 39, 46, 88,
    155, 156, 163, 217n33
    Iran and, 44, 168n8
    Iraq and, 56
    Jews in, 21
    oil from, 13
    Six Day War and, 135–6
    Turkey and, 17–18, 27, 88
strategic alliances, 3
Sudan, 2
Suez Canal, 13, 36, 49, 53, 117, 144,
    158–9
Suez War, 28, 36, 37, 38, 81–2, 116–18,
    157–9

Swiss Civil Code, 16
Syria, 26, 31, 41, 42, 59, 60, 86–7, 97,
    200n2

Tabor, Hans, 124, 126
Temple Mount attack, 111–12
Tesemma, G., 32
Toufanian, Hassan, 66
trade, 20, 22–3, 40, 85, 108, 120, 150,
    153
Truman, Harry, 9
Tudeh Communist party, 6
Tural, Cemal, 87
Turkey, 156, 165
    1956–1972, 81–97
    1973–1982, 98–115
    Arab relations, 18–19, 98–9
    coup of 1980, 104–10
    Cyprus and, 23–4, 88–91
    Democratic Party, 22, 23
    foreign policy of, 16
    Jewish community in, 18
    Lebanon War and, 110–15, 163
    pre-1955 relations with, 13–28
    Six Day War and, 91–7, 159–60
    Soviet Union and, 17–18, 27, 88
    Suez War and, 81–2, 157–8
    Syria and, 86–7, 200n2
    trade with, 22–3, 85, 108
    UNGA and, 91–7
    UNSC and, 86
    U.S. and, 87, 108
    Yom Kippur War and, 98–104,
        161–2
Turkmen, Ilter, 102, 105, 108–9,
    112–13, 163

Ülkümen, Salahattin, 16
UN Charter, 8, 131
UNGA Emergency Special Session,
    37–8
United Arab Republic (UAR), 41,
    47–8, 118, 120, 121, 125
United Nations, 4, 8, 24, 157

United Nations Emergency Force
  (UNEF), 38, 63
United Nations General Assembly
  (UNGA), 13, 91–7, 117, 135–40,
  168n1
  partition plan, 155
  Resolution 194, 19–20
  Resolution 2253, 137
  Resolution 2254, 137
  Resolution 2256, 137
  Resolution 2443, 93
  Resolution 2799, 139
  Resolution 3379, 63, 101, 115
  Resolution ES-997, 81
United Nations Relief and Works
  Agency (UNRWA), 95, 96, 100,
  102, 136
United Nations Security Council
  (UNSC), 11–12, 26–7, 37, 76, 86,
  124–35
  Resolution 106, 26
  Resolution 107, 11, 26
  Resolution 108, 26
  Resolution 242, 101, 128–9
  Resolution 248, 131
  Resolution 250, 131
  Resolution 251, 131
  Resolution 256, 133
  Resolution 258, 133–4
  Resolution 262, 134
United Nations Truce Supervision
  Organization (UNTSO), 11, 172n50
United States
  interests of, in Middle East, 3
  Iran and, 5, 9, 72–3, 74, 191n37
  Israel and, 19–20, 65–6, 79–80, 84
  Korean War and, 23
  Turkey and, 87, 108
  Yom Kippur War and, 59

Vala, Muhandes, 39
Velayati, Ali Akbar, 74, 80

War of Independence (Israeli, 1948),
  7–8
war risk insurance, 20
Water Resources Development
  Company, 42–3
Weizmann, Chaim, 17
West, ties with, 20–1, 23, 46, 88
West Bank, 64
White Revolution, 45–6, 183n61
Wingate, Orde, 31–2
World War I, 16
World War II, 16, 17, 31–2

Yemen, 31, 118
Yifru, Ketama, 137
Yishuv, 13–14, 16
Yom Kippur War, 59–67, 98–104,
  141–2, 145, 161–2
Young Turks, 15
Yugoslavia, 24, 156

Zahedi, Ardeshir, 47, 48, 49, 50
Zionism, 7, 14, 30, 41, 72, 75, 79, 101,
  142, 146, 202n32

www.ingramcontent.com/pod-product-compliance
Lightning Source LLC
Chambersburg PA
CBHW050424280326
41932CB00013BA/1986